Deploying OpenLDAP

TOM JACKIEWICZ

Apress®

Deploying OpenLDAP

Copyright (c)2005 by Tom Jackiewicz

ISBN-13 (pbk): 978-1-59059-413-1
ISBN-10 (pbk): 1-59059-413-4

Printed and bound in the United States of America (POD)

Lead Editor: Jim Sumser

Technical Reviewers: Massimo Nardone, Oris Orlando

Editorial Board: Steve Anglin, Dan Appleman, Ewan Buckingham, Gary Cornell, Tony Davis, John Franklin, Jason Gilmore, Chris Mills, Dominic Shakeshaft, Jim Sumser

Project Manager: Laura E. Brown

Copy Edit Manager: Nicole LeClerc

Copy Editor: Kim Wimpsett

Production Manager: Kari Brooks-Copony

Production Editor: Laura Cheu

Compositor: Linda Weidemann

Proofreader: Nancy Sixsmith

Indexer: John Collin

Artist: Kinetic Publishing Services, LLC

Cover Designer: Kurt Krames

Manufacturing Manager: Tom Debolski

Distributed to the book trade in the United States by Springer-Verlag New York, LLC, 233 Spring Street, 6th Floor, New York, New York 10013 and outside the United States by Springer-Verlag GmbH & Co. KG, Tiergartenstr. 17, 69112 Heidelberg, Germany.

In the United States: phone 1-800-SPRINGER, fax 201-348-4505, e-mail orders@springer-ny.com, or visit http://www.springer-ny.com. Outside the United States: fax +49 6221 345229, e-mail orders@springer.de, or visit http://www.springer.de.

For information on translations, please contact Apress directly at 2560 Ninth Street, Suite 219, Berkeley, CA 94710. Phone 510-549-5930, fax 510-549-5939, e-mail info@apress.com, or visit http://www.apress.com.

*This book is dedicated to all those who suffered while I grew up
from a bright and curious kid to the bitter, stubborn, and outspoken
person I've become, especially my dad, Zdzislaw Jackiewicz.*

Contents at a Glance

Contents

▓CHAPTER 3   **Implementing Deployment, Operations, and Administration Strategies** 47

▓CHAPTER 4   **Installing OpenLDAP** 65

About the Author

TOM JACKIEWICZ is currently responsible for global LDAP and e-mail architecture at a Fortune 100 company. Over the past 12 years, he has worked on the e-mail and LDAP capabilities of Palm VII, helped architect many large-scale ISPs servicing millions of active e-mail users, and audited security for a number of Fortune 500 companies.

Tom has held management, engineering, and consulting positions at Applied Materials, Motorola, TAOS, and WinStar GoodNet. Jackiewicz has also published articles on network security and monitoring, IT infrastructure, Solaris, Linux, DNS, LDAP, and LDAP security. He lives in San Francisco's Mission neighborhood, where he relies on public transportation plus a bicycle to transport himself to the office—fashionably late.

About the
Technical Reviewers

Born under Vesuvius in southern Italy, **MASSIMO NARDONE** moved to Finland more than eight years ago, where he now works and lives. He holds a master's of science degree in computing science from the University of Salerno, Italy, and has more than nine years of work experience in project management and the mobile, security, and Web technology areas for both national and international projects. Massimo has worked as a technical account manager, project manager, software engineer, research engineer, chief security architect, and software specialist for many different software houses and international telecommunication companies. Massimo is also a visiting lecturer and supervisor at the Networking Laboratory of the Helsinki University of Technology (TKK) for the course "Security of Communication Protocols." As a software engineer, he mainly develops Internet and mobile applications involving different technologies, such as Java/J2EE/WebLogic, ASP/COM+, WAP, SMS, PKI, and WPKI. As a research engineer, he participated in different research projects involving PKI, WPKI, WAP, sim applications, SMS, SIP, SAML, BS7799, TTS, security, NGN, and mobile applications. In his role as chief security architect, he has been researching security standards and methods, as well as developing a security framework model for different companies. He researches, designs, and implements security methodologies for Java (JAAS, JSSE, JCE, and so on), BEA WebLogic, J2EE, LDAP, Apache, Microsoft SQL Server, XML, and so on. He's an expert on the security standard BS7799 and the protocols PKI and WPKI, where he holds two international patent applications.

ORIS ORLANDO, born in Naples, Italy, in 1971, has been interested in computer science since the '80s. His first computer was a Computer Intellivision Module that developed programs written in the limited-edition BASIC language. At the end of the '80s, he began to use 8086 machines. In 1989 he enrolled at the University of Salerno, in Italy, for computer science. During his university career, he developed many applications for small businesses and used the BBS before the Internet became prominent. He graduated in 1997 from the University of Salerno. In December 1997 he began working for Siemens Nixdorf for two years as an analyst/programmer (Java, C, PL/SQL, CGI, HTML) in the Web environment. In 1999 he came to work for Bull H.N. For two years he worked with the technical team; in the third year he became a project leader in the security department, and this year he's a project manager. He has had significant experience with Unix, Windows, Linux, DOS, computer programming, security, and databases (Oracle and LDAP), and he's certified for the BS7799 security standard.

Acknowledgments

I'd like to thank all those who have helped me go from bitterly screaming about LDAP (among other things) to finally writing it down, including Lane Davis, my mentor; Darin Wayrynen, whose late-night sessions inspired me to get into this systems stuff; Strata Rose, of whom I'm still in awe after working with her on SMTP and LDAP environments; Susan Surapruik, my better half, who, with great patience and understanding, has dealt with my opinionated rantings for so many years; and all those who have helped me in the search for the perfect chopped liver sandwich in the Bay.

And thanks to everyone involved in this project who put this together and dealt with any of the pain usually associated with geeks such as me.

Preface

A few years ago I was at an industry conference and saw a session about designing LDAP directories. At this time, LDAP was a relatively new technology, and even though I was already significantly exposed to it, I wanted to see what others had to say about the topic. With an open mind and a thirst for knowledge, I attended the session. From the first few words mumbled by the instructor to the very end, my jaw hung wide open, and I began to realize that although people were familiar with the APIs and how to use a few basic tools, no one really knew how to deploy LDAP. The same is true today.

What This Book Covers

The goal of this book is to show you the types of decisions you'll need to make about your OpenLDAP environment before even downloading any software. I discuss discovering information about your current environment, consolidating data, planning for data creation and migration, and planning the most useful directory infrastructure possible. Once I've covered those topics, I dive into the configuration files and the base set of tools. Finally, I discuss integrating LDAP into your current environment and the available APIs you'll be using. I chose OpenLDAP as the platform because the open-source community encourages standardization and doesn't focus on the proprietary features of commercial systems. Whether or not OpenLDAP is your choice for a directory within your organization, the lessons you'll learn about directory design and integration will be useful.

Who This Book Is For

This book will help programmers and system administrators deploy OpenLDAP as cleanly and efficiently as possible. This book is for someone thinking about deploying LDAP six months from now and for people who are responsible for maintaining LDAP today.

Source Code

Source code and scripts are provided in the generic shell, Perl, C, and Java to complement the text and give you a running start. You can find them on the Apress Web site at http://www.apress.com in the Downloads section.

Introduction

Welcome to the world of directories. Much like the fabled database administrator, you'll be walking into a realm of often-complex data structures, mangled sources of information, and a buzzword-happy executive wanting to push your infrastructure into uncharted territory. Fortunately, many others have already gone down this path and have already made the initial mistakes for you.

A *directory* is basically a subset of the all-too-generic term *database*. It's a specialized database with well-known methods of accessing and presenting information. Essentially, it's a simple database used to hold straightforward information that's accessed by simple methods from easy-to-understand clients written using solid, yet basic, programming interfaces. Directories, in the generic sense, have gone wherever the implementers' imaginations have taken them. In the beginning, a database or some source of information was used for straightforward lookups for a single, simple task. That is, some applications required the ability to maintain data and, without input (or guidance) for any place, create a general format that fit its particular need—and only its particular need. These are application-specific directories. Vendors have their own methods of implementing and storing this data. An example in use today is the Name and Address Book in Lotus Notes. In a really bad scenario, these could just be text files that store local information in a format that only the parent application can use.

One of the key limitations of these directories is the inability to share information between different systems. When information is updated in a directory containing a person's employee status, for example, it would have to be updated across multiple environments. Lightweight Directory Access Protocol (LDAP) and directories in general have been optimized for the various tasks I'll be discussing. They give you higher performance on reads and on retrieving data than they would on writes. Therefore, certain dynamic information (that requires a significant amount of updating) isn't the best candidate for storage within LDAP.

X.500

X.500 is the model used to define directories services in the Open Systems Interconnection (OSI) world. While considered outdated in the corporate world (and among those using newer technology that doesn't depend on legacy applications), X.500 and X.400 e-mail systems still have their places in the realm of intelligence, military, and aviation. This is primarily because of the slow pace of upgrades and extensive testing requirements within those industries. A good sign of LDAP adoption is that currently products exist that serve as X.500-to-LDAP gateways; in addition, some products are capable of interacting with the data structures of both X.500 and LDAP. X.500 has been around for more than a decade, but adoption has been slow for the international standard because it's complex and because its client half, Directory Access Protocol (DAP), is a hefty load for personal computers. LDAP creates a simple protocol for updating and searching directories running on Transmission Control Protocol/Internet Protocol (TCP/IP). LDAP standards have evolved to offer various extensions, including whois++ and the Simple Object Lookup (SOLO) service to support wide-area searches. Future extensions will make LDAP the Internet directory service of choice.

Naming Services

Like directory services, naming services such as Yellow Pages (yp), Domain Name Service (DNS), or Network Information Service (NIS)/Network Information Service Plus (NIS+) store information in a central place. Systems or applications can then use this information to facilitate further communication across the network. However, unlike directories, the primary focus of a naming services is machine data (hostnames, Internet Protocol [IP] addresses, Media Access Control [MAC] addresses), system-level access permissions, and system-level group membership (for example, print services). Centralized naming services enable each independent host to look to a central repository for data instead of having to maintain local copies of information.

Yellow Pages

In the mid-1980s, Sun added the Yellow Pages–distributed naming service to the Solaris operating environment to complement the advances of its Network File System (NFS). The overall goal was to create a complete environment that enabled stand-alone workstations to use a minimal set of protocols to access information stored centrally on other servers. That is, a workstation containing no local resources—except for a physical monitor, a keyboard, some memory, and a network interface—is able to remotely access enough configuration information to connect to the network and access remote resources. Sun was apparently ahead of its time with this idea because the concept of "the network is the computer" never caught on until the economic boom of the late 1990s and early 21st century. Because of trademark violations, Sun gave up the Yellow Pages name and replaced it with NIS. Yellow-page searches generally find all entries in the directory whose attributes satisfy some search criteria. For example, an e-commerce application may want to search for all companies that manufacture digital audio components. A Web application may want to search for all users with signing authority more than $5,000 in department 3320. Yellow-page capabilities are especially needed for e-commerce, as potential customers need a way to find all vendors of a given part, for example. Companies deploying these types of applications must select their directory with care. Some directory services are more scalable than others are, and organizations must accurately gauge their application requirements to select a directory that's capable of handling their anticipated load. Another yellow-page issue is the eventual adoption of Uniform Resource Names (URNs) on the Internet.

NIS

As mentioned, NIS eventually replaced Yellow Pages. NIS makes network administration more manageable by centralizing information necessary for administration of hosts. NIS stores information about the network, machine names and addresses, users, and network services in the NIS namespace via NIS maps. These maps replace the standard /etc services on your local Unix machine.

Some current NIS implementations rely on NIS protocols with LDAP back ends. This is often seen as a transition step between dependence on NIS and full LDAP support.

In an NIS environment, systems can have the following roles:

Master server: This is a system that stores the master copy of the NIS database files, or *maps*, for the domain in the /var/yp/*DOMAIN* directory and propagates them at regular intervals to the slave servers. Only the master maps can be modified. Each domain can have only one master server.

Slave server: This is a system that obtains and stores copies of the master server's NIS maps. These maps are updated periodically over the network. If the master server is unavailable, the slave servers continue to make the NIS maps available to clients. Each domain can have multiple slave servers distributed throughout the network.

Client: This is any system that queries NIS servers for NIS database information. Clients don't store and maintain copies of the NIS maps locally for their domain.

NIS+

NIS+ is a more dynamic version of NIS that's able to better scale across your organization. Some current NIS+ implementations rely on NIS protocols with LDAP back ends. This is often seen as a transition step between dependence on NIS+ and full LDAP support.

NIS+, a component of ONC+ in SunSoft's Solaris 2.0 and beyond, is an enterprise naming service designed to replace the widely installed ONC NIS in customer environments. NIS+ is a secure and robust repository of information about network entities (such as users, servers, and printers) that enables efficient administration of enterprise client-server networks. Administration tasks, such as adding, removing, or reassigning systems and users, are facilitated through efficiently adding to or modifying information in NIS+. An important benefit of NIS+ is scalability; it will simplify administration of small networks as well as enterprise-wide networks containing tens of thousands of systems and users. As organizations grow and decentralize, NIS+ continues to provide administrative efficiency.

DNS

DNS is the standard repository for hostname-to-IP translation, as well as other relevant host information that can provide a standardized translation table. Unlike other systems that keep adapting to change, it's commonly known that DNS works. By *works*, this means you have no real reason to update the type of service provided by DNS and give it LDAP support. This is a topic you'll probably run across frequently during your LDAP implementation.

Relational Model

You must understand the fundamentals of the relational database model during your implementation of a directory. The relational model is concerned with three aspects of data: the structure (or objects) that's used in the database, the integrity of the data being stored, and the manipulation of the information. Having a basic understanding of a database will show you that there's a fundamental difference between what can be stored in a database and what should or shouldn't be stored within a directory. Similarities, or even directory equivalents, of the information will also help guide your implementation.

In a relational database model, objects have a complex relationship to each other. This is unlike a well-defined directory, but it has its uses. Similar to a directory, a relational database has strongly typed and structured information. The advantages of a relational database are its ability to deal with this complex set of data. LDAP itself has a great deal in common with object-oriented programming languages. You can think of each entry in LDAP itself as an object. The main difference is that an entry within LDAP can inherit values from multiple object classes.

LDAP Standards

LDAP is a term that's almost as generic as *database*. LDAP can mean different things in different, or the same, contexts. LDAP can mean many different things depending on the intention. A good reference to LDAP standards is available at http://www.mozilla.org/directory/standards.html.

As a protocol, the first implementation of LDAP was developed at the University of Michigan in 1992. The whole concept behind LDAP was to create a TCP-based gateway to DAP, thus eliminating the need to maintain state. As a protocol, the specific methods of access to this directory are defined, such as the ability to bind, unbind, and perform operations. The data itself may not necessarily be a factor in this particular definition.

As a data definition, LDAP is the simplification and optimization of the X.500 data structure. LDAP uses the X.500 data model, based on a hierarchical structure of information. At the top is the highest level of the organization, with more data being stored in leaves hanging off branches of this tree.

As an implementation, LDAP may be someone's view of how the protocol and data can be combined as an implementation. You can think of this as the directory package known as OpenLDAP.

I'll discuss all things LDAP, including the protocol, the definition of data, and the specific implementation.

What problem was LDAP trying to solve? When LDAP was conceptualized, the problem statement may have been focused on the outdated OSI model, the overly complex data definitions, or the complexity of the systems required to access this information. The solution was a TCP-based gateway to DAP. Over a short period of time, the first version of LDAP came into being with the release of RFC 1487, *X.500 Lightweight Directory Access Protocol*.

LDAP v2, which stabilized all the brainstorming sessions and came up with a concrete foundation, is defined in RFC 1777, *Lightweight Directory Access Protocol*, and RFC 1778, *The String Representation of Standard Attribute Syntaxes*. With these, a new era of directory services began. The current version of the LDAP protocol, LDAP v3, was completed in 1997.

To further understand the initial development of LDAP, it may be helpful to discuss the timelines of X.500, the definitions and related protocols LDAP was supposed to supercede, and the current direction of LDAP.

The following is a brief timeline of X.500 and LDAP:

1989: The first X.500 software package (Quipu) was released.

1990: The first version of the X.500 standard was published.

1992: Software developers at the University of Michigan released the first LDAP software.

1993: The LDAP specification was detailed in RFC 1487.

1995: The first stand-alone LDAP server (slapd) shipped as part of the University of Michigan's LDAP 3.2 release.

1996: LDAP was chosen as the Internet directory service protocol of choice by industry software vendors.

1997: *PC Magazine* named LDAP v3 the winner of its Award for Technical Excellence at the fall 1997 COMDEX.

1998: Netscape shipped its first commercial LDAP v3 directory server.

1998: OpenLDAP 1.0 was released.

1999: A Sun-Netscape alliance was formed. The best software from both sides of the spectrum was combined. It took time for everything to work together, but the final results pushed LDAP into a new realm of stability. LDAP software from this era (for example, Netscape Directory Server 4.*x*) is still in use today.

2000: OpenLDAP 2.0 was released.

2002: Current releases of OpenLDAP (in other words, those being maintained) were released in June, starting with OpenLDAP 2.1. Version 2.2 followed in December.

It may seem that all is well and good with LDAP. The defined problem was solved, and the key, which was based on structured simplicity, was still intact. In the following RFC overview, I'll discuss the evolution of X.500 and LDAP and where each of these directory models and implementations went right and ultimately may have lost their paths:

November 1991: RFC 1274, *The COSINE and Internet X.500 Schema*, was released. This RFC specifies an Internet Activities Board (IAB) standards-track protocol for the Internet community. The document suggests the X.500 directory schema, or *naming architecture*, for use in the COSINE and X.500 pilots. The schema is independent of any specific implementation. As well as indicating support for the standard object classes and attributes, it also defines a large number of generally useful object classes and attributes. This document also proposes a mechanism for allowing the schema to evolve in line with emerging requirements. It also includes ways of carrying out this vision.

November 1991: RFC 1275, *Replication Requirements to provide an Internet Directory using X.500*, was released. This RFC considers certain deficiencies of the 1988 X.500 standard, which need to be addressed before an effective open Internet directory can be established using these protocols and services. The only areas considered are primary problems, to which solutions must be found before a pilot can be deployed. The RFC concerns itself with deficiencies that can be addressed only by using additional protocols or procedures for distributed operation.

November 1991: RFC 1279, X.*500 and Domains*, was released. This RFC considers X.500 in relation to the Internet. It emphasizes a basic model of X.500 that provides a higher level and a more descriptive naming structure. In addition, it proposed a mapping of domains into X.500, which gives a range of new management and user facilities beyond those currently available. This specification proposes an experimental new mechanism to assess and manage domain information on the Internet. It has no intention of providing an operational replacement for DNS.

Early on, the creators of the X.500 protocol standard intended that X.500 and DAP, based around OSI, will take over the Internet and replace TCP/IP. They also hope a more standardized schema will improve these chances. Later, it was proven that an open schema standard is a better choice for today's world. Unfortunately, the nonstandardization of schemas is also a major deficiency in LDAP today. Go figure!

March 1992: RFC 1308, *Executive Instruction to Directory Services Using the X.500 Protocol*, was released. This document briefly discusses the deficiencies in the currently deployed Internet directory services and then illustrates the solutions provided by X.500. This RFC is a product of the Directory Information Services (pilot) Infrastructure Working Group (DISI). It's a combined effort for the User Services and OSI Integration Areas of the Internet Engineering Task Force (IETF).

March 1992: RFC 1309, *Technical Overview of Directory Services Using the X.500 Protocol*, was released. This document is an overview of the X.500 standard for people not familiar with technology. It compares and contrasts directory services based on X.500 with several of the other directory services currently in use on the Internet. This RFC also describes the status of the standard and provides references for further information on the X.500 implementations and technical information. The primary purpose of this paper is to illustrate the vast functionality of the X.500 protocol and show how it can provide a global directory for human use and can support other applications that would benefit from directory services.

By this time, the Internet was growing at a phenomenal rate; it had thousands of new users each month. New networks were added almost every day! And people were already talking about the deficiencies in X.500. Important directory services at this time were the Whois service and DNS. Unfortunately, while people were proposing that the centralization of information is a good thing, RFC 1309 discusses that centralization of information is a bad thing. Once again, you can see why X.500, especially as a driver, is obsolete.

February 1993: RFC 1430, *A Strategy for Deploying an Internet X.500 Directory Service*, was released. This document describes an overall strategy for deploying directory services on the Internet, based on the OSI X.500 directory service. It then describes, in more detail, the initial steps that need to be taken to achieve these goals and how work already undertaken by the IETF working groups is working toward these goals.

The goals of this RFC were to take away all other directories (such as Whois and DNS) and replace then with X.500, or rather, DIXIE (which stands for *Directory Interface to X.500 Implemented Efficiently*), which is a TCP/IP gateway to X.500. Another loss is that X.400 is discussed here as a standard Internet message-handling service. Unfortunately for them, SMTP was already the protocol of choice. This RFC also discusses other goals, including interfacing current relational databases (RDBMS) into the X.500 model. Imagine turning X.500 into a full-fledged and complex database engine that's optimized for complex data types. Unfortunately, others had already filled this need.

December 1993: RFC 1558, *A String Representation of LDAP Search Filters*, was released. Tim Howes, one of the creators of LDAP from the University of Michigan, defines a network representation of a search filter transmitted to an LDAP server. Version 1 of the LDAP protocol is already out at this time and is simply a TCP gateway to DAP.

While Time Howes was defining simple search filters so that people would actually start being able to use the functionality of LDAP, the OSI side of the standards world was still overreaching in its goals and attempting to incorporate traditional TCP services and simpler directory-based systems into its framework. The concept of small programs or tools used to perform a single task well was completely lost by this time, and the focus was more on the creation of an all-encompassing directory system to replace just about everything that existed. You can see this type of focus in the RFCs I'm discussing.

May 1994: RFC 1617, *Naming and Structuring Guidelines for X.500 Directory Pilots*, was released. This document defines a number of naming and structuring guidelines focused on white-page usage. Alignment to these guidelines is recommended for directory pilots. This is the time that current technology approaches.

March 1995: RFC 1777, *Lightweight Directory Access Protocol*, was released. This document specifies an Internet standards-track protocol for the Internet community. The protocol described in this document provides access to the X.500 directory while not incurring the resource requirements of DAP. This protocol is specifically targeted at simple management applications and browser applications that provide simple read/write interactive access to the X.500 directory and is intended to be a complement to DAP itself. Here, many of the current advantages are defined as follows:

- Protocol elements are carried directly over TCP.

- Many protocol elements are encoded as ordinary strings.

- A lightweight encoding scheme is used.

March 1995: RFC 1778, *A String Representation of Standard Attribute Syntaxes*, was released. This document defines the requirements that must be satisfied by encoding rules used to render X.500 directory attribute syntaxes into a form suitable for use in the LDAP system, and then it defines the encoding rules for the standard set of syntaxes.

March 1995: RFC 1779, *A String Representation of Distinguished Names*, was released. This specification defines a string format for representing names, which is designed to give a clean representation of commonly used names while being able to represent any distinguished name. At about the same time, OSI was practically dead, so new standards for making this complex X.500 model user-friendly started to occur. Now the OSI directory infrastructure based on X.500 has user-friendly naming as a goal. This is one of the final nails in the coffin of X.500.

March 1995: RFC 1781, *Using the OSI Directory to Achieve User-Friendly Naming*, was released. While all the X.500 evangelists and pro-OSI (anti-TCP?) crowd was starting to define what it can be used for, the LDAP community was getting ready to define LDAP as a standard and clarify any open-ended standards, as you can see in the following RFCs.

June 1995: RFC 1798, *Connectionless Lightweight Directory Access Protocol*, was released. This new protocol provides access to the directory while not incurring the resource requirements of DAP. In particular, it avoids the elapsed time that's associated with connection-oriented communication, and it facilitates using the directory in a manner analogous to DNS. It's specifically targeted at simple-looking applications that require reading a small number of attribute values from a single entry. It's intended to be a complement to DAP and LDAP. The protocol specification draws heavily on that of LDAP.

August 1995: RFC 1823, *The LDAP Application Program Interface*, was released. Having an API is always an important step in the adoption of the any system. Without one, you're limited to what you can accomplish. Finally, the LDAP system you know today is finally born with the creation of an API in August of 1995. This document defines a C language application program interface to LDAP. The LDAP API is designed to be powerful yet simple to use. It defines compatible synchronous interfaces to LDAP to suit a wide variety of applications. You can find a good reference for LDAP RFCs at http://www.directory-info.com/LDAP/DirectoryRFCs.html.

June 1996: RFC 1959, *An LDAP URL Format*, was released. This defines the URL format.

June 1996: RFC 1960, *A String Representation of LDAP Search Filters*, was released. This RFC defines the various supported features of LDAP (AND, OR, NOT, and so on) into specific text strings that can be used universally.

October 1996: RFC 2044, *URF-8*, was released. This is a transformation format of Unicode and ISO 10646. Needless to say, while the LDAP community is coming up with practical RFCs for actually using the new protocol (and encouraging development within the global community), the LDAP/OSI/X.500 crowd was creating new encoding formats for theirs. While it's always necessary to clarify any components of a system that raise concerns, it's more important to actually make the system usable. Imagine if the same life cycle were necessary for automobiles. Without realizing that a car needed wheels to run, people would be creating standards for four-cylinder transmissions—which is useless until the car has the basic ability to function.

January 1998: RFC 2164, *Using an X.500/LDAP Directory to Support MIXER Address Mapping*, was released. MIXER defines an algorithm for using a set of global mapping between X.400 and RFC 822 addresses.

October 1997: RFC 2218, *A Common Schema for the Internet White Pages Services*, was released. This document defines a common schema for use by the various white-page services. This schema is independent of specific implementations of the white-page service. This document specifies the minimum core attributes of a white-page entry for an individual and describes how new objects with those attributes can be defined and published.

January 1998: RFC 2247, *Using Domains in LDAP/X.500 Distinguished Names*, was released. This document defines an algorithm by which a name registered with DNS can be represented as an LDAP distinguished name.

December 1997: RFC 2251, *Lightweight Directory Access Protocol*, was released. This is v3, which supports all protocol elements of LDAP v2 (as defined in RFC 1777).

December 1997: RFC 2252, *Lightweight Directory Access Protocol (v3) Attribute Syntax Definitions*, was released. This document defines the standard set of syntaxes for LDAP v3 and the rules by which attribute values are represented as octet strings for transmissions of LDAP. The syntaxes defined in this document are references by this and other documents that define attribute types. This document also defines a set of attribute types that LDAP servers should support.

December 1997: RFC 2253, *Lightweight Directory Access Protocol (v3) UTF-8 String Representation of Distinguished Names*, was released. This RFC standardizes the strings that can be used for showing a DN.

December 1997: RFC 2254, *A String Representation of LDAP Search Filters*, was released. This is a follow-up to RFC 1960; it explains LDAP search filters with more clarity.

December 1997: RFC 2255, *The LDAP URL Format*, was released. This is a follow-up to RFC 1959; it defines the URL format with more clarity.

December 1997: RFC 2256, *A Summary of the X.500 User Schema for Use with LDAP v3*, was released. This RFC is a start for porting existing X.500 user schemas into an LDAP-compliant format.

March 1998: RFC 2293, *Representing Tables and Subtrees in the X.500 Directory*, was released. This shows how tables and subtrees can be stored within the X.500 directory structure.

March 1998: RFC 2294, *Representing the O/R Address Hierarchy in the X.500 Directory Information Tree*, was released. This document defines a representation of the O/R Address hierarchy in the directory information tree. This is useful for X.400/RFC 822 (SMTP) address mappings and mail routing. At this stage of the game, once again, X.500 is trying to be an all-in-one solution to every data storage problem in existence. The original Unix philosophy of "do one thing, do it well" is fully lost by this point, as the OSI crowd ties to define more things that can be, in a very complicated way, stored in X.500.

March 1998: RFC 2307, *An Approach for Using LDAP As a Network Information Service*, was released. This document describes an experimental mechanism for mapping entities related to TCP/IP and the Unix system into X.500 entries so that they can be resolved with LDAP. It proposes a set of attribute types and object classes, along with specific guidelines for interpreting them. The intention is to assist the deployment of LDAP as an organizational name service.

September 1998: RFC 2377, *Naming Plan for Internet Directory–Enabled Applications*, was released. Once standards have been established and X.500 is removed from the road maps of typical organizations, you can take multiple routes involving LDAP without having to worry about the restricting nature of X.500. The OpenLDAP project was started as a collaborative effort to develop a robust, commercial-grade, fully featured, and open-source LDAP suite of applications and development tools. The first release of OpenLDAP (1.0) was in August 1998. Since then, OpenLDAP has kept the integrity of LDAP, and the future of directories, by adhering to the open-source philosophy, by keeping the project within scope, and by ensuring that all developers involved in the project adhere to open standards and not develop proprietary methods for commercial gain. In other words, the OpenLDAP project (and open-source initiatives in general) serves as the protector of standards from exploitation by private vendors.

In the timeline of LDAP, you can see rapid advancement of the technology as well as integration with a key number of popular components. The focus on the technologies must be commended because, whether by luck of a keen eye for the future, many important components of modern infrastructure are addresses and posed for LDAP integration.

April 1999: RFC 2559, *Internet X.509 Public Key Infrastructure*, was released. The protocol described in this document satisfies some of the operational requirements within the Internet X.509 Public Key Infrastructure (IPKI). Specifically, this document addresses requirements to provide access to Public Key Infrastructure (PKI) repositories for the purpose of retrieving PKI information and managing that same information. The mechanisms described in this document are based on LDAP, as defined in RFC 1777, which defines a profile of that protocol for using within IPKI and updates encodings for certificates and revocation lists from RFC 1778.

June 1999: RFC 2587, *Internet X.509 Public Key Infrastructure Schema*, was released. The schema defined in this document is a minimal schema to support PKIX in an LDAP v2 environment.

May 1999: RFC 2589, *Lightweight Directory Access Protocol (v3), Extensions for Dynamic Directory Services*, was released. This document defines the requirements for dynamic directory services and specifies the format of request and response extended operations for supporting client-server interoperation in a dynamic directory environment.

May 1999: RFC 2596, *Use of Language Codes in LDAP*, was released. This includes preparations for all LDAP implementations to accept language codes. This is the first step to LDAP's global appeal.

September 1999: RFC 2696, *LDAP Control Extension for Simple Paged Results Manipulation*, was released. Now that data is in the directory, this RFC takes great care that it's able to be retrieved efficiently.

October 1999: RFC 2713, *Schema for Representing Java Objects in an LDAP Directory*, was released. This shows Sun's influence in LDAP. Unfortunately, the scope of LDAP is changing.

October 1999: RFC 2714, *Schema for Representing CORBA Object References in an LDAP Directory*, was released. Once again the scope of RFCs for LDAP are moving into territories already explored (and lost) by X.500.

April 2000: RFC 2798, *Definition of the inetOrgPerson LDAP Object Class*, was released. This is one of the most basic object classes used to define person data that exists. It's a good step toward redefining LDAP as a directory once again.

May 2000: RFC 2829, *Authentication Methods for LDAP*, was released. To function for the best of the Internet, it's vital that security functions be interoperable. Basic threats to an LDAP directory service include unauthorized access via data-fetching operations, unauthorized access to reusable client authentication information via illegal monitoring, spoofing, and others. These concerns, and more, are discussed in this RFC, thus moving it toward an area of more secure access.

May 2000: RFC 2820, *Extension for Transport Layer Security*, was released. This document describes the StartTLS extended request and extended response themselves, describes how to form the request, describes the form of the response, and enumerates the various result codes the client MUST be prepared to handle.

June 2000: RFC 2849, *The LDAP Data Interchange Format, Technical Specification*, was released. This document updates the LDAP Interchange Format (LDIF) used for communication with the directory.

August 2000: RFC 2891, *LDAP Control Extension for Server-Side Sorting of Search Result*, was released. This document explains new server-side features for optimizing LDAP information searches.

February 2001: RFC 3062, *LDAP Password Modify Extended Operation*, was released. This document describes LDAP extended operation, which is intended to allow directory clients to update user passwords.

April 2001: RFC 3088, *OpenLDAP Root Service*, was released. This is an experimental LDAP referral service run by the OpenLDAP project. The automated system generates referrals based upon service location information published in DNS SRV RRs (location of service resource records). This document describes this service.

May 2001: RFC 3112, *LDAP Authentication Password Schema*, was released. This document describes schemas that support user/password authentication in an LDAP directory, including the authPassword attribute type. This attribute type holds values derived from the user's password(s) (commonly using a cryptographic-strength one-way hash). authPassword is intended to be used instead of userPassword.

September 2002: RFC 3377, *Light Directory Access Protocol (v3), Technical Specification*, was released. The specification for LDAP v3 comprises eight RFCs that were issued in two distinct subsets at separate times—RFCs 2251 through 2256 first and then RFCs 2829 and 2830. RFC 2251 through 2256 don't mandate the implementation of any satisfactory authentication mechanisms and hence were published with an "IESG note" discouraging implementation and deployment of LDAP v3 clients or servers implementing update functionality until a proposed standard for mandatory authentication in LDAP v3 is published. RFC 2829 was subsequently published in answer to the IESG note. The purpose of this document is to explicitly specify the set of RFCs comprising LDAP v3 and formally address the IESG note through the explicit inclusion of RFC 2829.

September 2002: RFC 3383, *Internet Assigned Numbers Authority (IANA) Considerations*, was released. This document provides procedures for registering extensible elements of LDAP. This document also provides guidelines to IANA that describe conditions under which new values can be assigned.

A good level of initial growth resulted in LDAP being picked as the directory of choice for managing commonly used data. Unfortunately, with its new popularity came abuse from multiple sides. System architects, now seemingly disconnected from current needs, have moved LDAP into the same area of complexity as the X.500 model. Too much clarification of information and the addition of extensions not necessary for a functional directory structure have the potential to leave LDAP a shell of its initial self. Many people now see LDAP as losing the vision of the problems it was supposed to solve and see it going toward where X.500 ultimately failed.

The movement of LDAP into various areas of the infrastructure, from e-mail systems to PKI support, is one of the reasons for LDAP's current growth and popularity. A good part of this has to do with luck in adopting technologies that have stuck. While the initial concept of LDAP was used as a starting point for data storage, there was, initially, a lack of additional supporting layers and standard schema. Everyone liked LDAP, but no real framework existed. The luck that LDAP had wouldn't have lasted if the technologies chosen had been replaced by something else. Imagine what would have happened if LDAP had provided more support for COBOL, dBase schema, and mechanisms for integrating with Livingston Portmasters for dial-up Internet service providers. LDAP would have been equated with those technologies, and it wouldn't have been adopted appropriately because these technologies are no longer part of a core infrastructure. For LDAP to be taken seriously, it needs to work with technology that's readily available and commonly used.

■■■

## CHAPTER 1

Assessing Your Environment

In a perfect world, the people installing, administering, and planning Lightweight Directory Access Protocol (LDAP) deployments for your company are involved from the beginning of setting up your entire infrastructure. Unfortunately, it's more common that the implementation of a directory infrastructure within your company is already in place by the time you come on board. While often a frustrating scenario, your ability to determine the existing state of information within your company will help you plan your installation and data layout for the phases in which you're involved. If you're tasked with installing directory services, you can be assured that currently some directories are already prevalent within your environment. One of the key goals of a directory has become the centralized storage of useful information.

In this chapter, I discuss the process of assessing your existing infrastructure to discover possible sources of data for your LDAP system. I also cover the potential uses of your directory. Finally, I cover some of the mistakes that others have made while deploying directory services so you can avoid making the same ones.

Gathering Information

If you want to have a useful and reliable directory, you must make sure the current directories in your infrastructure don't have more useful or accurate information than you have. If they do, what benefit would someone gain from using your directory? For example, people have no reason to use your new directory for e-mail address lookups if the current X.500 directory or Lotus Notes Name and Address Book contain more accurate information.

All data within the directory you're creating will have an original and authoritative source of data. For new information, which may not even be currently accessible, you'll need to take into account its origin so that you can determine an appropriate path of data flow. One of your first goals should be, through the discovery phase of your particular project, to determine where the data currently exists. That task may not be as easy as it sounds. What if people are currently accessing one system to obtain an e-mail address, but behind the scenes a different department is running the real source of data?

The initial result may look something like Table 1-1.

Table 1-1. *Origin vs. Source*

Data	Origin	Source/Access Method
Name	Human resources department	Oracle database/Define query. PeopleSoft database/Define query.
E-mail	Lotus Notes Name and Address Book	Lotus Notes database/Define query.
Phone	Telecom department	Unknown database.
Badge	Security department	Lotus Notes database/What's the original source of this data?
Customer data	Multiple groups	Multiple sources/Multiple definitions of data.

As you can see, even when a data source is available, it may not always be the correct place to obtain information. However, I can't stress enough how important it is to obtain information as close to the source as possible. The fewer dependencies on interim data stores, the better. A typical environment may have the data existing on one system (an Oracle table), crude procedures for extracting data and putting it into another system (a different Oracle table with different access rights), and yet another procedure that makes the data available to you via another directory interface. In this scenario, you aren't only dependent on the primary data source but also on all the steps that are involved in you pulling it from another directory three steps away. You should avoid situations such as these.

You'll need to evaluate the overall workflow of any data creation process in order to get the best results for the system's architecture. It's a good idea to understand the workflow associated with the new hire process to help you make decisions. To illustrate, the new employee workflow may look something like this:

1. The applicant is hired.

2. The applicant data is inputted into the human resources (HR) database. The data includes the following: name, birthday, Social Security number, photo, department, and payroll information.

3. The applicant data is passed from HR to security. The data includes the following: badge name, badge information, security clearance, roles, and responsibilities.

4. The applicant data is passed from security to the information technology (IT) department. The data includes the following: standard logins, passwords, and account data.

As you can see, each step in hiring a new employee (or contractor) within your organization has a specific set of inputs and a specific set of output. This is useful in knowing which values are owned by which organization and which databases may be involved when retrieving information for your directory. If you make the wrong decision, such as obtaining someone's name from the IT department instead of the HR department, you could get unknown results if HR changed the name and the value wasn't appropriately reflected in the target systems. Your ability to map information successfully is based on these decisions.

Name

In typical cases, your HR department is the first group responsible for keeping track of a name. Someone's name is often stored in multiple values depending on the look of the data. You could use the `GivenName` attribute, which I'll discuss in later chapters, to store someone's first name. You could then map this value to `FirstName`. You could use the `sn` attribute to store someone's last name. You could then map this value to `SurName` and `LastName`.

Understanding all the values you'll need to use is important. Maintaining consistency across all environments, so that applications interfacing with your system understand what they're getting, is one of the most important parts of the directory design process.

The following are some of the names you'll run across:

Legal name: This is the legal name, as taken by HR, and will most likely exist on someone's driver's license, Social Security card, or other form of legal identification. Often, this name isn't one that's commonly used throughout the enterprise for identification; it may be used only on legal documents such as payroll. For example, Wojciech Tomasz Jackiewicz, my legal name, would exist as part of this data set.

Preferred name: The preferred name may be a nickname that someone prefers to use. Tom Jackiewicz would exist in this set of data. Depending on internal policies, you can define this during the initial interview process (thus passed onto other applications for provisioning) or later, once all the accounts have already been provisioned. However, it's unwise to ignore this field for all the Wojciechs (who go by Tom) of the world.

E-mail name: E-mail addresses require uniqueness more so than other systems. Because a computer, not a human, does the processing, it's necessary to maintain complete uniqueness here. The e-mail name may be, depending on the format chosen by your company, a combination of the first name, middle initial, and last name. I may become Tom W. Jackiewicz in this set of data.

Application specific: Once your directory has been integrated with a number of components (especially utilizing some level of synchronization), you can ensure that the name field within some of your applications will be writable by the user. That is, if I have access to Application X, which has a feed from LDAP, and Application X pulls in my common name (which is usually some form of the first name plus the last name with some delimiter) or `cn` attribute, a good chance exists that the user interface will allow me to modify this information. It's always recommended that feeds are either two-way (in which changes in valid applications are propagated back to LDAP) or one-way and read-only (in which the data that's pulled from LDAP is read-only and can't be modified by any entity other than LDAP). However, this isn't always the case; sometimes names are modified, and the result will be a phone call asking why the name keeps being changed (via LDAP), why it isn't updated in another application, or, in a worst case scenario, why the application (after deciding that this will become the primary key) no longer functions correctly.

Names are also split between first, middle, last, and a combination of all these in different applications. It's necessary to note which applications require splitting, which ones are combined, and what the specific format of the information is. If you're going to maintain consistency, make sure that `cn: Jackiewicz, Tom` always exists in that specific format and no other, or the data will not longer be appropriately parsable. All this information is stored in object classes that group the various types of data. Some object classes you may use are `organizationalperson` or `inetorgperson`.

E-mail

One of the driving factors behind the fast adoption of LDAP standards was the ability to interface LDAP and e-mail systems. Up until the late 1990s, the ability to filter, route, rewrite, and utilize e-mail systems in a large scale (in other words, across multiple systems working as a single entity) was typically based on customizations to the e-mail server (such as sendmail). Hosting e-mail across multiple hosts often required a user to have an e-mail address based on a three- or four-part domain name. That is, if Tom Jackiewicz were to have an account on ISP.COM, and the service provider wanted to utilize multiple servers, his account may be `tjackiewicz@HOST4.ISP.COM`. Susan Surapruik, using the same service provider, may end up as `susan@HOST2.ISP.COM`. This created e-mail addresses that were difficult to remember but easy for computers to route across multiple systems.

Although tools were often created to better route `tjackiewicz` and `susan` (and give them e-mail addresses at just ISP.COM), no accepted methods existed for doing this from one system (or independent entity) to another. Fortunately, LDAP came to the rescue by providing e-mail systems with a repository for e-mail information stemming from the e-mail address, routing methods, final destination, and other e-mail–related configuration information.

As you can see, e-mail, in the case of LDAP, is a story of two sides. As a system administrator, you can see that during the processing of an e-mail by a Mail Transfer Agent (MTA), LDAP goes beyond standard Domain Name Service (DNS)–based processing of the e-mail. As an end user, you may see that LDAP can be used as a centralized address book to look up other users' e-mail addresses (as well as other information). LDAP should be used in both of these ways, even relying on each to share information.

You may also encounter X.400 systems. X.400 is the set of standards from International Organization for Standardization (ISO) and the International Telecommunications Union (ITU) that describes a messaging service. The transport of e-mail is the primary application. X.400 exists as X.400/84 and X.400/88, which are standards described in the ITU-TU Red Book and Blue Book. They're named as such because of the years that the standards were created (1984 and 1988, respectively). X.400/84 has been defined to run over a standard Open Systems Interconnect (OSI) stack (X.25, TP0, BAS Session); thus, most implementations, and all that pass conformance tests, are able to run over an X.25 network. If you have an e-mail address in the form of `TomJackiewicz@mail.YourCompany.com`, realize that this really isn't your true address in an X.400 environment. X.400 uses directory services to create maps between your e-mail address and something that looks remarkably like a distinguished name (DN). For example, the previous e-mail address may map to `C=com;ADMD=;PRMD=yourcompany;O=lab;OU=mail;S=Jackiewicz;G=Tom`, which is a far cry from what you're accustomed to typing. Other mapping possibilities exist, all of which rely on directory services.

Phone

The primary goal for deploying directory services is, more often than not, the creation of a phone directory within your environment. While the task may not seen difficult to accomplish, creating this environment will often involve gaining access to an old legacy mess of information. Phone systems, unlike modern components of your infrastructure, are built so well that they often work for many decades. Where new systems may be modern and have appropriate interfaces for accessing information, you'll probably have to brush up on RSTE/E (an old operating system that's the predecessor to VMS) and a series of dead scripting languages in order to pull information from the telephone database.

In many environments, this job is done for you in a number of ways. Unfortunately, this will also create problems, because accessing information away from the direct source often creates data ownership and maintenance issues.

The format of the telephone number must also be standardized and maintained. Some companies rely on extensions, and others use the full telephone number. Still others may choose different formats (see Table 1-2).

Table 1-2. *Phone Formats*

Data	Number
Extension	3261
Telephone number	555-3261
Global telephone number	1-408-555-3261
Global telephone number, presentation	(408) 555-3261
Global telephone number, presentation 2	1+408- 555 3261

It's important to maintain consistency across all the information. However, realize that various applications may need the various telephone number formats currently in use. An application will not change its format, and it doesn't always have the ability to manipulate information (for example, removing the area code or performing regular expression parsing against your data). For this reason, keep track of all the formats in use, determine which applications need a certain format, and provide the appropriate information. Meta-directories and other methods of parsing information may be necessary if, for example, the original source of the data provides information in a particular format but other sources, which may be outdated, provide invalid data in another format.

PKI Information

Public key infrastructure (PKI) is a comprehensive system of policies, processes, and technologies that enables users of the Internet to exchange information securely and confidentially. PKI is based on the use of *cryptography*—the scrambling of information by a mathematical formula and a virtual key so that only an authorized party using a related key can decode it.

PKI uses pairs of cryptographic keys provided by a trusted third party known as a certification authority (CA). Central to the workings of PKI, a CA issues digital certificates that positively identify the holder's identity. A CA maintains accessible directories of valid certificates and a list of certificates it has revoked.

PKI brings to the electronic world the security and confidentiality features provided by the physical documents, handwritten signatures, sealed envelopes, and established trust relationships of traditional, paper-based transactions. These features are as follows:

- **Confidentiality**: Ensures that only intended recipients can read files

- **Data integrity**: Ensures that files can't be changed without detection

- **Authentication**: Ensures that participants in an electronic transaction are who they claim to be

- **Nonrepudiation**: Prevents participants from denying involvement in an electronic transaction

PKI includes a CA and digital certificates, each containing a private and public key. These elements work together based on defined certificate policies within your company. Certificates, based on X.509 technology, as well as other components of your infrastructure, are commonly stored in LDAP. Determine if and how PKI is used within your environment, and view the existing layout of its LDAP infrastructure. Having independent LDAP systems work together is often extremely difficult if the information contained within the system doesn't match. This is especially true of security systems.

Badge

We've moved away from the model of entry that requires a large set of keys to access certain buildings, rooms, and cabinets. A more modern physically security infrastructure is in place throughout corporate America, and it often requires computerized badges and access lists. No uniform standard for badges is available; therefore, it's up to you to determine what you can obtain from your existing system, what you want to obtain, and what can be appropriately be used outside its home. Because this is in the realm of security, red tape and political hurdles are involved in obtaining access to the system. Once you succeed in gaining access, you'll encounter various pieces of information.

- **Primary key**: Because of the age of some badge systems, the primary key may be poorly derived by nonstandard methods. That is, a badge system is more likely to rely on a name rather than an employee number.

- **Badge ID**: Physical badge IDs are often the primary key used for data on the system. They're typically the serial number associated with a given badge.

- **Badge name**: The name of the badge owner may be included in the database.

- **Access information**: While it's often stored in proprietary formats, unreadable and unusable by outside applications, access information includes what can and can't be accessed. Often, area maps of the office aren't included as part of this and could be useful for other applications.

- **Expiration date**: Especially true for contractors, the expiration date is a good piece of information to obtain from any badge system.

The overall key is to find out what data may be usable outside the specific system you're using. If you can think of a use for the data, others integrating with your application can probably think of a few more uses.

Customer Data

The scope of a directory server, in recent years, has extended beyond that of the internal enterprise. External-facing systems, customer records, supplier information, and other noninternal sources of information are now part of the overall scope of most deployed LDAP systems. Larger companies are now sharing information with competitors and forming alliances that require sharing data electronically.

Often, security profiles for vendors, suppliers, and customers may need to be provisioned and maintained within your directory. Individual contacts from each of the new sources of data may also need to be included, depending on the overall need (see Table 1-3).

Table 1-3. *External Sources of Data*

Potential Need	Resulting Data	Approach
Vendor profiles for contact list	Storing vendor information, including location, delivery address, and contacts	DN: CN=Vendor? Other relevant information
Vendor profiles for a delivery system	Storing vendor information, including specific identification codes (primary keys in other databases) used to identify vendor	DN: VENDORID=VendorId Other relevant information
Vendor contacts (specific users managing specific projects and sets of information)	Storing vendor contacts, underneath a vendor profile, of specific users	Vendor branch created Specific vendor branch created dn: uid=X, ou=VENDORID, ou=VENDOR

You can see the progression of the vendor data. Where it may be a project that someone quickly dives into in order to create profile information within your directory, it's good to know all the ways various applications could be used in order to create the appropriate hierarchy. For instance, you may not consider having profiles for vendors stored in separate organizational units underneath a vendor hierarchy if the original scope of the project includes only vendor contacts.

Having to rework your directory after the profile information is created one way requires a significant amount of reworking of your data and will also slow down future projects. Make sure you have all the information you need from the beginning to make the correct choices for your deployment.

Looking at existing systems and analyzing the data that's currently in use will give you a good start for creating appropriate profiles within your directory. You should use the same approach for creating external data that you'd use for creating internal data. Unfortunately, external data is often stored in competing systems and has independent profiles. For example, if Intel is a vendor, it may have certain information stored in a database that's tracking the network cards your company is purchasing. As a strategic partner, Intel may have different profile information (and, as a result, different primary keys for identification) stored in another database. These two sets of data, when merged, will often create difficult-to-manage situations and competing results of data. You need to consider all this when maintaining a clean directory.

Other systems may even contain data that's inappropriate for storing in your directory. For example, a parts inventory may exist in your company that requires complex searches. In this case, it may not be the best idea to store the information in a directory. This is because the structure of the information doesn't logically fit into the provided namespace; further, the queries that would be required from an inventory system are more complicated than those that can be defined and processed easily by LDAP.

Examine your goal, your scope, and your plan appropriately, or the end result may be a directory that's unmanageable.

Creating an Ongoing Process

An initial implementation of a directory without a maintenance plan is much like cleaning a room full of dishes during the lunch hour rush, going home for the day, and being shocked that the dishes are dirty again. Maintaining a directory that incorporates existing company information is often an ongoing process that requires not only the importing of company data but the procedures for future synchronization or, if desired, migration. The first step, as previously discussed, is to identify the data sources and the information contained within them that would be beneficial if stored within a directory. The initial step of obtaining this information is often the easiest. The ability to maintain a record of the changes and propagate them to your directory requires a significant amount of work. Multiple approaches exist.

Changing Application Sources

In a typical scenario, you'll be obtaining your initial set of data from existing applications. These applications will rely on back-end data sources, usually consisting of text files or proprietary systems that don't have the advantages of LDAP. The initial migration of the data from the source system to a directory may be relatively simple and involve obtaining a text dump of the existing data, parsing it, and importing it into your directory. Unfortunately, if you want to have this data available in your directory in the first place, you'll probably need some external processes and systems to make sure it's accurate. This creates a scenario where a dynamic set of data exists (see Figure 1-1).

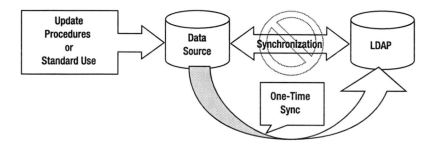

Figure 1-1. *Initial creation of data from a dynamic source*

This figure shows that while a one-time synchronization occurs, you have no true method of appropriately obtaining any of the changes that may have occurred within the data source (by means of an external update procedures or through typical application use) after the initial synchronization. This creates a gap in the data you have in your directory, which demonstrates why you need LDAP as a central repository in the first place.

You'll encounter many scenarios during the discovery phase of your OpenLDAP implementation. For example, you'll encounter various sources of data that you won't know how to deal with, departments that won't give you appropriate access to information, and outdated systems that certain customers will insist need to be imported into your directory. You'll need to deal with each case on an individual basis. What may seem like a simple method of retrieving and mapping data could turn into a sea of red tape and headaches. Therefore, plan for the previous scenarios when mapping your data and design your layout.

User-Facing Applications

User-facing applications are phone directories or other systems that contain information typically used by nonadministrators. Users will often access a Web-based or graphical user interface (GUI) front end for this application and be accustomed to a base set of information stored in a particular way. This type of application is just a front end to a back-end database—whether or not other applications use this information.

Depending on the particular applications, users may be able to modify this information. Imagine the scenario where Susan Surapruik wants to look up the information for Tom Jackiewicz. She could access a user-facing application called PhoneBook by entering the uniform resource locator (URL) http://PhoneBook.YourCompany.Com. Although it's often true that people may be the best source for information about themselves, they're often unaware of the interdependencies between the data. If Susan Surapruik were to update her location in the phone directory based on her working in the Campbell satellite office (instead of San Francisco), what would happen if HR and payroll used this particular field for the payroll record and *Campbell* didn't return an appropriate match?

Be careful when looking at these applications; you should understand where the data originates and how it's used. The ultimate solution for systems such as these—that is, simple user-facing applications where data is presented and where the presentation interface (user interface) is the only one available—would be to change the source of the data. When a new directory is deployed within your organization, the directory itself often meets the data needs of other, smaller, back-end systems (see Figure 1-2). This removes the proprietary method used by the user interface (or the application itself) to access information in the original source. The replacement stores information in the OpenLDAP directory directly and uses standard LDAP calls to access the information. By changing the source of the data, you may require synchronization methods to populate the information in the original source.

Figure 1-2. *Changing the source of your data*

It's also important to evaluate your existing environment. For instance, you may decide that while LDAP can be used immediately for authentication, automounter maps are going to stay in files or maps for now. Evaluate possible server choices. For instance, you could use Novell's eDirectory, Sun's SunONE Directory Server software, or OpenLDAP.

Start with the your potential clients' applications. As a suggestion, you can first test that the clients can actually do what they claim they'll do, and then you can spend time porting applications, cleansing and moving data, and maintaining a directory server.

Middleware

In this particular case, I'll consider *middleware* to be any application that utilizes existing information and adds its own unique data set to it. Take, for example, an application that manages supplier and vendor interaction. The original set of data used to create profiles for this application may currently exist in a database somewhere within your organization. On top of this basic set of data, new roles and information (often proprietary and used only by this middleware application) would need to be added. The union of the data that already exists elsewhere, plus this new set of information, would be necessary for your application to function appropriately.

The methods of changing the source of data from some database to a directory would apply here as they would for a user-facing application. However, you'd need to add various roles that may be contained within this system. Whether the additional information can comfortably fit into the existing directory you have is up to you. No real guidelines exist for this except to say that if you have independent role information for multiple integration projects, your system would be cluttered with information that can be used only by a minimal number of applications, and a directory may not be the best place to store this information.

However, standardizing role information and leveraging a good framework for the initial design enables you to store role information for multiple systems in the directory and have this information be used across multiple systems.

Back-End Systems

Outside the world of middle management and PowerPoint presentations, groups of people (presumably in dusty caves) actually utilize information for something other than pop-up windows. Having an appropriate source of information for e-mail addresses, locations, and other such things helps various systems. Many system administrators utilize scripts to generate this information and store it in other formats. For example, e-mail services, often relying on sendmail or qmail, use directories to generate their access lists. The difficulty in dealing with some of these systems is that you have no direct way to access information via LDAP. This is changing as time moves on, but programmers and system administrators often don't complain about the lack of software compliance and just create their own interfaces. These scripts, which may currently be tied into an incorrect (but somewhat accurate) data source, may benefit you if they were rewritten to utilize the directory for synchronization. While it may be nice to have the `/etc/mail/vir-tusertable` directory for sendmail stored directly in LDAP, an easier chore would be to generate file in its original format, based on LDAP information (see Figure 1-3).

Figure 1-3. *LDAP as a source for "well-known" file formats*

Similar scripts have existed for integration with NIS/NIS+, Web server access lists, and other "well-known" services that already have a standardized and accepted format for storing information. This is often the choice when a system has many utilities already in use that can check for the integrity of the generated files but not necessarily the integrity of the data stored in LDAP. As you push toward storing and managing information in a directory, this will be less common.

Because migrating current directory services to LDAP may not be a trivial or risk-free undertaking, you may decide to run and maintain proprietary directory services in parallel with LDAP for some period of time. (Although this is certainly not textbook advice, it may be practical.) This may also be necessary when you need to keep some of the proprietary services that can't be supported with LDAP running for some time. Another common reason for running LDAP and other directory services in parallel may be a shortage of skills or staff personnel. Table 1-4 shows the types of applications you may encounter in the wild and their potential problems.

Table 1-4. *Types of Applications You'll Encounter*

Application Type	Example Solution(s)	Problems
User-facing application. Users are able to modify data, and LDAP support as sync source.	A user facing application such as a phone directory. Users have the ability to update their records.	If a user can directly see information, they often have a desire to update it. This will have unknown repercussions on other systems that may depend on this information. Problems can arise if the data shown isn't kept in sync with the real source.
User-facing application. Users are unable to modify data.	A user-facing application such as a phone directory. Users don't have the ability to update information.	Read-only systems have fewer problems. But problems can arise if the data shown isn't kept in sync with the real source.
Middleware. Users or administrators able to modify information.	A midlevel application, such as a supplier/vendor interaction application that may be tied to a Web server. Users need special information (or roles) specific to this particular application to interact.	Role information, derived a number of ways, can often be tied to individual applications and doesn't comply with any set standards. That is, manual role additions are more difficult to keep track of than roles derived based on certain values. Problems can arise if the data shown isn't kept in sync with the real source.

(Continues)

Table 1-4. *Types of Applications You'll Encounter (continued)*

Application Type	Example Solution(s)	Problems
Middleware. Users and administrators are unable to modify information.	A midlevel application, such as a supplier/vendor interaction application that may be tied to a Web server. Users need special information (or roles) specific to this particular application to interact.	Role information is derived from a combination of synchronized data. Problems can arise if the data shown (and used to derive roles) isn't kept in sync with the real source.
Back-end systems. Users and Administrators are able to modify information, or users and administrators are unable to modify information.	A back-end application, such as an e-mail database for a monitoring application.	Problems can arise if the data isn't kept in sync with the real source. Because this system has minimal visibility, problems can often be reported only by a small subset of users. For simplicity (and because of a lack of audits), information may be manually updated rather than relying on the original source.

Understanding Meta-Directories

Because the term *meta-directory* is so generic, you can find entire libraries dedicated to the concept of a meta-directory—and many of the references would lead you in different directions. The term *meta-directory services* is a label for a class of enterprise directory tools that integrate existing, or *disconnected*, directories by addressing both the technical and political problems inherent in any large-scale directory integration project. A meta-directory is the question mark in Figure 1-4. Technically, meta-directory services consolidate subsets of the information in multiple directories, including data on people, groups, roles, organizational units, locations, and other resources. This consolidation creates a *join*, or unified view, of the different directories in an organization. The meta-directory makes that unified view accessible via LDAP and Web-based access protocols. In general, a meta-directory scenario in use at many companies today involves centralized registration of network operating system (NOS) accounts; synchronization of e-mail addresses; publication of people data through LDAP servers; and attribute synchronization with telephone directories, HR systems, and access management systems such as firewalls or authorization servers. An emerging scenario is one in which a meta-directory links directory-enabled networks (DENs)–compliant, policy-based network access and routing controls with the user account information in a NOS directory, such as Novell Directory Server (NDS) or Active Directory.

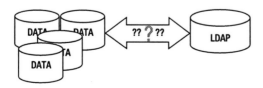

Figure 1-4. *The role of a meta-directory*

A meta-directory is an intermediate layer between one set of data and another. It's used, in a number of different ways, as a joiner of information so that the available set of data can be utilized outside its source. That is, each application may store information in its own method (a database implementation, a directory, flat text files in a number of formats, and so on) using its own data model so that it can be used effectively by a given application. However, because the information contained within the data set you're looking at may be useful for other applications, deploying a meta-directory solution would help in retrieving, normalizing, and using this data.

As discussed previously, you'll be relying on a number of sources of information in order to create a useful OpenLDAP implementation.

The "system," "method," or "procedure" used to *extrapolate*, or derive, data from one data source before importing it into your LDAP directory is covered by the concept of a meta-directory that I'll discuss in a moment. In short, it's the solution for obtaining data from one source and importing it into another.

I've discussed the importance of standardizing information across your enterprise. A name should be consistent across all systems, a number should be in the same format, and terms should be standardized. When referring to a business category in PeopleSoft, for example, it's a good idea to keep the same term when implementing your LDAP directory. Unfortunately, this isn't always the case, for whatever reason. A meta-directory *layer* will be able to connect to various sources of data, read information in the format native to the remote application, and manipulate it for use within your LDAP directory.

In a typical meta-directory scenario, you'll have the following components:

Connector: A *connector* is the technology (whether advanced or not) that relies on realistic programming interfaces or is just a simple Perl script that enables your meta-directory to access data on another system. The connector is just an enabler or a mechanism that gains you access to a given resource much like a key or a combination can gain you access to a house. Depending on which vendor you choose or whether you program your own solution, you'll see connectors for many of the common technologies available today. The typical lag for a commercial connector is usually a few months after an initial version of software has been released. That is, if you're working with version 8.2 of a database, you'll see that connectors are available up to version 8.1. This is to be expected. However, realize that the typical deployment scenario of many large applications give integration candidates time to adjust and engineer appropriate solutions.

Connectivity to a system has a basic set of prerequisites. You must have some sort of available interface for accessing the information. While this is quite a generic statement, realize that it's often difficult to, out of the box, create any sort of a connector to a spreadsheet. That is, the spreadsheet would have to be copied from one host to another, and no standard interfaces are available to request a system for the data contained within the spreadsheet.

Rules and rule sets: When working with any data in any environment, it's necessary to define a set of criteria for obtaining, parsing, and moving information. Once a connector establishes itself to a data source, it relies on defined rules and rule sets to know what to do. The various components of this are as follows:

- Join or match rule: This is the criterion that shows how to connect information from your data source to another. That is, this includes the discovery of primary keys between systems and a rule to obtain this set of information.

- Rule: A rule with a meta-directory can be as simple as "pull value X, map to value X" (or the atomic mapping of information to something complex that manipulates the information and maintains status between runs).

- Rule sets: Rule sets are the combination of rules. These are then typically associated with the data that needs to be utilized.

A rule as an individual statement isn't useful until it's associated with a rule set. The rule set is then associated with the connector view.

Connector view: A *connector view* is the "view" that you have into an application's data. For a system relying on Oracle, for example, the connector view may have access to a table showing information in a specific format. The table may use EmployeeNumber as a primary key and, underneath this record, may have various attributes that are used by an application.

Looking at this data, you may the following set of information:

- EMPLOYEE_NUMBER: 013838

- FNAME: TOM

- LNAME: JACKIEWICZ

- TAG: 539

- DEPT: IT09

- EADDRESS1: TOM_JACKIEWICZ

- EADDRESS2: YOURCOMPANY.COM

Your first goal in establishing connectivity, as a connector view, to your target system is to determine what data needs to be pulled from the host and made usable to LDAP.

Target connector view: The same concepts that apply to the connector view apply to the target connector view. In fact, the target connector view is just the final connector view. That is, upon connecting to and retrieving data from the regular connector views and then processing and normalizing information, the end result is that it's being written to your LDAP system. Therefore, just like any other system, a meta-directory will need to know of your LDAP system and establish the appropriate connectivity—even if all it's doing is writing to your system blindly.

Meta-view: Whether this is a requirement based on the particular implementation of a meta-directory solution you're using, the concept is the same. This is the "work area" where information is stored, whether in a temporary directory or in memory, before it's effectively processed, parsed, and moved to your target system.

You should understand that a meta-directory architecture, as shown in Figure 1-5, doesn't replace existing applications. Instead, it serves as the glue to tie together systems in a structured and manageable way. The overall role of a structured meta-directory system is to take away the many scripts that may be used in your current environment and replace them with a central source of data management. The overall value of doing this really depends on the organization, but you should definitely explore this.

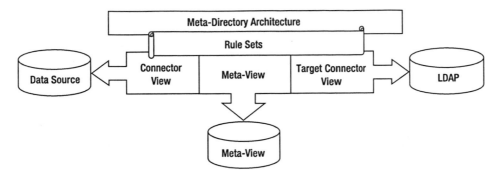

Figure 1-5. *Meta-directory architecture*

To evaluate meta-directory products, you should check several general categories of directory integration functions.

- The virtual directory administration client, which allows administrators to use a single GUI tool to manage information in multiple directories

- Directory synchronization, which allows companies to synchronize two or more directories using object and attribute creation and deletion

- The information broker, which enables real-time connectivity by allowing a directory server to access data in another directory server on behalf of a client or server

- The join, which enables full relationship management through sophisticated synchronization and replication features, creating a unified directory infrastructure

Avoiding Mistakes

One of the most powerful aspects of directories is that they give you the flexibility to do what you want with them. This can be both a positive and a negative ability, depending on how it's utilized. One of the problems with the original X.500 directory implementations was the inability to adjust the directory for its contents. That is, the directory itself needed to be created in such a way that it was always up to standards, whether or not this was necessary for the data being stored. The objects within a directory needed to be, in order to maintain compatibility with other systems, described with such detail that it was often prohibitive for certain people to utilize them. By removing some of the complexity of data that was necessary for base functionality, LDAP entered an area that was inaccessible to X.500—the end user, system administrator, and manager tasked with a basic goal. By allowing data to be stored in any reasonable (but still based on the hierarchical) method, LDAP could be used for any application.

Unfortunately, many mistakes were made because of this flexibility.

LDAP As Oracle

When LDAP became the latest industry buzzword, and Oracle (or any other full database implementation) was considered too large of a project for a simple implementation, the inevitable happened. Many vendors realized that to gain acceptance of their products, and to show they were at the bleeding edge of the industry, they needed to implement LDAP support.

While this looked like a good idea, the problem was the way it was implemented. When you see a raw view of the data stored in Oracle, you see it as a series of tables, columns, and metadata that's used to create a searchable archive. Each element in the system has the potential of having a relationship with another object that isn't necessarily directly connected to it. Metadata maps these relationships.

Take, for instance, a software company that stores information in Oracle. To meet with some of its customers' compliance issues, support for LDAP in the latest version is necessary. Instead of revisiting the structure of the information contained within its Oracle implementation and changing it to work better in an LDAP environment, information is directly put into an LDAP system the same way it would be if it were Oracle. The end result is a mess, as demonstrated in the following code. For this example, you'll start with the knowledge that someone has the employee number 91358. Based on this data, find out as much information as possible about this person from the LDAP system.

```
$ ldapsearch -h ldaphost -p 389 -D "cn=directory manager" -w password
-b dc=Your,dc=Company uid=91358 erparent

dn: erglobalid=5368616861693268173,ou=0,ou=people,erglobalid=00000000000000000
 000,ou=PRODUCT,dc=Your,dc=Company
name: Tom Jackiewicz
firstname: Tom
lastname: Jackiewicz
uid: 91358
erparent: erglobalid=13132326925877942114,ou=orgChart,erglobalid=0000000000000
 0000000,ou=PRODUCT,dc=Your,dc=Company
```

Upon completion of the first query, you can gather a certain set of data that may be useful to you. But wait, it looks like the query you generated provided you only with basic information about Tom Jackiewicz—most of which you already knew. The query did provide you with an erparent attribute that may be useful.

```
$ ldapsearch -h ldaphost -p 389 -D "cn=directory manager" -w password
-b dc=Your,dc=Company
uid=91358 erparent="erglobalid=13132326925877942114,ou=orgChar
t,er globalid=00000000000000000000,ou=PRODUCT,dc=Your,dc=Company" erparent

dn: erglobalid=1855207254792657305,ou=0,ou=people,erglobalid=00000000000000000
 000,ou=PRODUCT,dc=Your,dc=Company
erParent: erglobalid=13132326925877942114,ou=orgChart,erglobalid=0000000000000
 0000000,ou=PRODUCT,dc=Your,dc=Company
```

The result of performing multiple queries against this database will lead you across various seemingly disconnected sets of data (which are outside the standard structure you're accustomed to with LDAP). Upon traversing multiple trees and gathering pieces of information from various sources, you may end up finally gathering all the data for which you're looking.

If you were looking for someone's account in Windows NT, their badge, their legal name, and their other information that's stored in multiple types of systems (or not associated with a single account), for example, you would have to perform a significant amount of queries to obtain the valid information (see Figure 1-6).

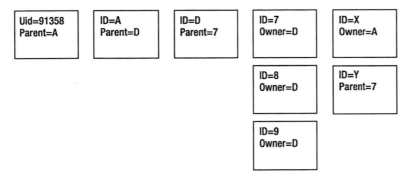

Figure 1-6. *Types of queries*

What's shown in this figure is that one initial starting point can generate multiple objects. To obtain information that may be contained in the fifth tier in the figure, you'd need to perform multiple queries. The first query would be against uid=91358, in order to find a parent. Subsequent queries would be for ID=A, ID=(Parent of ID=A), and so on. You can finally retrieve the information you're seeking after multiple queries against the system. While this is fine for databases, it's a poor use of LDAP and requires too many queries to obtain a simple set of data. Figure 1-7 shows an example of the information that you could retrieve during each of the tiers.

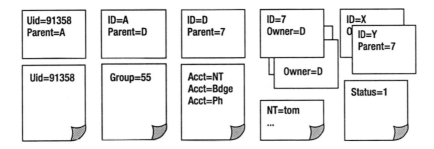

Figure 1-7. *Retrieving information*

In the first tier (uid=91358), you have information on the uid. In the second tier, you obtain that this person is a member of group 55 (group=55). The third tier may provide you with the information that this person has Acct=NT, Acct=Bdge, and Acct=Ph. From this you derive, among other information, that this person has the NT login of tom (NT=tom). A final query from the fifth tier shows you that this person is active (Status=1). To obtain all this information, you had to query the system more times than you would have liked—at least five times, depending on how far in depth you went on the search results (some searches returned more than a single entry that could then be explored further).

New implementations of software on top of LDAP rarely have to rely on a structure that requires this level of querying (though you may be surprised). Instead of the previous structure, it's more common, and usually a better idea, to store information under a single DN.

```
$ ldapsearch -h ldaphost -p 389 -D "cn=directory manager" -w password
-b dc=Your,dc=Company uid=91358

dn: erglobalid=5368616861693268173,ou=0,ou=people,erglobalid=00000000000000000
 000,ou=PRODUCT,dc=Your,dc=Company
uid: 91358 \
group: 55 \
Acct: NT \
Acct: Bdge \
Acct: Ph \
NT: Tom \
Status: 1 \
```

You can obtain the information you previously queried using multiple searches, in this example, using a single query. Consider this sort of structure for your own implementations of software that utilize an LDAP structure. As the size of your object base (whether this is users or parts) grows, it will be beneficial to maximize the amount of data that can be retrieved using a single query.

Unfortunately, the difficulty of working systems that integrate LDAP in this way often lands outside your control. If you have no control over the way a system utilizing LDAP stores information, you have no quick solution for making it compliant. Many vendors, from Tibco to IBM, use such methods of storing and accessing information. The only hope for true integration with products such as these is using meta-directories that create the appropriate connections and mapping data between your LDAP environment (utilizing your own standard LDAP mappings) and the product LDAP environments. Maintaining the mappings of information without products such as these adds to the complications of the environment and will be difficult to maintain.

LDAP As a Sync Source

The poor man's method of LDAP compliance is often referred to as *LDAP as a synchronization source*, in that LDAP queries are performed by one system, and the values are parsed and then stored in another system, with no regard to the actual LDAP structure that exists at the source. This is a common way for applications that use other directories (or even databases) within the back-end configurations to allow some level of LDAP compliance. Typical applications, which are all listed within the vendor documentation as "Fully LDAP Compliant," will require that you go through certain configuration options that are then used to populate another database.

Whether the configurations you'll be dealing with are available via a GUI, a Web page, or a configuration file, the basic ideas will be the same. You'll be prompted for a host, a port, a base DN, and a search filter. Some configurations let you enter a list of attributes to retrieve and configure in order to map to their application database. Upon entering this data, through some mechanism, the application connects to the specified LDAP host and performs a query (see Figure 1-8).

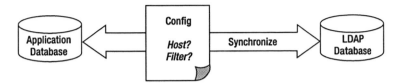

Figure 1-8. *LDAP synchronization*

In this figure, you can see that through some generic method, application data is synchronized with the LDAP database. The values used to synchronize this data are inputted into a user interface. To fully understand this type of LDAP integration, imagine a scenario where an application needs to utilize person data within your company. This application may already exist in the form of a telephone book, a portal, or something else that requires users to log in. Without some level of integration with an LDAP system, active users in your company (which are stored in the LDAP database) aren't in sync with the user base (stored in application database) that's being used by the application. The process that currently exists may be manual or scripted. The authoritative source of users may provide a text file to the application, and a process could exist that converts this to a series of database calls to input data into the application database. While this method may work, it doesn't scale as more applications are added because of the proprietary interfaces that are always used. This is where LDAP comes in. Using a standard mechanism (LDAP calls) against a standard system (the LDAP database), a nonstandard application is able to retrieve an authoritative user base and import it into the application database for use.

At a high level, this is a reasonable solution. The database ends up with users that exist in LDAP, thus meeting any policies requiring integration with LDAP. Unfortunately, when a synchronization model is part of an already existing application (or one a generation or two removed from the original application), coming up with a real design is often beyond the scope.

Imagine the scenario where your application uses the custom attributes First Name, Last Name, Employee Number, and UID within its own database. These may be mapped to firstname, sn, empnum, and uid, respectively, within your LDAP directory. This wouldn't cause many problems; however, if data doesn't match appropriately or ends up being split between data sources, the tasks become more difficult. What if, after a synchronization, the application needs to add new attributes and values to the data source that don't currently exist in LDAP? This splits the authority of the data into two, which becomes difficult to maintain.

However, the biggest problem with a synchronization method is requiring a full export and import of the data whenever a synchronization process is initiated. The time it'd take to retrieve just the changes between the last-scheduled synchronization process and the current time is minimal. Even performing a synchronization for a directory of 100 entries may not consume too much time. Unfortunately, as companies grow and directories increase in size, the synchronization process may need to retrieve 50,000 records complete with all attributes.

To fully demonstrate the complexity and speed at which an integration such as this can happen, I'll show you a typical environment. The user base you're dealing with is 50,000 users. The identity data within this system consists of ten attributes per user (from LDAP) and five attributes added to the system later, which may or may not be derived based on LDAP data (see Figure 1-9).

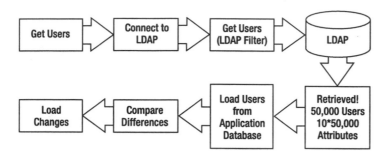

Figure 1-9. *Example of a typical environment*

In this example, you can see that you can retrieve all the users in the LDAP database, which contains 50,000 records and, because of the attributes, 500,000 lines of data. Information is then compared between the data that already exists in the application, and relevant values are updated. The application also contains five attributes of non-LDAP data (which means 250,000 extra lines of data) that need to be taken into account. In some cases, the non-LDAP data (such as local groups, custom groups, and specific application roles) is derived from information that's contained in LDAP. For example, if a user has an LDAP attribute pertaining to a certain business category, this attribute may be used to create mappings in the target application. The comparisons of all this data and the mappings that need to occur as a result often translate into many hours for the synchronization process.

A method of integration such as this has no easy solution. Often the only mechanism available for LDAP synchronization is via an application-specific interface. Cutting out the middleman and directly writing to the application database may be an option when the data stored is easily understood, but this, once again, becomes a good reason to look into metadirectories for mapping of information. It's unfortunate that many vendors choose to use LDAP synchronization models such as this one.

Shortsighted Deployment

Like anything else, LDAP can be deployed quickly and end up as a usable mess or a completely unusable data source because of lack of planning. Many applications will be potentially using your system. Take into account the data sources you have (during the integration phases) to fully understand what your system will need to look like in order to consider all applications that will be integrating with it. When approaching the initial designs of your directory information tree (DIT) and schema, keep in mind that the requirements in the beginning may not appropriately scale in the long run. A common scenario you may run across during your implementations is the lack of separation of organizationalunits. For example, take the scenario where you have a base DN of dc=Your,dc=Company with only a single level of ou=People below it. Queries will start at the top (dc=Your,dc=Company) and traverse your tree. If in the future you decide to add separate branches for application configurations, as well as trees for suppliers and other types of users outside your regular employee base, you'll need to modify all existing search queries. That is, if you start with ou=People and alongside you add ou=Suppliers, existing applications that currently set the search to start at the base DN will traverse both the ou=People and ou=Suppliers trees needlessly. Create some level of logical separation so that your filters and search scopes won't need to be regularly updated to keep up with the data that's stored in your directory.

Often you'll see that some integrated applications choose to create a DIT structure based on specific application needs. It's all too common to have the base DN followed by ou=MyApplication, underneath which all the users in your company will exist. As more applications integrate in the future, they will be reading a tree that looks like it has been designated for just a particular application. Try to keep trees generic and the formats of data standard to not give that impression.

It's all too common of a scenario during integration to have multiple user bases (that contain the same set of information) existing multiple times in the directory (see Figure 1-10).

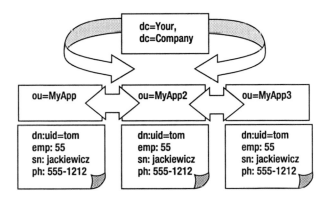

Figure 1-10. *Example tree*

As you can see, multiple user trees are in use in this DIT, all containing the same set of data. This is because each application has chosen to use its own specific structure and can't utilize the trees and data in use by the other applications. In this case, the size of your directory has tripled because it contains redundant information.

> **Tip** You can't use LDAP for everything. Realize that the best use of LDAP is for identity information of a relatively static nature. Putting dynamic nonidentity data into a directory can lead only to heartache.

Summary

Depending on when your involvement in designing your LDAP environment begins, it's always good to understand that a significant amount of work should go into creating your environment at any stage. The more planning that goes into your LDAP environment, the more use you'll get out of it. Understand the layout of data within your company, the methods of retrieving it, and the mistakes others have made in the same situations. The less structure and fewer constraints you're initially given during the initial phases of deployment, the more opportunity you have to create a robust and usable environment.

■■■

## CHAPTER 2

Understanding Data Definitions

The core of fully understanding Lightweight Directory Access Protocol (LDAP) and OpenLDAP lies in the definition of the data components. A lack of understanding of these definitions is akin to considering yourself a mechanic but never looking under the hood. I'll discuss the various components of LDAP used to make your system run. An understanding of the specifics of schemas and the standards used to define and support these data types and operations are key to being well-versed in LDAP. I'll also discuss the methods and standards used to create information outside the LDAP world (using object identifiers [OIDs] and Abstract Syntax Notation One [ASN.1]), cover LDAP-specific schema, and provide an overview of the methods used to manipulate this information.

A *schema* is a definition of what data can be stored within a system. That is, it's a set of rules by which information in a directory can determine whether data is valid. A schema is important because it not only defines an object, but also helps maintain the integrity of the data stored within your directory. A well-defined schema also can help create useful, duplicate-free data, and applications can use schemas to expect information in specific ways. A schema is constantly and consistently checked by the directory server while creating, modifying, deleting, or accessing any data within the directory. Schema definitions determine how a set of values will be treated.

In addition to schemas, I'll discuss the layout of your directory information tree (DIT) and other data elements such as LDAP Interchange Format (LDIF) and how to index information. After reading this chapter, you'll understand the layout of data in terms of LDAP and the specifics as they apply to your OpenLDAP directory. I'll also discuss OIDs, which are the global identifiers used to identify information consistently across the LDAP space. These identifiers extend beyond just LDAP and will be (or at least should be) used with all your enterprise applications.

Defining Your Schema

A schema consists of attribute names, attribute types, and attribute syntax, all held together and defined as valid data using object classes. The attribute must also be defined further to include various restrictions (or lack of) on using this data. Unfortunately, the history within LDAP to date has yielded rather ill-defined object classes and attribute definitions that are not well understood in deployments. A common schema design and object class deployment will greatly increase the utility of a directory deployment for applications and interinstitutional authorizations, white pages, and application deployment.

Before going into the OpenLDAP schema details, I'll start by saying that the schema design is critical to the planning process. Depending upon the complexity of the directory, you may need lots of planning or little at all. If all you want to provide is a simple white pages service, then this document should meet your needs. Beyond white pages, you need to answer at least the following questions:

- What are the needs of an application?

- What your goals are for the application?

- Where will the data reside?

- What will be the system of record?

- Who can change it?

- How frequently will it change?

- Should it be visible?

The schema ties together all the definitions, object classes, attributes, and any information necessary for defining your data. OpenLDAP, as other implementations, takes into account standards and provides a base set of information (core information) that will be used by your directory. Table 2-1 shows what files need to be modified in order to update your schema definitions within OpenLDAP. Not only does this provide a standard set of information that will provide you with a starting point for utilizing your directory, it ensures that you maintain compatibility across other LDAP systems. Using include lines within configuration files gives you the ability to separate configurations into their own files for cleanliness. The following is an example of this:

```
include /usr/local/etc/openldap/schema/
```

Table 2-1. *OpenLDAP's File Structure for Schema*

File	Description
Core.schema	Required OpenLDAP core
Cosine.schema	Cosine and Internet X.500 schema
Inetorgperson.schema	InetOrgPerson default schema
Misc.schema	Experimental schema
Nis.schema	Network Information Services schema for NIS/NIS+ integration
Openldap.schema	OpenLDAP project schema

I'll use the Openldap.schema file to demonstrate the overall format of schema files that you'll be using during your deployment (see Listing 2-1).

Listing 2-1. *OpenLDAP Schema Definitions, Start of Record*

```
# $OpenLDAP: pkg/ldap/servers/slapd/schema/openldap.schema,v 1.17 2001/12/07 23:
36:11 kurt Exp $
#
# OpenLDAP Project's directory schema items
#
# depends upon:
#        core.schema
#        cosine.schema
#        inetorgperson.schema
#
# These are provided for informational purposes only.

objectIdentifier OpenLDAProot 1.3.6.1.4.1.4203

objectIdentifier OpenLDAP OpenLDAProot:1
objectIdentifier OpenLDAPattributeType OpenLDAP:3
objectIdentifier OpenLDAPobjectClass OpenLDAP:4
```

The objectIdentifier is always listed at the top as an organizational component of schema files.

Further along in the file, you can see specific definitions of data outside the headers or initial definitions, as shown in Listing 2-2.

Listing 2-2. *OpenLDAP Schema Definitions, Object Classes*

```
objectClass ( OpenLDAPobjectClass:3
    NAME 'OpenLDAPorg'
    DESC 'OpenLDAP Organizational Object'
    SUP organization
    MAY ( buildingName $ displayName $ labeledURI ) )

objectClass ( OpenLDAPobjectClass:4
    NAME 'OpenLDAPou'
    DESC 'OpenLDAP Organizational Unit Object'
    SUP organizationalUnit
    MAY ( buildingName $ displayName $ labeledURI $ o ) )

objectClass ( OpenLDAPobjectClass:5
    NAME 'OpenLDAPperson'
    DESC 'OpenLDAP Person'
    SUP ( pilotPerson $ inetOrgPerson )
    MUST ( uid $ cn )
    MAY ( givenName $ labeledURI $ o ) )
```

```
objectClass ( OpenLDAPobjectClass:6
    NAME 'OpenLDAPdisplayableObject'
    DESC 'OpenLDAP Displayable Object'
    MAY displayName AUXILIARY )
```

Individual object classes are then listed, along with their schema requirements. That is, the object class of OpenLDAPorg has a superior object class of organizationalUnit and *may* have the attributes of buildingName, displayName, labeledURI, and o.

When designing your schema, you need to take into account how applications intend to utilize your directory environment and what new attributes and object classes may be required for new application functionality. Therefore, in this chapter, you'll see how to define object identifiers, attributes, and object classes in your schema file.

Understanding Schemas

As mentioned earlier, a schema ties together all the definitions, object classes, attributes, and any information necessary for defining your data. OpenLDAP, as like other implementations, takes into account standards and provides a base set of information (core information) that your directory will use. Chapter 3 discusses specific details.

You can analyze the other default schema files that come with OpenLDAP to get a greater sense of the organization of schema.

In addition to the core components available to you, you'll want to extend the schema to support additional syntaxes, matching rules, attribute types, and object classes. You'll then need to include the new schema definitions in your slapd configuration files.

You can use the objectclass and attributeTypes directives within configuration files to define schema rules within the directory. Local schema shouldn't mix with the existing schema within your system, however. You should use a local file, such as local.schema, to contain localized schema. In more complicated environments, creating multiple files for each new object class defined could separate this even more. In a typical environment, schema files may exist for the structure shown in Table 2-2.

Table 2-2. *Example of Customized Structure for Your Organization*

Schema File	Description
Local.YourCompanyPerson	Schema for internal objects
Local.YourCompanyExternalPerson	Schema for external (for example, customers, vendors, and so on) objects
Local.YourCompanyMeta	Schema for meta-directory interaction, such as the mappings between various data sources and directory objects

ASN Schema Format

LDAP uses ASN.1 to keep track of schema and many internal components of the directory. Like Extensible Markup Language (XML), ASN.1 is a standard way to format information to enable its use across multiple systems.

ASN.1 is an international standard. The benefits of a standard are that it's vendor-independent, platform-independent, and language-independent. It's a language used for specifying data structures at a high level of abstraction that enables them to be used across a large number of different systems. It's supported by rules that determine the precise bit patterns to represent values of these data structures when they have to be transferred over a computer network using a variety of encoding methods. It supports a great number of tools in order to map the ASN.1 notation to data structure definitions in the parsing language of your choosing. A good place to start when looking at ASN.1 information is the home page of the ASN.1 Consortium (`http://www.asn1.org`). There you can find links to many of the tools available to create and parse ASN.1 data. Common tools include Asnp and Ecnp. ASN.1 extensions are also available for common editors such as emacs. Online translators that convert from Web-based XML to ASN.1 are also available.

The abstract syntax used by ASN.1 enables you to produce specifications without running into various encoding issues or the specific binary- or character-based realities of a protocol. That is, it's a common language, akin to Hypertext Markup Language (HTML), that, when used correctly, enables a single set of data to be interpreted by a number of systems with the same overall results.

Familiarity with ASN.1 isn't necessary for understanding LDAP, but is required if you want a better understanding of the data structures used to configure your system. Most of the core configurations for your directory will be stored in this format. You'll be able to modify these files by using a suite of tools or by directly manipulating the configuration files.

Object Identifiers (OIDs)

A globally unique OID defines each element of schema. Like your directory, OIDs are hierarchical. You may have run across OIDs if you've interacted with a network monitoring system, because Simple Network Management Protocol (SNMP) relies heavily on OIDs for its hierarchy. Table 2-3 shows the common branching of OIDs.

Table 2-3. *Common Branching of OIDs*

OID	Assignment
1.1	Organization's OID
1.1.1	SNMP elements
1.1.2	LDAP elements
1.1.2.1	AttributeTypes
1.1.2.1.1	MyAttribute
1.1.2.2	Object classes
1.1.2.2.1	myObjectClass

The original intention was that anyone would be able to obtain an OID if they requested one. IANA, ANSI, and BSI (which is for U.K. organizations) currently maintain OID registries.

OIDs are allocated in a hierarchical manner so that the authority for 1.2.3, for example, is the only one that can specify the definition for 1.2.3.4. The formal definition of an OID comes from the ITU-T recommendation X.208 (ASN.1). The dot notation in OIDs comes from the

IETF. The ITU thought it better to have notation using spaces and braces, with optional text tables, so that 1.3.6.1 would become something like this:

```
{iso(1) org(3) dod(6) iana(1)}
{1 3 6 1}
{dod 1}
```

The IETF considered this illogical and used a dot notation instead.

Following an OID tree is akin to following a hierarchical directory tree. Starting at the top, you'll find the highest common denominator that groups all elements below it (such as the organization name). Below that, you'll find subcategories and other details up to the final destination.

The OID structure follows the same hierarchical structure you'll be familiar with from your LDAP study. At the top is the head of the tree, and information becomes more detailed when expanded (see Table 2-4).

Table 2-4. *The OID Structure*

1	ISO-assigned OIDs
1.3	ISO-identified organization
1.3.6	U.S. Department of Defense
1.3.6.1	OID assignments for Internet
1.3.6.1.4	Internet private
1.3.6.1.4.1	IANA-registered private enterprise
1.3.6.1.4.1.1466	Mark Wahl (Critical Angle)
1.3.6.1.4.1.1466.115	LDAPv3 schema framework
1.3.6.1.4.1.1466.115.121	LDAPv3 syntaxes

It's possible to look up information on specific OIDs and related subtrees in various OID registries available on the Internet. The result of inputting 1.3.6.1.4.1.1466.115.121 will yield some basic information and, often, pointers to future references, including request for comments (RFCs). Figure 2-1 shows an example of a common interface you can use for performing these lookups. One such interface is available from France Telecom at `http://asn1.elibel.tm.fr/oid/search.htm`. Using this interface, you can search the OID tree by the branch, identifier, number, description, rules, or even the parties responsible for submitting and registering specific OIDs.

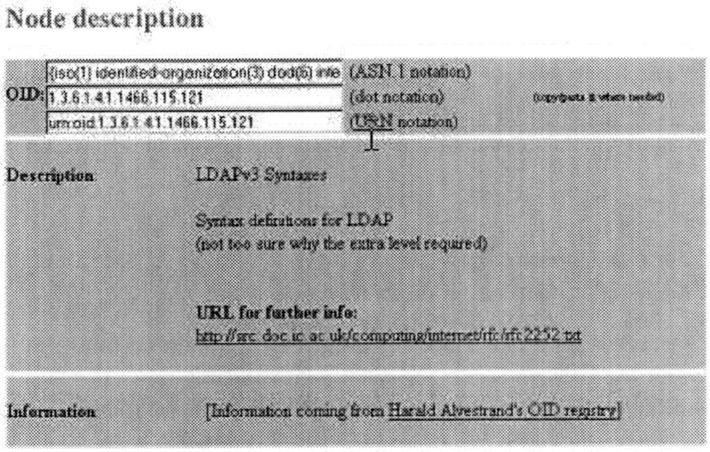

Node description

Figure 2-1. *A Web-based interface for OID lookups*

Attributes

You can use the attributeType directive to define and describe attribute information in your directory. The directory uses the RFC 2252 AttributeTypeDescription shown in Listing 2-3.

Listing 2-3. AttributeTypeDescription

```
AttributeTypeDescription = "(" whsp
Numericoid whsp      ; AttributeType identifier
[ "NAME" qdescrs ] ; name used in AttributeType
[ "DESC" qdstring ] ; description
[ "OBSOLETE" whsp ]
[ "SUP" woid ]; derived from the superior AttributeType
[ "EQUALITY" woid; matching rule name
[ "ORDERING" woid; matching rule name
[ "SUBSTR" woid ]; matching rule name
[ "SYNTAX" whsp noidlen whsp ] ; syntax OID
[ "SINGLE-VALUE" whsp ]; default multi-valued
```

```
[ "COLLECTIVE" whsp ]; default not collective
[ "NO-USER-MODIFICATION" whsp ; default user modifiable
[ "USAGE" whsp AttributeUsage ]; default userApplications
whsp " ) "

AttributeUsage =
  "userApplications" /
  "directoryOperation" /
  "distributedOperation" / ; DSA-shared
  "dsaOperation"      ; DSA-specific, depending on server
```

In Listing 2-3, whsp is a space, numericoid is a globally unique OID, qdescrs is one or more name, woid is either the name or the OID, and qdstring is a directory string.

Using the previous definitions, you can easily define a generic attribute as follows:

```
AttributeType ( 1.2.3.4.5.6 NAME 'YourCompanyAttribute'
  DESC 'MyCompany Attribute'
  EQUALITY caseIgnoreMatch
  SUBSTR caseIgnoreSubstringMatch
  SYNTAX 1.3.6.1.4.1.1466.115.121.1.15
  SINGLE-VALUE )
```

Attribute Name

As you may have guessed, an attribute name is the specific name of a single piece of data. That is, telephonenumber could be the attribute name representing someone's telephone number, for example. When accessing data, you'll always (or at least, should always) know that when you see this particular attribute name, you'll be dealing with the same type of data.

Although you can easily determine what type of data is held by the attribute named telephonenumber, this won't always be the case. You'll come across attribute names that you won't understand unless you're familiar with the particular data source, you're familiar with the application accessing the attribute, or you've created the attribute yourself.

In many cases, attribute names used by applications don't have the base requirement of being readable (or even usable) by a human traversing the directory. This is because a schema, and thus attribute names, traverse all layers of the directory, including internally used data. What applies to you, as an implementer of a specific directory infrastructure, applies to those who engineered the model originally.

In some cases, depending on the overall design of the system storing data, even having the same attribute name across different types of data will yield different results. For example, the cn attribute, typically used for the common name (which, depending on the directory, can mean many things), may store a person's first name in one branch of the tree or the Windows login name in the branch imported from an Active Directory system. Although a common practice, this is something you should avoid.

To reduce the potential for name clashes, the convention is to prefix names of attributes with an acceptable company prefix. For example, for a specific set of data, VendorData, in YourCompany, the resulting attribute name would be yourcompanyVendorData.

Additional Attribute Information

Additional data will be stored within an attribute definition. The generic information you'd need to define could include the following:

An OID that will uniquely identify the attribute across your organization or globally. These are strings of numbers that are (at the highest level) allocated by the ITU to make sure a namespace exists that your organization can work within to define more information. For example, if you were to be assigned 1.2.3.4, you'd be allowed to define data that would have the prefix of 1.2.3.4. You wouldn't be allowed to define data outside your specific prefix and have it recognized.

A set of matching rules and specifics about this data that can be used to process it. For example, you may want to know that you should ignore all the data within the telephonenumber attribute that isn't a number.

It's also helpful to know if an attribute is single-valued or multivalued. Many times it's useful to know whether the information returned is unique for the sake of data processing.

Attribute Syntax

Attributes need to be given a syntax that defines how they're to be used. This isn't only for your use (in that it helps to know that something is an integer, case sensitive, or a binary string), but it's also for the directory server when processing the information. You can read about the syntax for the specification of attributes in RFC 1778, *The String Representation of Standard Attribute Syntaxes*.

The syntax can be any of the following types:

Cis: This stands for *case ignore string*, which is a text string. The case of the letters contained within this string is completely ignored. This is case-insensitive data.

Ces: This stands for *case exact string*, which is a text string. The case is the letters contained within this string. This makes a difference when evaluating this data. This is akin to the Unix filesystem.

Tel: This stands for *telephone number*, which is a string that represents a phone number. This is just like a case ignore string except that spaces and delimiters are ignored during comparisons.

Int: This stands for *integer*. The data contained within this string contains integers and can be used within integer comparisons.

Dn: This stands for *distinguished name*. The data contained within this string is a DN. Attributes defined as distinguished names relate a specific set of data to another set. For example, the attribute manager would contain your manager's DN, thus allowing a logical connection between you and your manager. You can use DN information contained within entries to create another hierarchy of information within the directory outside the defined DIT.

Although these are generic attribute declarations, which are set based on the OID of the given attribute, you can expand the syntax of an attribute to include others. Table 2-5 shows that the standard hierarchy, 1.3.6.1.4.1.1466.115.121.1, is the start of standard LDAPv3 syntaxes.

Table 2-5. *OIDs for Attribute Syntax*

OID	Description
1.3.6.1.4.1.1466.115.121.1.3	Attribute type description
1.3.6.1.4.1.1466.115.121.1.5	Binary syntax
1.3.6.1.4.1.1466.115.121.1.6	Bit string syntax
1.3.6.1.4.1.1466.115.121.1.7	Boolean value
1.3.6.1.4.1.1466.115.121.1.8	Certificate
1.3.6.1.4.1.1466.115.121.1.9	Certificate list
1.3.6.1.4.1.1466.115.121.1.10	Certificate pair
1.3.6.1.4.1.1466.115.121.1.11	Country string
1.3.6.1.4.1.1466.115.121.1.12	DN
1.3.6.1.4.1.1466.115.121.1.14	Delivery method
1.3.6.1.4.1.1466.115.121.1.15	UTF-8 string
1.3.6.1.4.1.1466.115.121.1.16	DIT content rule
1.3.6.1.4.1.1466.115.121.1.17	DIT structure rule description
1.3.6.1.4.1.1466.115.121.1.21	Enhanced guide
1.3.6.1.4.1.1466.115.121.1.22	Facsimile telephone number
1.3.6.1.4.1.1466.115.121.1.23	Fax image
1.3.6.1.4.1.1466.115.121.1.24	Generalized time
1.3.6.1.4.1.1466.115.121.1.26	ASCII string
1.3.6.1.4.1.1466.115.121.1.27	Integer
1.3.6.1.4.1.1466.115.121.1.28	JPEG image
1.3.6.1.4.1.1466.115.121.1.30	Matching rule description
1.3.6.1.4.1.1466.115.121.1.31	Matching rule use description
1.3.6.1.4.1.1466.115.121.1.33	MHS or address
1.3.6.1.4.1.1466.115.121.1.34	DN plus UID
1.3.6.1.4.1.1466.115.121.1.35	Name form
1.3.6.1.4.1.1466.115.121.1.36	Numeric string
1.3.6.1.4.1.1466.115.121.1.37	Object class description
1.3.6.1.4.1.1466.115.121.1.38	OID
1.3.6.1.4.1.1466.115.121.1.39	Other mailbox
1.3.6.1.4.1.1466.115.121.1.40	Arbitrary octets
1.3.6.1.4.1.1466.115.121.1.41	Postal address
1.3.6.1.4.1.1466.115.121.1.43	Presentation address
1.3.6.1.4.1.1466.115.121.1.44	Printable string
1.3.6.1.4.1.1466.115.121.1.49	Supported algorithm
1.3.6.1.4.1.1466.115.121.1.50	Telephone number
1.3.6.1.4.1.1466.115.121.1.51	Teletex terminal
1.3.6.1.4.1.1466.115.121.1.52	Telex number
1.3.6.1.4.1.1466.115.121.1.53	UTC time
1.3.6.1.4.1.1466.115.121.1.54	LDAP syntax description

Matching Rules

The server uses matching rules to determine how data should be processed (see Table 2-6). Depending on the matching rule used within the attribute definition, the client knows what to expect, and the server knows how to treat any given request.

Table 2-6. *Matching Rules*

Name	Type	Description
BooleanMatch	Equality	Boolean
OctetStringMatch	Equality	Octet string
ObjectIdentifierMatch	Equality	OID
DistinguishedNameMatch	Equality	DN
UniqueMemberMatch	Equality	Name with optional UID
NumericStringMatch	Equality	Numerical
NumericStringOrderingMatch	Ordering	Numerical
NumericStringSubstringsMatch	Substring	Numerical
CaseIgnoreMatch	Equality	Case insensitive, space insensitive
CaseIgnoreOrderingMatch	Ordering	Case insensitive, space insensitive
CaseIgnoreSubstringsMatch	Substring	Case insensitive, space insensitive
CaseExactMatch	Equality	Case sensitive, space insensitive
CaseExactOrderingMatch	Ordering	Case sensitive, space insensitive
CaseExactSubstringsMatch	Substring	Case sensitive, space insensitive
CaseIgnoreIA5Match	Equality	Case insensitive, space insensitive
CaseIgnoreIA5OrderingMatch	Ordering	Case insensitive, space insensitive
CaseIgnoreIA5SubstringsMatch	Substring	Case insensitive, space insensitive
CaseExactIA5Match	Equality	Case sensitive, space insensitive
CaseExactIA5OrderingMatch	Equality	Case sensitive, space insensitive
CaseExactIA5SubstringsMatch	Substring	Case sensitive, space insensitive

The matching rules in Table 2-6 are important for describing attributes and for system indexing. The server must be made aware, via the schema definitions, how to treat an attribute so that it's evaluated appropriately.

Attribute Inheritance

Just like other data structures, attributes themselves can inherit information from superior, or parent, structures. This is useful when creating generic data types that all must follow a similar syntax. For example, assume that you have generic structures for a set of data that refers to a name. You'd want all other attributes associated with a name to inherit the same set of information so that you maintain consistency across your environment. That is, if a common name, or cn attribute, maintains certain characteristics, logic would lead you to believe that surname, or sn, would maintain the same characteristics.

For example, the following syntax describes the object name that represents the generic properties of a name:

```
AttributeType ( 2.5.4.41 NAME 'name'
  DESC 'name(s) associated with the object'
  EQUALITY caseIgnoreMatch
  SUBSTR caseIgnoreSubstringMatch
  SYNTAX 1.3.6.1.4.1.1466.115.121.1.15{32768} )
```

To expand on this definition and create a usable data structure, you could add the following:

```
AttributeType ( 2.5.4.3 NAME ( 'cn' 'commonName' )
  DESC 'common name(s) associated with the object'
  SUP name )
```

To not duplicate information provided for the definition of cn, you give only the name. The rest of the information is inherited from the superior (SUP) data type of name. When defining your own attribute standards, it's recommended that you take a similar approach within your organization. It makes standardizing data quick and easy—not just an afterthought.

Object Classes

The grouping of the attribute data is stored in an object class. An object class definition specifies what attributes should be included. Just like attribute definitions, the object class definition includes similar data, including the standard OID.

Standard object classes are part of the definition of both X.500 and LDAP systems. Certain standards are already set to ensure some level of compatibility across multiple LDAP systems. An object class, as a directive, is defined in RFC 2252, shown in Listing 2-4.

Listing 2-4. *RFC 2252's Object Class Description*

```
ObjectClassDescription = "(" whsp
  Numericoid whsp   ; Object class identifier
  [ "NAME" qdescrs ]
  ["DESC" qdstring ]
  ["OBSOLETE" whsp ]
  ["SUP" oids ]; Superior object classes
  [ ("ABSTRACT" / "STRUCTURAL" / "AUXILIARY" ) whsp ]
    ; Default structural
  [ "MUST" oids ]; Attributetypes
  [ "MAY" oids ]; Attributetypes
whsp ")"
```

In this case, whsp is a space, numericoid is a globally unique OID in numeric form, qdescrs is one or more name, qdstring is a standard directory string, and oids is one or more name and/or OID.

You'll notice that abstract, structural, and auxiliary object classes are available for definition and use. Each object class is always one of the following three types.

Abstract Object Classes

You use abstract object classes to derive other object classes, providing the common characteristics of such object classes. An entry can't belong to just an abstract object class. The object class top is an abstract object class used as a superclass of all structural object classes.

```
objectClasses: ( 2.5.6.0 NAME 'top' DESC 'Standard LDAP objectclass'
 ABSTRACT MUST
objectClass X-ORIGIN 'RFC 2256')
```

Structural Object Classes

A structural object class is defined in the structural specification of the objects (DNs) within the directory. Structural object classes are the standard type of object class used to group attributes describing standard entries within the directory. The structural object class of an entry controls the content of an entry.

```
objectClasses: (  2.16.840.1.113719.2.142.6.1.1
NAME 'ldapSubEntry'
DESC 'LDAP Subentry class, version 1'
SUP top
STRUCTURAL MAY ( cn )
X-ORIGIN 'LDAP Subentry InternetDraft' )
```

Auxiliary Object Classes

Auxiliary object classes specify data that supports the rest of the information provided by the standard data definition. For example, information related to a user's e-mail information can be contained in an auxiliary object class. Auxiliary object classes are descriptive of entries or classes of entries. Besides being a member of a structural object class, an entry may be a member of multiple auxiliary object classes.

The scope of data described by an auxiliary object class typically has a smaller scope than a structural object class does. Think of a structural object class as one that defines that an entry is a Person, yet an auxiliary object class expands upon that and also says that this Person uses Mail, has access to a Calendar, and provides other pieces of useful information. Auxiliary object classes are more dynamic. Typically, application access is stored in auxiliary object classes that are added to a smaller subset of DNs.

```
objectClasses: ( 2.5.6.15 NAME 'strongAuthenticationUser'
  DESC 'Standard LDAP objectclass'
SUP top AUXILIARY MUST ( userCertificate ) X-ORIGIN 'RFC 2256' )
```

Other Data Definition Information

I've discussed the types of information that are essential to running the core of the LDAP system. In the following sections I'll discuss the various methods of groups and how to define information in your system via roles, groups, and proprietary methods.

Groups

Just like groups in any other system that organizes sets of data, *groups* are the mechanism commonly used to organize and associate entries within your directory. A typical group entry contains a list of all the other objects (DNs) that are part of that particular designation. A directory has multiple types of groups (see Figure 2-2). With standard group configuration, the group is looked up first. Based on the contents of the group information, the members are then determined.

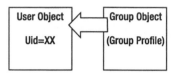

Figure 2-2. *Representation of group-to-user interaction*

Static Groups

Static group information is the most common type of group data you'll be using within your LDAP environment. A *static group* defines information that can stand alone and doesn't depend on any specific filters or further action upon obtaining the information. For example, by looking up a group defined as cn=Static Group, dc=Your, dc=Company, you have all the information present after your initial query. By referencing the following group, you can see that its members are Tom Jackiewicz and Big Snoop Dogg. No references within a static group definition point to other locations within your DIT.

```
dn: cn=Static Group,dc=Your,dc=Company
description: This is the description for Static Group
objectClass: top
objectClass: groupofuniquenames
uniqueMember: uid=Tom Jackiewicz, ou=People, dc=Your, dc=Company
uniqueMember: uid=Big Snoop Dogg, ou=People, dc=Your, dc=Company
cn: Static Group
```

Dynamic Groups

Dynamic groups specify a filter that's then used to evaluate group membership. The dynamic group cn=All Active may be a filter that searches for YourCompanyactivestatus=A across all branches of the tree. This specific example is as follows:

```
dn: cn=Dynamic Group,dc=Your,dc=Company
memberURL: ldap:///dc=Your,dc=Company??sub?
  (&(|(objectclass=YourCompanyPerson)
  (objectclass=groupofuniquenames))
  (YourCompanyActiveStatus=A))
description: This is the description for Dynamic Group
objectClass: top
```

```
objectClass: groupofuniquenames
objectClass: groupofurls
cn: Dynamic Group
```

Because of all the types of data that could be stored within your directory, you should make the groups apply only to relevant objects. In this example, you've limited the scope of the group not only to everyone whose YourCompanyActiveStatus=A, but to people containing the object class of YourCompanyPerson.

Combined Groups

Combined groups are a combination of static and dynamic groups. The following is possible by merging the previous entries:

```
dn: cn=Combined Group,dc=amat,dc=com
memberURL: ldap:///dc=Your,dc=Company??
    sub?(&(|(objectclass=YourCompanyPerson)
objectclass=groupofuniquenames))(YourCompanyActiveStatus=A))
uniqueMember: uid=Tom Jackiewicz, ou=People, dc=Your, dc=Company
uniqueMember: uid=Big Snoop Dogg, ou=People, dc=Your, dc=Company
description: This is the description for Combined Group
objectClass: top
objectClass: groupofuniquenames
objectClass: groupofurls
cn: Dynamic Group
```

In the example, the memberURL is evaluated first. Upon completion, you then add unique-Member values to the membership of the group.

Roles

Roles are a relatively new and unstandardized phenomenon in the world of modern LDAP implementations. Although they still organize or group information, just like standard group configurations, they do it in the opposite way. Instead of a group specifying its members, the user specifies to which group they belong (see Figure 2-3). With a role-based group configuration, the user is looked up first. Based on the user's profile information, data identifying the user as a member of a particular group is retrieved. The membership information then points to a particular group.

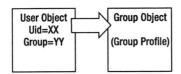

Figure 2-3. *Representation of role-based group-to-user interaction*

No standard definitions of roles are available that work in all environments.

Class of Service

Another nonstandard development in LDAP, but one that is catching on and that you should know, is Class of Service. Because one of the disadvantages of the various forms of group is the inability to agree among vendors, Class of Service was proposed as a solution for grouping sets of attributes (using proprietary mechanisms) while giving the appearance that they're part of the object being retrieved.

For instance, suppose you have a large number of employees spread across multiple offices. Each office has certain profile information, such as a mailing address, standard extensions, and such. It'd be useful to pull up a user's individual profile and have this information available during the first lookup, instead of having to rely on searching at the next group or role level to obtain information. Because each has a way to distinguish to which office they belong, you can create a simple profile that enables you to display attributes contained within the office profile in each user's individual entry. When the office profile is updated, the information is automatically displayed in each user's profile. This prevents you from having to maintain thousands of entries across multiple objects that display the same profile information.

To clients, the attributes contained with the user's profiles appear as standard attributes. It's unknown to the clients that these attributes really exist only as a Class of Service profile.

Understanding Distinguished Names (DNs)

The *primary key* is the unique identifier for the specific table within a database. A column or combination of columns will need to exist with a property that, at any given time, no two rows of the table contain the same value in that column or column combination. In other words, the DN will be the unique identifier of the system across which all other database elements are linked. The reason you could use one of more columns in a database is because in a database all data will be directly linked, using a single logical step, from one set of data to another. That is, the unique identifier serving as a telephone extension may sort one set of data, and a unique badge number can sort the other set. It's the combination of these elements that's uniquely identified by an employee number.

An example of a DN is as follows:

```
dn: uid=Tjackiewicz, ou=People, dc=Your, dc=Company
```

Schema Checking

Schema checking is an option used to maintain the integrity of your data. Whenever information within your directory is manipulated in any way, schema checking validates that the data within the entry adheres to all the object classes. Although it's common in many configurations to turn off schema checking for testing, this creates many more problems than it's generally worth. Schema checking is there to maintain integrity of your directory by making sure that all data within an entry is valid. The result of having schema checking turned off is often a significant amount of data in your system that doesn't belong.

The schema-checking option is one of the base configuration options available with your openldap.conf configuration file. I'll discuss the methods of utilizing this feature in detail in subsequent chapters.

Referential Integrity

Referential integrity is a set of rules that you can use to ensure that the relationship between entries within your directory is valid and that any changes to one set of data doesn't invalidate other information within your directory. Referential integrity is common in many databases but is typically (unfortunately) an afterthought for LDAP. LDAP vendors don't necessarily address referential integrity semantics, and each has its own way of addressing the issue. The more you dive into specific implementation of nonstandardized tools within the world of LDAP, the more locked into a particular vendor implementation you become. The typical response by OpenLDAP on the lack of referential integrity standards lets you know that for any object you create in a directory you're responsible for, no additional methods are being used to control this data. In many ways, OpenLDAP's focus on standards may be commended. However, some leadership would help ensure that important features are guided by a standards-based community rather than by commercial interests.

Common thought claims that referential integrity, at the transaction layer, hinders the light-weight nature of LDAP. LDAP specifies that manipulation to the data is atomic and that entries don't necessarily relate to each other. It has no allowance in the protocol specifications and standards set that allow manipulation of elements of the directory to have any effect on other entries.

If you desire some level of referential integrity in your system, it may be wise to use a relational database to initially store and process information (because at this point in time your data may be too complex) and then use LDAP to distribute the information.

Structuring the Directory Information Tree (DIT)

The beauty of directories lies in the hierarchical structure and the way entries in the directory relate to each other. In a standard database configuration, the primary key is the unique identifier for a table. It consists of a column or column combination that maintains uniqueness across the entire table. That is, no column or column combination can serve as a primary key if more than a single occurrence exists within the database. The primary key in an LDAP system is the DN. While the relationship between objects in a database can traverse multiple (yet well-defined) boundaries, in a directory each entry is a member of the tree and all the branches (or organizations) that lie above it (see Figure 2-4).

Figure 2-4. *DIT structure*

The top of the tree is called the *base DN*. In other words, it's the initial set of data that names the database. This component can either be the organization, defined as an o, or a series of domain components, which are defined by dc. Using the example of Your Company, you can define the base DN as o=YourCompany or dc=Your, dc=Company. The dc format is historically a remnant of the X.500 standards. The o format is part of the originally defined LDAP schema defined in early RFCs. Looking at various implementations of LDAP, the o format is typically linked hierarchically to the dc components that are used internally. In other words, o could be considered a link to the data as it's really represented—an obstruction of the data.

The value of your base DN is one of the first decisions you need to make during the architecture or installation of the system. Because a hierarchy is involved, every object in your directory can be traced back to the base DN. Thus, if you choose to change the value of this in the future, the values of all the data in your directory will change.

You have many ways to approach the overall architecture of your tree, depending on your company. Common (yet not necessarily correct) methods of organization are regional, functional, and group deployment of information. The following sections describe these in more detail.

Regional Deployment of Information

Regional deployment of information is extremely common for companies with more than one office. In the previous example, data is split between the United States and China. Many offices with global presence have split this into many organizations throughout the world. This is common, but also relies on a value indicator within the data itself to allow you to organize entries into each of these respective trees. A prerequisite of this is having the ability to map data as it comes into a variety of trees. Once this basic obstacle is passed, the future maintenance of the data requires minimal work.

Functional Deployment of Information

Functional deployment of information is, unfortunately, extremely common. This type of deployment splits branches of the tree among various functions, thus creating multiple accounts for the same person across different trees. That is, the Windows NT account of a person may exist in ou=WinNT while the dial-up information for a particular user exists in ou=Dialup. Imagine a company with 10,000 employees and 10 functional areas where accounts may exist. This would result in 100,000 DNs within your directory and would increase the overhead host of maintenance of your directory. The dynamic nature of some of this information would also require significantly more writes than a typical deployment segmented along more traditional lines. However, depending on your specific deployment and the size of your data, this can enable better maintenance and security rules based on the ability to create access control lists across branches of the tree and not individual attributes. Another drawback of this approach is that it would, in a best-case scenario, require the ability to map all the individual account information across multiple DNs to a primary account. A structure such as this is better suited for a relational database environment.

Organization by Business Function or Group

Organization along business lines is also common today. That is, you can organize Sales, Marketing, and other departments within your company (often defined by a financial hierarchy elsewhere) into separate trees. One good way to determine whether this will work for you requires trying to map out a tree of existing organizations. If this is too much work to do on paper, it may be too difficult to establish within a directory.

Introducing the LDAP Data Interchange Format (LDIF)

The format used for storing data in a directory system is defined as LDIF in RFC 2849, *The LDAP Data Interchange Format—Technical Specification*. This is comparable to an SQL statement because you can use it to generate statements for interfacing with an LDAP directory, describing LDAP information, or exporting it for use across all LDAP-compliant formats. This is a standard format that, regardless of the specific implementation or encoding methods used, you can use across all systems adhering to the defined standards.

A simple LDIF record looks like this:

```
dn: (RDN+tree)
objectclass: (Objectclass definitions)
attribute (Name): Value
```

In short, LDIF is the human-readable storage mechanism of entries in a directory or the translation of the back-end methods into a format that's easy to understand and manipulate. It serves as a buffer between the way the bits are stored for system use and the way they're usable by humans.

LDAP Operations

Additionally, you can expand records to include various commands for manipulating data within the directory. LDIF is the common language used to represent this information. You can add, modify, delete, and, in some cases, move data within a directory (see Table 2-7).

Table 2-7. *Available* Changetype *Operations*

Changetype Operation	Result
MODIFY	Modifies a set of data for an existing DN
ADD	Adds a new DN
DELETE	Deletes a DN
MODRDN	Moves the RDN from one tree to another
MODDN	If available, changes the DN of an entry

The changetype operations will need a full DN with which to work (RDN+tree). This is specified at the top of any legitimate statement. It lets the system know the DN that will be worked on.

These commands are represented as follows:

```
dn: (RDN+tree)
changetype: (CHANGETYPE OPERATION)
(ACTION) : (TARGET)
(DATA)
```

The following is a common example:

```
dn: uid=tjackiewicz,ou=People,dc=Your, dc=Company
changetype: add
objectclass: top
objectclass: inetorgperson
cn: Tom Jackiewicz
sn: Jackiewicz
uid: tjackiewicz
```

The changetype in this example is add. Once the changetype is specified, you'll see lists of object classes and attributes for input.

Changetype: add

A changetype of add specifies that you want to add a specific DN to the directory. Following the DN and the changetype operation, you'll need to specify a list of object classes and attribute names and values. To add an example to an empty system, use this:

```
dn: uid=tjackiewicz,ou=People,dc=Your, dc=Company
changetype: add
objectclass: top
objectclass: inetorgperson
cn: Tom Jackiewicz
sn: Jackiewicz
uid: tjackiewicz
```

The result of this LDIF statement is the previous entry, which I'll use for further examples.

Changetype: modify

You use the changetype operation of modify when you want to modify an entry. The modify in this case refers to attribute information within the entry itself. For example, this is the previously mentioned entry:

```
dn: uid=tjackiewicz,ou=People,dc=Your, dc=Company
objectclass: top
objectclass: inetorgperson
cn: Tom Jackiewicz
sn: Jackiewicz
uid: tjackiewicz
```

If you wanted to change the CN from Tom Jackiewicz to Thomas Jackiewicz, you'd also need to specify a specific operation to be performed on the attribute. In this case, you want to change, or replace, the value. The resulting operation is as follows:

```
dn: uid=tjackiewicz,ou=People,dc=Your, dc=Company
changetype: modify
replace: cn
cn: Thomas Jackiewicz
```

The end result, assuming the operation is successful, will change the CN attribute within this entry. When dealing with attributes that have multiple values (such as an object class), you'll also need to specify which values need to be modified.

```
dn: uid=tjackiewicz, ou=People,dc=Your, dc=Company
changetype: modify
replace: objectclass
objectclass: inetorgperson
objectclass: YourCompanyPerson
```

In this case, you replaced the object class of inetorgperson with YourCompanyPerson by specifying the existing object class on the first line and the replacement object class on the next. This will be useful when replacing sets of data stored using the same attribute, such as multiple telephone numbers, locations, and other such fields.

Changetype: modrdn

You can use the changetype operation of modrdn when the relative DN (RDN) needs to be changed. The ultimate goal of this operation is to change the naming key used to identify the entry. In this example, where the RDN is uid=tjackiewicz, you'd use this operation if you wanted to change tjackiewicz to tomjackiewicz, resulting in an RDN of uid=tomjackiewicz. Only the RDN can change here, as the object stays in the same location within the tree. Other elements of the full DN, such as the ou=People,dc=Your, dc=Company component that identifies the object's location within the tree, remain the same.

A common misconception is that the full DN of the entry, including its location within the tree, is able to change with this operation. Although that may be the case with certain implementations of LDAP, this isn't standards-based, and relying upon a full modification of a DN is inconsistent at best. To change the full DN of an entry, it's advised that the current DN be deleted and re-created in a different branch of the tree.

To use the modrdn operation, use the following statement:

```
dn: uid=tjackiewicz, ou=People,dc=Your, dc=Company
changetype: modrdn
newrdn: uid=tomjackiewicz
deleteoldrdn: 1
```

The postoperation deleteoldrdn will then take the binary flag of 0 to maintain the old DN, thus resulting in entries of uid=tjackiewicz and uid=tomjackiewicz, which both maintain the same set of data or the flag of 1 to delete the old object.

Chaining Operations

You can chain operations so that multiple operations can be performed on the same target DN. This provides a benefit because the target DN is specified only once, is imported into the server's memory, and is utilized for all the operations that need to be performed against that specific entry. This saves in server overhead. Imagine that you have 10,000 entries in a directory and need to add three object classes and five attributes to each. By chaining operations, it's possible to have only 10,000 changetype operations instead of 80,000. Like the overall model of Transmission Control Protocol/Internet Protocol (TCP/IP), it's the overhead of establishing the connection (or importing the target DN into memory) that causes the greatest delay.

One problem with chaining operations is that all the operations need to be valid (and not violate schema), or no operations are processed.

```
dn: uid=tjackiewicz, ou=People,dc=Your, dc=Company
changetype: modify
add: description
description: Description Field
-
add: invalidattribute
invalidattribute: invalidvalue
```

What you have in this scenario is an attempt to add description and invalidattribute. If adding a description field to the value is legitimate and doesn't violate schema, but adding an invalid attribute fails, both operations will result in a failure. This is the drawback of chaining operations.

Indexing Data

Indexes improve the search performance of your directory. Indexes are basically files stored on disk that are used by your directory. Individual index files are maintained for each database within the directory and for each specific attribute that's indexed. An individual index file can contain many types of indexes. Depending on the types of data in the directory and the methods that will be used to access this data, many indexes are available to you.

Presence index: This index lists entries that contain a particular attribute. For example, this will be used to determine whether this entry contains the attribute uid.

Equality index: This index lists entries that contain a specific attribute and value (for example, uid=tomjackiewicz).

Approximate index: This index allows searches for information that's approximately what's specified in the search filter. For example, a search for cn=Tom Jackiewicz would also allow cn=Thomas Jackiewicz or cn=Tom W Jackiewicz to be returned.

Substrings index: This index allows for wildcard searches within attribute values. For example, a search for uid=*ackie* would return uid=tomjackiewicz. It must be noted that a significant amount of overhead is required for this type of index; use it sparingly. Unfortunately, depending on which products you choose to interact with your directory, many vendors assume all directory entries have this entry. Performing a substring search against an attribute that doesn't contain this entry will result in significant resource utilization and slow return times for operations.

International index: This index is reserved for OID searches.

Browsing index: While not present in all directory implementations, this index increases the speed of displaying search branches within your tree.

To fully understand indexing, take into account the relative size of the data you're storing in your directory. Certain searches, because of their frequency of use, may be required to perform better than others. A query for a person's name will be used by multiple applications, from your phone books to e-mail system. However, doing a partial, substring, or wildcard search for a city starting with *San Fr* may be something considerably less common (and discouraged). Indexing allows you to cache certain information that's required for lookups on a regular basis and incurs the system overhead that this would entail. The fundamental advantage of an index is that it speeds up retrieval. However, the overhead that this takes can be measured in more than just the amount of memory that needs to be allocated. Each update performed will also need to write out data to the index cache if the values being updated are indexed. This will decrease the speed up updates across your system.

With a system with a significant amount of data, you need to consider many things when determining whether to index an attribute. For example, in a dynamic organization, you should consider whether you want to index the department number contained within a person's entry. Because of the dynamic nature of your organization, this data often changes. Whenever a change occurs to the indexed attribute representing a department number, the update to the data is slower than it'd be if no index were used.

Because of the cascading nature of LDAP systems, you'd have good reason to create different indexes on different types of hosts. For master systems, which are the ones primarily used to update data, a minimal amount of indexes may be necessary to speed up the update speed. For systems that look outwardly at clients, such as random consumers existing in a replicated environment, the number of indexes could be greater. This is because updates aren't performed directly on the consumers but forwarded to the master hosts (see Figure 2-5).

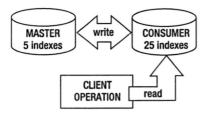

Figure 2-5. *Workflow of client operations in a replicated environment*

Summary

You should now be able to understand the various data types and formats that will be used within your OpenLDAP deployment. Your understanding of OIDs, ASN.1 notation, schemas, and LDIF will help you get the most out of later chapters. Your understanding of changetype operations will allow you to manipulate data within the directory to serve your needs.

■ ■ ■

## CHAPTER 3

Implementing Deployment, Operations, and Administration Strategies

For many, simply installing software on a system signals the end of the project. But for system administrators, the process of maintaining an installation, troubleshooting it, and debugging it—*administering*—has just begun. In management's perfect world, software runs itself, nothing ever breaks, and you can just let something sit untouched until it has outlived its usefulness. This isn't the case—your fun is just beginning.

It will benefit you to understand the basic concepts of environment deployment, name standardization, and system optimization in order to best run an OpenLDAP environment. In this chapter, I'll discuss the basics of environment setup and describe some of the tools required to successfully run an OpenLDAP environment.

Separating Your Environments

Environment separation, which is your ability to physically or logically isolate environments, is often quite difficult to accomplish at a well-established company but is achievable at the beginning. Without having any level of separation within your environment, you reduce your ability to expand without having to rearchitect your existing systems. That is, your environment may be so flat that adding new components to your system will have a negative impact on your existing environment. Although you may not always be able to do something about the problem, it's necessary to view the topography of the network you'll be using to understand complexities in your OpenLDAP deployment.

Unlike an isolated system, OpenLDAP often relies on network services and data stored outside its own host. The potential for multiple environments that are configured to share a common set of data to corrupt or cause disruption is high. You can prevent the overlapping of data between a system being used for testing and one that's running in a production state by appropriately separating the two environments. This separation will allow you to perform tests of varying levels of impact without disrupting existing services. Imagine needing to perform an upgrade on a development system that's tied to your production environment. Your ability to do this will be hindered because any errors that are made will be introduced into your production environment. How you implement the separation will depend on the goal of each environment. In a typical organization, an environment could be split into one (or even many) groups.

The following are common environments:

- **Development**: In this environment, standard development on your systems takes place. Development can mean many things depending on your organization.

- **Staging**: After software is developed or new system configurations are established, they're commonly moved from a development environment to a staging environment.

- **Production**: The final move of new software or new system configuration is into the production environment.

The following are some other common environments:

- **Engineering**: Engineering work is performed in one environment.

- **Quality assurance**: The result of engineering work goes through the quality assurance (QA) procedures. Depending on the type of tasks being performed, QA environments often have a completely different set of network services, such as Domain Name Service (DNS) and Simple Mail Transfer Protocol (SMTP) servers.

- **Operations**: Upon approval by the QA department, information is passed onto operations. This is where all engineering products that have passed QA end.

All these types of environments can be divided into even more environments depending on the size and scope of your infrastructure. You could have hosts for internal access, external access only, external access by internal resources, internal access by external resources, demilitarized zones (DMZ) systems, and so on. The ability to manage these different infrastructures relies on the appropriate separation of the resources and valid (and current) documentation. It's also common to separate different departments so that consistency can be maintained on that (or any other) level. That is, it may be a good idea to have your finance department on a different network segment than the help desk because of the sensitive nature of the data going over the wire.

Regardless of the names used for each of these environments, the idea is the same. You separate different sets of hosts that aren't meant to specifically interact with each other into different network segments and split them into different domains or DNS zones.

Imagine a common scenario where YourCompany's resources exist in a single local area network (LAN) with the DNS name of YourCompany.com (see Figure 3-1). All machines are within the same domain, have random ranges of Internet Protocol (IP) addresses, and can access the same information on the LAN.

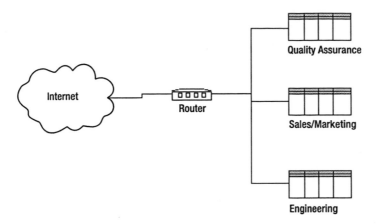

Figure 3-1. *Typical network separation, logical networks*

What you see in Figure 3-1 is a simplified network utilizing a single router. All environments are in the same network. In some cases, production systems and the DMZ (if the illusion of one exists) just hang off the same physical layer.

What happens if interns with no security clearance are brought in to do data entry for one department? The interns would have access to the entire network and could actually view network traffic within the entire environment. What happens when traffic patterns between departments differ (or when someone is doing some performance and load testing)? What happens when the performance required for external-facing systems isn't achievable because of out-of-control internal network traffic?

Many people realize that there needs to be physical separation between environments on the network level and have created complicated, and often high-performance, network topologies to take advantage of the technology readily available today. Companies may use expensive Layer 3 switches, virtual LANs (VLANs), and oddball packet-shaping tools, only to have their architectures defeated by inadequate planning. What's often overlooked is the logical separation between environments on the system side. It seems that while the world of networks has been advancing at a rapid pace, the concept of naming, often put solely in the domain of system administrators, has been at a standstill. Networks will be separated by a number of different layers—all controlled by a single DNS server and single domain name. What happens when YourCompany.com needs different levels of security based on different environments yet you have no easy way to group the information?

Let's assume that YourCompany.com has created a LAN environment that allows for easy scalability. At first it relied on a single connection out to the Internet with limited network hardware. Because of a good level of initial planning, the architects didn't just dive into the network architecture and create a large mess that would take months (or years!) to clean up. An environment was created with logically and (somewhat) physically separated networks to eventually create an appropriately scalable LAN. Nothing is worse than attempting to create a controlled network environment only to have it become a mess.

In this configuration (see Figure 3-2), YourCompany.com has each environment hanging off the same physical network connected by routers, hubs, or switches, giving the illusion of a physically segmented network. In this newly created environment, YourCompany.com realized that by segmenting areas into physically separate LANs, all changes would be controlled through individual switches, hubs, or routers. If the company later needs to increase performance for a particular department or change a network configuration, it can do this through the network devices themselves.

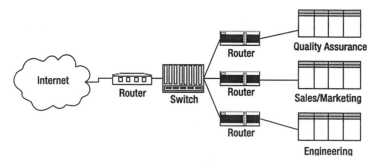

Figure 3-2. *Typical network separation, physical networks*

In addition, YourCompany.com has created separations in DNS for all the networks—for example, eng.YourCompany.com and 192.168.30.0/24, as well as qa.YourCompany.com and 192.168.20.0/24. This allows for changes per environment and gives you the ability to delegate control of naming each environment to its own administrators and servers as the environment grows. This setup gives you no immediate performance benefits but becomes invaluable as the company needs major architectural changes in the future.

Setting Up Classes of Hosts

Ultimately, you'll be deploying more than just a generic OpenLDAP host within your infrastructure. As the infrastructure grows, you may have multiple hosts mastering data, with some hosts responsible just for replicating data, and a number of different classes of consumers used for different purposes. It's important to be able to differentiate each of these hosts.

Master host: The *master host* (or, in some cases, hosts) is the primary host that's mastering data. This host is typically not accessible to the end user and most clients. Typically, master hosts have only the indexes necessary for standard operations to reduce overhead. That is, you may not want to have the same number of indexes on the master host than that of a consumer used by the phone book. Having the telephone number indexed on a master host would negatively impact update performance.

Replica head: The *replica head* is the host in the infrastructure serving as a buffer between the master and the various consumers. Its only responsibility is to replicate data across the environment. The same rules for indexing that apply to master hosts would apply to replica heads.

Application host: An *application host* could be a standard host that exists even outside of your standard system but maintains the base schema and configurations you've standard-ized throughout your environment. That is, a vendor may need to sit on top of a Lightweight Directory Access Protocol (LDAP) system and add various configurations you wouldn't want to exist throughout your LDAP infrastructure. The vendor installs an LDAP host, but for the sake of future integration, it'd be wise for even this host (or set of hosts) to maintain at least the same base distinguished name (DN), schema, and naming schema that your produc-tion systems do.

Consumer: A *consumer* is a standard host, configured as an LDAP consumer, that main-tains all the standard configurations for use by known applications. Because different types of queries are performed against the system, it'd be wise to investigate the types of queries that each set of applications may perform and then distribute their loads across a number of different systems.

Depending on the size of your environment, you may have multiple classes of con-sumer hosts for different purposes. These hosts often exist to handle certain types of con-trolled queries. By *controlled*, I mean that you know the specific types of applications that are integrated, or querying, your environment. Standard consumers that pull a small range of data may have a different set of configurations than consumers used to query larger por-tions of data (in other words, those used for application synchronization). Table 3-1 shows an example.

Table 3-1. *How Applications May Use LDAP*

Type of Application	Type of Query	Scope of Search	Target Host
Phone book	Simple queries	Very specific Indexed Returns 0 to 25 entries	Consumer 1
Limited scope application	Specific queries on department	General queries, specific scope Indexed Returns up to 250 entries	Consumer 1
Synchronization application	Queries entire user population	Large scope Unindexed Returns entire database	Consumer 2
Uncontrolled application	Random, unknown queries	Unknown scope Indexed and unindexed Returns random information	Consumer 2

Table 3-1 has different types of LDAP interactions split into Consumer 1 and Consumer 2. For certain applications, where the types of queries are relatively static, or at least have low over-head, the applications are pointed to one set of consumers, Consumer 1. The type of informa-tion being pulled is known, and little chance exists of a query hindering system performance so much that other applications suffer.

The second type of application, one that's a bit more dangerous to deploy in your environ-ment, has the advantage of accessing data from Consumer 2. Applications can query your entire database and even utilize all your LDAP server's system resources, but they won't impact the other, friendlier applications. Depending on the number of "abusive" applications you have in your environment, you may want to create multiple consumer groups.

Using Naming Conventions

Lack of naming standards for components within the LDAP environment is one of the biggest problems facing today's administrators. I'll stress the importance of these standards in this section to make sure they don't become an afterthought during your OpenLDAP deployment.

When your system is healthy and all components of your infrastructure are working correctly, it becomes extremely easy to overlook naming as a critical part of your system. By *naming*, I'm referring to the implementation of naming conventions within your enterprise for everything from hosts to disks, including the appropriate labeling of cables. When something goes wrong, it can mean the difference between a quick fix and a score of mistakes attempting to figure out how everything is connected and what roles each host on your network plays. You need to envision an appropriate naming convention for all components that have any relation to your systems, including routers, disks, filesystems, and even cables. However, this book sticks to the naming of hosts, as these other components are in the realm of system administration and are beyond the scope of this book. Many references are available that demonstrate best practices in name standardization. You can start with the white papers available from Sun Microsystems, request for comments (RFCs), and industry-standard Web sites.

People have argued about how to name hosts since, well, the first host needed a name. The following sections describe the two main sides to the issue of how to name a host—creative and logical.

■Note RFC 2345, *Domain Names and Company Name Retrieval*, discusses complications related to naming conventions and DNS. The document proposes a company-name-to-URL-mapping service based on Whois in order to explore whether an extremely simple and widely deployed protocol can succeed where more complex and powerful options have failed or, as it usually the case, have been excessively delayed. You should read this interesting document to gain a deeper perspective of the issues facing the lack of unity on the Internet today.

Using the Creative Convention

You've probably seen creative naming for hosts and other devices for years. The creative namers are those responsible for TheyKilledKenny, neptune, and RedJumpSuiteWithTwoBrainsInMyHair—along with various abuses of naming standards focusing on underscores and special characters. The overall idea is that the name of a host should be easy to remember and not be confused with other hosts. No one will confuse neptune and Jupiter, but hosts with similar names (with different numbers, as I'll discuss later) are often thought to be a problem point. This side argument is that nobody expects to learn much about a person by their name (names are just arbitrary tags), so the same concept applies to computers.

One of the problems with creating naming is the inability to debug systems using the smallest amount of tool sets available. If one has to rely on a set of spreadsheets, previous knowledge of the hosts, and other tools in order to understand the host infrastructure, it'd be difficult to, in a panic, quickly discover and resolve problems. Look at the following traceroute example:

```
$ /usr/sbin/traceroute pillow.host.com
traceroute to pillow.host.com (192.168.10.31), 30 hops max, 38 byte packets
gino.host.com (192.168.10.3)  0.390 ms  0.315 ms  0.266 ms
fershizzle.host.com (192.168.10.18) ...
b00gab00ga.host.com (192.168.10.99) ...
ILIKEMEAT.host.com (192.168.10.105) ...
Pillow.host.com (192.168.0.31) ...
```

While slightly amusing ("Dude, they've got a host named fershizzle!"), the output of the traceroute is rendered almost useless. By looking at this output, it isn't possible to tell what each of the devices is, the role each plays within the infrastructure, and how to start approaching the problem you're attempting to debug.

RFC 1178

RFC 1178, *Choosing a Name for Your Computer*, shows one method for choosing appropriate names, as well as inappropriate names, for various hosts within your infrastructure. It shows simple guidelines for names that you should avoid. By choosing good names for hosts, you can avoid many problems in host identity, confusion, and conflict.

Don't use terms already in use, such as reserved words. For example, choosing hostnames based on things commonly in use during your daily speech is inappropriate. For example, say a distributed database had been built on top of several computers. Each one had a different name. One machine was named up, as it was the one that accepted updates. "Is up down?" doesn't make the context of up obvious and creates a "Who's on first?" scenario.

The following are other recommendations:

Don't choose a name after a project unique to that machine: If a machine is originally provisioned for a single purpose, and it's named after that specific purpose, a great deal of confusion could arise in the future if the initial scope changed. As I discuss other naming conventions, you'll learn obvious solutions for when this happens (which is actually quite desirable at times). However, realize that it's difficult to choose generic names that stay valid.

Don't use your own name: Even if a computer is sitting on your desk, it's a mistake to name it after yourself.

Don't use long names: Although it may be hard to quantify, experience has shown that names longer than eight characters simply annoy people. Most systems allow prespeci-fied abbreviations, but why choose a name that you don't need to abbreviate in the first place? This removes any chance of confusion.

Avoid alternate spellings: Although it'd be a nice tribute to those from the eastern block of Europe, having a host named after the Polish spelling of Warsaw (Warszawa) isn't the best name for a host. Spelling varies, such as those used by gangstah rappyhz t' hizzify theirrr fershizzle awrnt n3sessar1leee rell-uh-vent.

Avoid domain names: In particular, name resolution of nonabsolute hostnames is problematic.

Avoid organizational (domainlike) names: That is, domain names are either organizational or geographical. Naming yourself after something that conjures up images of something else could lead to confusion. The name Tahiti sitting in a data center in Topeka may be misleading.

Don't use antagonistic or otherwise embarrassing names.

Don't use digits at the beginning of the name.

Don't use special, nonalphanumeric characters in a name.

Don't expect case to be preserved: Hostnames shouldn't require case sensitivity. However, in all files, directories, and databases, you should decide on a standard format for names (in other words, keeping them all lowercase or uppercase) and preserve that consistency.

Rules for proper hostnames, according to RFC 1178, are as follows:

Use words/names that are rarely used: While words such as *typical* and *up* aren't necessarily computer jargon, they're just too likely to arise in a discussion and throw off one's concentration while determining the correct referent. Words such as *lurch* and *squire* would cause less confusion.

Use theme names: Naming groups of machines in a common way is popular and enhances communality while displaying depth of knowledge and imagination. A simple example is to use colors. You should avoid certain finite sets, such as the seven dwarfs or good white rappers, because your infrastructure is likely to grow beyond this set. Mythical places, people, elements, and others are more scalable. Avoid using famous Russian cricket players.

Use real words: Random strings are inappropriate for the same reason they're so useful for passwords. They're hard to remember.

Don't worry about reusing someone else's hostname: You should avoid extremely well-known hostnames since they're understood in conversations as absolute addresses even without a domain (for example, uunet and InterNIC).

And, remember, there's always room for an exception.

Most people don't have the opportunity to name more than one or two computers, but site administrators name large numbers of them. By choosing a name wisely, both users and administrator will have an easier time remembering, discussing, and typing the names of the computers.

The process of changing your hostname is, according to all your system manuals, extremely easy. However, you'll find that lots of obscure software has rapidly accumulated that refers to computers using their original names. You'd have to find and quickly change all the references to your old hostname. Everything from e-mail systems to backup software needs to be informed of the new hostname. So while the process of changing the name is often quick and easily, the repercussions are often severe and can cause great headaches. Pick hostnames, and stick with them. This will save you a great deal of time.

RFC 2100

RFC 2100 illustrates in a humorous way the need for name standardization (see Listing 3-1).

Listing 3-1. *Why People in IT Aren't Poets*

```
The Naming of Hosts is a difficult matter,
        It isn't just one of your holiday games;
    You may think at first I'm as mad as a hatter
        When I tell you, a host must have THREE DIFFERENT NAMES.
    First of all, there's the name that the users use daily,
        Such as venus, athena, and cisco, and ames,
    Such as titan or sirius, hobbes or europa--
        All of them sensible everyday names.
    There are fancier names if you think they sound sweeter,
        Some for the web pages, some for the flames:
    Such as mercury, phoenix, orion, and charon--
        But all of them sensible everyday names.
    But I tell you, a host needs a name that's particular,
        A name that's peculiar, and more dignified,
    Else how can it keep its home page perpendicular,
        And spread out its data, send pages world wide?
    Of names of this kind, I can give you a quorum,
        Like lothlorien, pothole, or kobyashi-maru,
    Such as pearly-gates.vatican, or else diplomatic-
        Names that never belong to more than one host.
    But above and beyond there's still one name left over,
        And that is the name that you never will guess;
    The name that no human research can discover--
        But THE NAMESERVER KNOWS, and will usually confess.
    When you notice a client in rapt meditation,
        The reason, I tell you, is always the same:
    The code is engaged in a deep consultation
        On the address, the address, the address of its name:
                    It's ineffable,
                    effable,
                    Effanineffable,
                    Deep and inscrutable,
                    singular
                    Name.
```

Using the Logical Convention

Logical naming is the idea that a host or a device on the network should have names based on the function of the host, plus a combination of other factors, including the location. You have many ways to approach this topic.

Data Center Layout

Many well-organized companies have large data centers that take care of all their data-processing needs. These large data centers, which were the "next big thing" during the escalation of technology to the level it's at today, are well organized based on the physical location of the rack of equipment being used. You can use lessons learned from these major data centers deployments to guide you when you're establishing your naming practices.

A data center, on paper, is a grid comprised of X, Y, and Z coordinates. The grid is formed using the computer room tiles or some other identifying feature. Often, a pole or support location (with a unique number) is also used. Based on the physical location of a particular server within the data center, you can generate a coordinate. If a particular coordinate is 24B8, which may represent that a server is located at tiles 24 and B and located 8 units high (on the rack itself), you can incorporate this particular designation into the hostname.

The end result, depending on the rest of the naming convention being used, could be DC05-SUN-24B8.

Pure Function

Another way to approach hostnames is based on the role that the particular host plays within your enterprise. Every system you deploy plays a particular role, and in many cases, these roles can be split into multiple groups, as shown in the following lists.

For example, a mail services system may have incoming and outgoing mail transport functions and mail storage in several locations. The hosts could be named as follows:

- MTI01, for [M]ail[T]ransport[I]ncoming01

- MTO05, for [M]ail[T]ransport[O]utgoing05

- MSSC09, for [M]ail[S]torage[S]anta[C]lara09

- MSCH03, for [M]ail[S]torage[CH]ina03

An LDAP application with master, replica head, and slave hosts in various locations could use names such as these:

- LDAPMCH, for [LDAP][M]aster[CH]ina05

- LDAPRHS, for [LDAP][R]eplica[H]ead[S]eattle01

The idea is to be able to determine the role based on the hostname. You can tell this naming system is in use when you see hostnames such as LDAP-RH-05.

Function and Major Designation

A variation of functional-based naming also combines other relevant information into the name of a host. This information can be the location within the data center, the location within the rack, its significance within the architecture, or some other designation. The resulting hostname is always cryptic, but to those familiar with the naming convention used, it's relevant and often helpful.

Reaching a Compromise

While the debate will continue, a compromise exists. The big misconception is that a host can have only one name—which is either logical or creative. This isn't the case. Within DNS, multiple names for a host exist in the form of A or CNAME records. CNAME records are "canonical name" records in DNS, which often represent the true name or alias of a host. Within your DNS configurations, you may see this:

```
www          IN     A       216.240.45.70
toaster      IN     CNAME   www
```

This shows that the A record for the particular host is set to www, and the CNAME is toaster. Debates surround whether the A record or CNAME record should be used to represent the true name of a host or the alias, but I'll leave that up to you to determine.

The overall idea is that a naming scheme can take advantage of aliases to enable the use of multiple names for different purposes.

Following Standard Procedures

The following are some basic requirements for standard procedures:

- You should have a set of standard operating procedures for everything deployed within your environment.

- You should have standard procedures for every component.

- Every set of procedures should adhere to the standards.

Additionally, a set of standard operating procedures should exist for everything deployed within your environment. Any set of procedures should adhere to the standards set within your organization. Standard procedures should exist for every component within your infrastructure where there are options. That is, if there is more than one way of doing something, you should document it. And even if there's only one way of doing something, a base set of documentation should exist to ensure that every task is accomplished correctly.

Using the Standard Host Specifications

Documents should exist that list the type of servers used for your LDAP environment. Standardization on the vendor, the model, and the specific internal configurations will always ensure parity within your environment. Maintaining consistent system configurations will alleviate any problems you may have in future debugging sessions; in addition, hardware that's the same will react the same. Many times a specific system problem results from a different physical network card being configured on a host. Always maintain consistent configurations for the same class of host (see Table 3-2).

Table 3-2. *Document-Relevant System Information*

Host Class	System Type	OS Version/Patch Level	Network Information	Vendor Data
MASTER	SUNW, Sun-Fire-880; 8192MB RAM	5.8 Generic_108528-26	192.168.0.1/ 255.255.255.0/MAC address, and so on	PO 12345, Information necessary to reorder, and so on
CONSUMER	SUNW,UltraAX-i2; 1024MB RAM	5.8 Generic_108528-13	...	...

Using the Standard Host Installation

It's necessary to know more than just the base hardware specifications of a host. A host with the same basic hardware profile will react differently based on the installation of the operating system, postinstallation parameters, and configurations at other levels. You'll need to document the base host parameters in detail, including the following:

Base image or installation instructions: Many system administrators take advantage of automated installation features available to most modern operating systems. Solaris has Jumpstart, and Linux has Kickstart. Other organizations have a junior system administrator to perform the tasks of automating and standardizing basic operating system installations.

Postinstallation parameters: Once the base image of a host is deployed and the system is accessible, a considerable amount of work needs to be done to configure a host for a particular task. Appropriate documentation shows what postinstallation parameters need to be included as part of a specific host deployment.

An example (using Solaris as a starting point) of such a reference document may include the set of information that would be configured in various operating system–related files. In the /etc/system file, you may have the following set of data configured:

```
set rlim_fd_cur=8192
set rlim_fd_max=8192
set eri:adv_autoneg_cap=0
set eri:adv_100T4_cap=0
set eri:adv_100fdx_cap=1
set eri:adv_100hdx_cap=0
set eri:adv_10fdx_cap=0
set eri:adv_10hdx_cap=0
```

The startup script S69inet (in /etc/rc2.d) may contain the following Transmission Control Protocol (TCP) parameters that optimize the TCP performance of your host:

```
ndd -set /dev/tcp tcp_deferred_ack_interval 5
ndd -set /dev/tcp tcp_smallest_anon_port 8192
ndd -set /dev/tcp tcp_strong_iss 2
ndd -set /dev/tcp tcp_ip_abort_interval 60000
ndd -set /dev/tcp tcp_ip_abort_cinterval 10000
ndd -set /dev/tcp tcp_rexmit_interval_initial 500
ndd -set /dev/tcp tcp_keepalive_interval 600000
```

```
ndd -set /dev/tcp tcp_time_wait_interval 30000
ndd -set /dev/eri adv_autoneg_cap 0
ndd -set /dev/eri adv_100T4_cap 0
ndd -set /dev/eri adv_100fdx_cap 1
ndd -set /dev/eri adv_100hdx_cap 0
ndd -set /dev/eri adv_10fdx_cap 0
ndd -set /dev/eri adv_10hdx_cap 0
```

The specific parameters may be different depending on your host and the specific interfaces used. Some hosts would use /dev/eri, and others would use /dev/hme. Also, these settings may change from host to host.

Only specific services would need to start up within your environment to comply with security standards that are in place. These could be as follows:

```
K21mwa
K28nfs.server
README
S01MOUNTFSYS
S05RMTMPFILES
S20sysetup
S21perf
S30sysid.net
S40llc2
S60random
S68arm
S69inet
S70hplwdce
S71ldap.client
S71rpc
S71sysid.sys
S72autoinstall
S72inetsvc
S73cachefs.daemon
S73nfs.client
S74autofs
S74syslog
S74xntpd
S75cron
S75flashprom
S75savecore
S77sf880dr
S80PRESERVE
S80lp
S88sendmail
S88utmpd
S92volmgt
S93cacheos.finish
S94ncalogd
```

```
S94vxnm-host_infod
S94vxnm-vxnetd
S95ncad
S95vxvm-recover
S96vmsa-server
S98efcode
S98opensshd
S99audit
S99iplanet
S99local.ldap
s99dtlogin
```

It's always necessary to document every parameter that may differentiate the installation of your host from the standard installation. Oracle installations will have a special set of requirements, and DNS servers may have their own, so LDAP should have a basic set of post-configuration parameters to ensure it's working appropriately and configured in a specific way. Each of these parameters need to be documented and understood by everyone so there won't be any future conflicts or wrong ideas about the system configuration. Also remember that with each revision of the operating system, you need to reexamine these parameters.

Using the Standard Application Installation

It's just as important to understand, and automate, all the specific application configurations you've created. The default installation for any application is simple enough, but the customizations required for an application to run within your environment usually aren't.

Running the Application

The OpenLDAP server, slapd, is designed to run as a stand-alone application. This allows it to take advantage of caching, manage concurrency issues with underlying databases, and conserve system resources. Typically, you invoke slapd during system startup out of the /etc/rc scripts. Upon startup, slapd normally forks and disassociates itself from the invoking tty. If configured, the process will print its process ID into a .pid file for convenience.

Starting the Application

In general, you run slapd like this:

```
/usr/local/etc/libexec/slapd [<option>]*
```

Other command-line options are available; the latest options for preferences are available in the 8C man pages for the application. The general syntax is as follows:

```
/usr/local/libexec/slapd [-[4|6]] [-T (a|c|i|p)]
[-d debug-level] [-f slapd-config-file]
[-h URLs] [-n service-name] [-s syslog-level]
[-l syslog-local-user] [-r directory]
[-u user] [-g group] [-t] [-c cookie]
```

where /usr/local/etc/libexec is determined by configure and where <option> is one of the options described in the following sections—or in slapd (8). Unless you've specified a debugging level (including level 0), slapd will automatically fork and detach itself from its controlling terminal and run in the background.

Stopping the Application

To kill slapd safely, you should give a command like this:

```
kill -INT `cat /usr/local/var/slapd.pid`
where /usr/local/var is determined by configure.
```

Killing slapd by a more drastic method (with the -9 switch, for example) may cause information loss or database corruption. Your operating system may also have the pkill utility available. This gives you the ability to kill a process based on the pgrep output of the process listing.

Using Command-Line Options

The following command-line options are available to slapd and can impact how the server runs:

-4: Listen on Ipv4 addresses only.

-6: Listen on Ipv6 addresses only.

-d <debug level>: This turns on debugging as defined by the debug level. If this option has been specified, even with a zero argument, slapd won't fork or disassociate itself from the invoking tty. Some generation operation and status messages are printed for any value of the debug level specified. This operation is taken as a bit string, with each bit corresponding to a different kind of debugging information.

-s <syslog-level>: This option tells slapd at which level debugging statements should be logged to the syslog (8) facility.

-n <service-name>: This specifies the service name for logging and other purposes. This defaults to the basename of argv[0], or slapd.

-l syslog-local-use: Selects the local user of the syslog (8) facility. Values can be LOCAL0, LOCAL1, and so on, up to LOCAL7. The default is LOCAL4. However, this option is permitted only on systems that support local users with the syslog (8) facility.

-f slapd-config-file: Specifies the slapd configuration file. The default is /usr/local/etc/openldap/slapd.conf.

-h URLlist: slapd will by default serve ldap:/// (LDAP over TCP on all interfaces on the default LDAP port). That is, it will bind using INADDR_ANY and port 389. You can use the -h option to specify LDAP (and other scheme) uniform resource locators (URLs) to serve. For example, if slapd is given -h "ldap://127.0.0.1:9009/ ldaps:/// ldapi:///", it will bind 127.0.0.1:9009 for LDAP, 0.0.0.0:636 for LDAP over TLS, and LDAP over IPC (Unix domain sockets). Host 0.0.0.0 represents INADDR_ANY. A space-separated list of URLs is expected.

The URLs should be LDAP (ldap://), LDAP over TLS (ldaps://), or LDAP over IPC (ldapi://) without a DN or other optional parameters, except an experimental extension to indicate the permissions of the underlying socket on those operating systems that honor them. Support for the latter two schemes depends on selected configuration options. You can specify hosts by name or by Ipv4 and IPv6 address formats. Ports, if specified, must be numeric. The default ldap:// port is 389, and the default ldaps:// port is 636. You indicate the socket permissions for LDAP over IPC by x-mod=-rwxrwxrwx, x-mod=0777, or x-mod=777, where any rwx can be - to suppress the related permission (note, however, that sockets honor only the w permission), and 7 can be any legal octal digit, according to chmod (1).

-r directory: Specifies a chroot jail directory. slapd will chdir (2) and then chroot (2) to this directory after opening listeners but before reading any configuration file or initializing any back end.

-u user: slapd will run slapd with the specified username or ID, and that user's supplementary group access list as set with init-groups (3). The group ID is also changed to this user's GID, unless the -g option is used to override.

-g group: slapd will run with the specified group name or ID.

Note On some systems, running as a nonprivileged user will prevent passwd back ends from accessing the encrypted passwords. Note also that any shell back ends will run as the specified nonprivileged user.

-t: slapd will read the configuration file (the default if none is given with the -f switch) and check its syntax, without opening any listener or database.

Implementing Logs

The ability to store, view, monitor, and analyze log files will make or break the success of your application. Configuring or running an application blind (in other words, with no use of log files or low log levels) is dangerous because you're running without the ability to foresee potential problems or warning messages.

OpenLDAP log file configurations are set in your slapd.conf configuration file. I'll use /var/log/slapd-log for these examples. The information stored in this file is determined by the log level at which your server is running. This information can be useful in tracking what operations are performed against your server and your server's response to them. You can keep track of the types of applications connecting to your system and track the queries that are performed. This can ultimately give you ideas on system or application tuning.

To demonstrate the format of information, let's perform a search against your server. I'll ask for all entries that contain an objectclass (filter of objectclass=*) and return the cn and uid attributes.

```
$ ldapsearch -b "dc=Your,dc=Company" -x "objectclass=*" cn uid
```

The resulting entry in your log file is as follows:

```
Feb 17 12:49:53 ldaphost slapd[4359]: daemon: conn=7448 fd=43 connection from
 IP=127.0.0.1:40629 (IP=:: 389) accepted.
Feb 20 12:49:53 ldaphost slapd[4359]: conn=7448 op=0 BIND dn="" method=128
Feb 20 12:49:53 ldaphost slapd[4359]: conn=7448 op=0 RESULT tag=97 err=0
text=Feb 20 12:49:53 ldaphost slapd[4359]: conn=7448 op=1 SRCH
 base="ou=people,dc=Your,dc=Company" scope=2 filter="(objectClass=*)"
Feb 20 12:49:53 ldaphost slapd[4359]: conn=7448 op=1 SEARCH RESULT tag=
101 err=0 text=
Feb 20 12:49:54 ldaphost slapd[4359]: conn=7448 op=2 UNBIND
Feb 20 12:49:54 ldaphost slapd[4359]: conn=-1 fd=43 closed
```

The best thing you can do upon initially configuring your server is to perform various operations against your new host (using command-line utilities such as ldapsearch) and viewing the log file. You'll the see how the OpenLDAP server interprets your command-line options. In the process of installing new applications or configuring existing applications for LDAP interoperability, it's always a good idea to view the log files and see exactly what the application is doing.

The following is a log file that shows a user's authentication:

```
Feb 20 12:53:14 ldaphost slapd[4359]: daemon: conn=7453 fd=43
connection from IP=127.0.0.1:40648 (IP=:: 389) accepted.
Feb 20 12:53:14 ldaphost slapd[4359]: conn=7453 op=0 BIND
dn="CN=MANAGER,DC=YOUR,DC=COMPANY" method=128
Feb 20 12:53:14 ldaphost slapd[4359]: conn=7453 op=0 RESULT
 tag=97 err=0 text=
Feb 20 12:53:14 ldaphost slapd[4359]: conn=7453 op=1 SRCH
base="dc=Your,dc=Company" scope=2 filter="(uid=tjackiewicz)"
Feb 20 12:53:14 ldaphost slapd[4359]: conn=7453 op=1 SEARCH
 RESULT tag=101 err=0 text=
Feb 20 12:53:14 ldaphost slapd[4359]: conn=7453 op=2 SRCH
base="ou=Group,dc=Your,dc=Company" scope=1
filter="(&(objectClass=posixGroup)(|(memberUid=tjackiewicz)
(uniqueMember=uid=tjackiewicz,ou=People,dc=Your,dc=Company)))"
Feb 20 12:53:14 ldaphost slapd[4359]: conn=7453 op=2 SEARCH
 RESULT tag=101 err=0 text=
Feb 20 12:53:14 ldaphost slapd[4359]: conn=7453 op=3 SRCH
base="ou=People,dc=Your,dc=Company" scope=1
filter="(&(objectClass=shadowAccount)(uid=tjackiewicz))"
Feb 20 12:53:14 ldaphost slapd[4359]: conn=7453 op=3 SEARCH
RESULT tag=101 err=0 text=
```

Each connection to the server is assigned a number so that you can trace multiple entries belonging to the same action.

Summary

Upon reading this chapter, you should now be able to deploy a functional and optimized environment and run a base configuration of your OpenLDAP directory server.

CHAPTER 4

■■■■

Installing OpenLDAP

This chapter covers how to install OpenLDAP, including choosing the version for you, obtaining the distribution, and creating your base configurations. It also introduces some of the utilities that are included in the base distribution. The installation instructions provided in this chapter are for the latest release of OpenLDAP available at the time of this writing—version 2.2.4. You can regularly check the OpenLDAP project Web site (http://www.openldap.org) for updated installation instructions and any changes that may have occurred. This installation guide should serve as a base set of installation instructions to help you but shouldn't be used as a definitive source for all forthcoming releases.

Choosing a Distribution

OpenLDAP is available for free from many sources. The OpenLDAP project distributes Lightweight Directory Access Protocol (LDAP) in only its source code form. It's up to you to compile your own copy or obtain a precompiled set of binaries from another distribution site. OpenLDAP has the following development and release types:

OpenLDAP release: This is the latest release of the OpenLDAP software for general use. It should be used by those familiar with the code itself or those wanting to stay on the bleeding edge of technology. This release has had minimal public testing.

OpenLDAP stable release: This is the release determined through general use to be the most stable. This release has gone through significant testing by the OpenLDAP project and the public.

OpenLDAP test releases: These are beta (or alpha, gamma, and so on) releases sometimes made available by developers. These releases are meant for testing purposes only and are commonly released so that significant new features can be tested.

Update releases and patches: These are also sometimes made to update and fix problems in previous releases when a full release isn't warranted.

Depending on where you obtain it, you can get OpenLDAP as source code (which is how it's primarily released and maintained) or as a package of binaries for the platform on which you choose to run it. The procedures for each type of installation will differ based on the operating system and version you'll be using. Regardless, the postinstallation configuration parameters, which are what this chapter concentrates on, will be the same throughout.

Setting Up Your System

OpenLDAP requires that certain software be available on your host for it to compile successfully. If the software it's looking for doesn't exist on your default host, you must make sure to install it. You'll need the following software:

C development environment: Obviously, in order to compile code written in C, it's necessary to have a compiler and a standard set of libraries installed on your system. By default, Linux distributions come with a compiler. Solaris often requires the installation of a compiler outside the standard operating system installation. If you're lacking a compiler in your environment and the standard set of necessary libraries, look into the installation of the GNU Compiler Collection (GCC). Visit http://www.gnu.org for more information.

OpenSSL: OpenSSL is required to be able to use OpenLDAP with Secure Sockets Layer (SSL) support within your system. The OpenSSL project is a collaborative effort to develop a robust, commercial-grade, full-featured, and open-source tool kit implementing SSL version 2/3 and Transport Layer Security (TLS) version 1, as well as a full-strength general-purpose cryptography library. Visit http://www.openssl.org for more information.

Berkeley Database (Berkeley DB) from Sleepycat: Sleepycat is the back-end database used to store information in OpenLDAP and provides the base set of libraries necessary for OpenLDAP to function. Berkeley DB is the most widely used application-specific data management software in the world. It's used for mission-critical applications throughout the world and is the back-end storage system for many applications you've probably used. Visit http://www.sleepycat.com for more information.

If, during your installation process, you get complaints about other missing components, please refer to the installation instructions included with the specific distribution of OpenLDAP that you're using.

Choosing a Special User

OpenLDAP can't be run as root. For this reason, you'll need to create a special user (such as *nobody*) with no shell privileges for slapd. The user should have no password (in other words, locked out with *), no valid shell, and no privileges in any way. The shell /bin/false is commonly used as a false shell. You need to ensure that it exists in /etc/shells for it to be valid on the system.

Obtaining the Distribution

For the examples in this book, you'll use /tmp as the base directory for storing all the installation files for OpenLDAP.

```
root@linuxhost# pwd
/tmp
```

Once you've verified your starting point, you'll need to obtain the source code. Listing 4-1 demonstrates this using File Transfer Protocol (FTP).

Listing 4-1. *Obtaining the Source Code via FTP*

```
root@linuxhost# ftp ftp.openldap.org
Connected to www.openldap.org.
220 boole.openldap.org FTP server (Version 6.00LS) ready.
500 'AUTH GSSAPI': command not understood.
Name (ftp.openldap.org:root): ftp
331 Guest login ok, send your email address as password.
Password: user@linuxhost
230- Copyright 1998-2002, The OpenLDAP Foundation, All Rights Reserved.
230- COPYING RESTRICTIONS APPLY, see:
230-    ftp://ftp.openldap.org/COPYRIGHT
230-    ftp://ftp.openldap.org/LICENSE
230 Guest login ok, access restrictions apply.
Remote system type is UNIX.
Using binary mode to transfer files.
ftp> cd pub
250 CWD command successful.
ftp> ls
200 PORT command successful.
150 Opening ASCII mode data connection for '/bin/ls'.
total 12
drwxrwxr-x   5 2000  20     512 Dec 31 04:18 OpenLDAP
drwxr-xr-x  12 0     65533  512 Dec 14 19:58 UMich-LDAP
lrwxrwxrwx   1 0     65533    8 Apr  7  2003 openldap -> OpenLDAP
drwxr-xr-x   2 2000  20     512 Aug 24  2002 tools
226 Transfer complete.
ftp> cd OpenLDAP
250 CWD command successful.
ftp> ls
200 PORT command successful.
150 Opening ASCII mode data connection for '/bin/ls'.
total 44
-rw-r--r--   1 2000  2000  2241 Dec 31 18:20 COPYRIGHT
-rw-r--r--   1 2000  20    2214 Dec  4 23:02 LICENSE
-rw-r--r--   1 2000  20    1258 Jul  6  2003 MIRRORS
-rw-r--r--   1 2000  20     848 Dec  4 23:05 README
lrwxrwxrwx   1 0     20      13 Apr  7  2003 openldap-alpha -> openldap-test
lrwxrwxrwx   1 0     20      13 Apr  7  2003 openldap-beta -> openldap-test
lrwxrwxrwx   1 0     20      13 Apr  7  2003 openldap-gamma -> openldap-test
drwxr-xr-x   2 2000  20    4608 Dec 31 04:17 openldap-release
lrwxrwxr-x   1 2000  20      35 Dec 31 04:18 openldap-release.tgz -> openldap-rel
ease/openldap-2.2.4.tgz
drwxr-xr-x   2 2000  20    2048 Dec 18 03:03 openldap-stable
lrwxr-xr-x   1 0     20      44 Dec 18 03:04 openldap-stable.tgz
 -> openldap-stable/openldap-stable-20031217.tgz
drwxr-xr-x   2 2000  20    1024 Dec  1 04:22 openldap-test
226 Transfer complete.
```

In Listing 4-1, you can see the various versions of OpenLDAP available to you. Versions exist for a number of operating systems, and you'll see different types of releases, as discussed earlier. Once you've identified the version you want to download, you can proceed with the following code:

```
ftp> binary
200 Type set to I.
ftp> mget openldap-release.tgz
mget openldap-release.tgz? y
200 PORT command successful.
150 Opening BINARY mode data connection for 'openldap-release.tgz' (2429622 bytes).
226 Transfer complete.
2429622 bytes received in 0.89 seconds (2.7e+03 Kbytes/s)
ftp> quit
221 Goodbye.
```

You should by now have successfully downloaded a copy of the OpenLDAP source code. To verify that the version of OpenLDAP you've obtained is an original and hasn't been tampered with, check the supplied signature with the Pretty Good Privacy (PGP) key available on the OpenLDAP Web site.

■**Note** You can also obtain OpenLDAP from http://www.openldap.org using a Web browser or from a Concurrent Versions System (CVS) tree. The method of obtaining the binaries (or source code) depends on your preference.

Performing the Base Installation

Now you must prepare for the base installation of the distribution by running the following code on your target installation host:

```
root@linuxhost# ls openldap-release.tgz
openldap-release.tgz
root@linuxhost# mkdir ol
root@linuxhost# mv openldap-release.tgz ol
root@linuxhost# cd ol
root@linuxhost# gzip -d openldap-release.tgz
root@linuxhost# tar xvf openldap-release.tar
openldap-2.2.4/
openldap-2.2.4/doc/
openldap-2.2.4/doc/man/
Complete output of 'tar' removed
..
```

Once you've uncompressed and untarred the source code, it's a good idea to review the provided documentation. You should review the COPYRIGHT, LICENSE, README, and INSTALL documents contained within the distribution. COPYRIGHT and LICENSE provide information on acceptable use, copying, and the warranty of the OpenLDAP software distribution.

Now you're ready to start the process of installing the software. Because you downloaded and extracted the installation to the /tmp directory, you should move the contents to a base installation directory of /usr. If you don't do this, variables related to the software HOME path will be set to /tmp. It's here that you'll either pass the stage without an error or realize that something may be missing on your system. You may want to modify the options passed to the configure script to fine-tune your system environment. The configure script accepts many command-line options that enable or disable optional software features. Usually the defaults are fine, but you may want to change them for a number of reasons. For example, you may want to include or exclude certain libraries depending on how your base operating system is configured. However, this will rarely be necessary if you're keeping up-to-date with the latest releases and patch levels of your operating system. To get a compete list of options that configure accepts, use the -help option, like so:

```
root@localhost# ./configure -help
```

You'll see a large number of options listed here. Don't be alarmed if you aren't familiar with all the options listed. You won't have to deal with a majority of them. However, flexibility is always one of the goals of open-source software, so enough rope is always given to the system administrator—enough to hang yourself and enough to get out of a hole. The direction you want to go is up to you. The script relies on environment variables for determining compiler and linker options. Table 4-1 describes some of the important ones.

Table 4-1. *Environment Variables for Compiler and Linker Options*

Variable	Description	Example
CC	C compiler	gcc
CFLAGS	C flags	-O -g
CPPFLAGS	CPP flags	-I/path/include -DFOO=42
LDFLAGS	LD flags	-L/usr/local/lib
LIBS	Libraries	-llib
PATH	Command path	/usr/local/bin:/usr/bin:/bin

Ensure that your environment variables are set appropriately before continuing with the installation procedure. If you had to install various sets of libraries on your system as a prerequisite for installing OpenLDAP, you have a good chance that your environment is lacking some vital information necessary for the installation to work.

Take note of where the include and lib files for your prerequisite applications have been installed and set them appropriately. If you're linking against shared libraries that reside in nonstandard locations, you'll need to tell the dynamic linker where to find them; otherwise the resulting executable files will not run. The stops are operating system-dependent but usually involve setting environment variables (or modifying /etc files) before attempting to run the programs. In most environments, this involves modifying LD_LIBRARY_PATH. You may also need to modify /etc/ld.so.conf. Refer to your operating system manuals or consult your system administrator if you have problems.

```
root@linuxhost# cd openldap-2.2.4/
root@linuxhost# ./configure
Copyright 1998-2003 The OpenLDAP Foundation. All rights reserved.
Restrictions apply, see COPYRIGHT and LICENSE files.
Configuring OpenLDAP 2.2.4-Release ...
checking host system type... i686-pc-linux-gnu
Complete output of './configure' removed
..
```

One common error that's often encountered is a script that complains that the Berkeley DB version is incompatible.

```
Full output of command removed
checking for db.h... yes
checking for Berkeley DB link (default)... no
checking for Berkeley DB link (-ldb42)... no
checking for Berkeley DB link (-ldb-42)... no
checking for Berkeley DB link (-ldb-4.2)... no
checking for Berkeley DB link (-ldb-4-2)... no
checking for Berkeley DB link (-ldb-4)... no
checking for Berkeley DB link (-ldb4)... no
checking for Berkeley DB link (-ldb)... yes
checking for Berkeley DB thread support... yes
checking Berkeley DB version for BDB backend... no
configure: error: BDB: BerkeleyDB version incompatible
```

This is one of the most common errors you'll encounter during your installation. To remedy the situation, install the Sleepycat DB libraries. These libraries are available through Sleepycat Software at http://www.sleepycat.com. However, other situations may arise because of various features (whether you want them or not) not being compatible with the system on which you're installing OpenLDAP.

The configure program is part of a GNUs Not Unix (GNU) suite of tools used to standardize the configuration of utilities you'll use on your Unix-based systems. It takes the place of proprietary configuration programs that differ from program to program and from platform to platform. The options that can be used with the configuration utilities are beyond the scope of this book and will likely change as new versions are released. Refer to the man pages for specific configuration options you may find useful for your particular deployment. You can configure nearly everything you can think of via files or via the command line with the configure program and associated tool kits.

Compiling OpenLDAP

Once you've resolved all the errors, you're ready for the next step. Run the following:

```
root@linuxhost# make depend
Making depend in /tmp/ol/openldap-2.2.4
Entering subdirectory include
Full output of command deleted
...
```

This command constructs the dependencies. Now you're ready for the actual compilation of the software. Run the following:

```
root@linuxhost# make
Making all in /tmp/ol/openldap-2.2.4
Entering subdirectory include
Full output of command deleted
...
```

Once you've compiled the software and you've received no errors, you can test the results with the following:

```
root@linuxhost# make test
cd tests; make test
Full output of command deleted
...
```

Now you're ready for the actual installation. Run the following:

```
root@linuxhost# make install
Making all in /tmp/ol/openldap-2.2.4
Entering subdirectory include
Full output of command deleted
...
```

Upon the successful installation of your system, all you really have in place are a set of libraries that can't be accessed (and used) and subdirectories full of various binaries that aren't yet configured. It's from this point on that you'll need to modify all the relevant configuration files to create an OpenLDAP server that will suit your specific needs.

Creating a Local Database

Upon the successful installation of your base OpenLDAP distribution, you're left with an empty directory and a large virtual box of tools. For you to have a functional directory server, you need to install a directory. You have a number of options you can use depending on your particular scenario.

For small deployments, or if this is a stand-alone instance, creating a database manually may be sufficient. For larger infrastructures, using LDAP tools to create and maintain your directory remotely is a more appropriate method.

For these examples, you'll be working with a standard set of assumptions about your infrastructure, as shown in Table 4-2.

Table 4-2. *Environment Assumptions*

Token	Value	Explanation
Suffix	"dc=Your,dc=Company"	This is the base distinguished name (DN).
Directory	/usr/local/var/openldap-data	This is where the index files will reside.
rootdn	"cn=Directory Manager"	This is your directory administrator, equivalent to the root or administrator of your systems.
rootpw	Password	This is the password for your rootdn.

You need to create all the directories specified in Table 4-2 with the appropriate permissions so that slapd can write to them. Additionally, the first accounts you'll be using to modify information in your directory should be treated as root accounts—that is, you have full control of the directory using these accounts. These are special accounts that are hard-coded externally within your configuration files and will also have the ability to modify your directory.

Finally, you should make sure the database definition within your slapd configuration file contains the index definitions you want; use the following code:

```
index {<attrlist> | default} [pres,eq,approx,sub,none]
```

For example, to index the cn sn, uid, and objectclass attributes, you can use the following index directives:

```
index cn,sn,uid pres,eq,approx,sub
index objectClass eq
```

This creates presence, equality, approximate, and substring indexes for the cn, sn, and uid attributes and an equality index for the objectClass attribute. Note that not all index types are available with all attribute types. While it'd be easy to overdo the indexing on your system and add all types of indexes for every attribute you have available, this method would soon be self-defeating, as the system resources you have available will not be utilized appropriately.

Once you've configured things to your liking, you can start slapd, connect to your new directory with your LDAP client, and start adding entries to your null database. The initial set of data you'll need to add is the base organizational information (the base DN) and the Directory Information Tree hierarchy. Create an LDAP Interchange Format (LDIF) file containing this information and save it, as it will be used to create the base of all your future systems. A sample LDIF may look like this:

```
# Base Configuration for Your Company
dn: dc=Your,dc=Company
objectclass: dcObject
objectclass: organization
dc: Your
o: Your Company
description: Your Company dot Com
```

```
# Standard INTERNAL Organizational Units
dn: ou=Internal, dc=Your,dc=Company
objectclass: organizationalunit
ou: Internal
description: Internal Components

# Standard EXTERNAL Organizational Units
dn: ou=External,dc=Your,dc=Company
objectclass: organizationalunit
ou: External
description: External Components
```

You can use the ldapadd or ldapmodify commands, which are explained in the next section, to add these entries to your directory. This method is generic enough to work for almost all LDAP implementations. This is because standard LDAP methods are used along with standard LDAP application programming interfaces (APIs). The target systems are treated as generic LDAP hosts, and no implementation specific tools are used.

Figure 4-1 demonstrates the difference between using LDAP-based tools versus those that depend on the implementation.

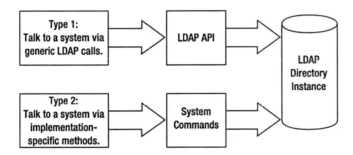

Figure 4-1. *Communication via LDAP API versus implementation-specific methods*

The next section demonstrates a real example of communication via specific implementation methods. Although communicating with your directory using system tools may be quicker, it may not scale and may change between implementations and versions.

Creating an Offline Database

Another method of database creation is to do it offline, using the standard slapd database tools that interact directly with the database files. That is, you can skip the standard LDAP APIs and use proprietary methods (specific to OpenLDAP as an implementation of LDAP). This method is best if you have a large number of entries to create and if it'd be time prohibitive to simple add them while the system is running. This is typically the case for systems that are being restored from backup or when you're converting an existing directory (from another vendor or version) to OpenLDAP. This method of database creation requires localized access to tools that read the slapd configuration files and an input file in LDIF format. Database files are written directly to the system using nonstandard methods that are proprietary to OpenLDAP. Ensure that your base configuration files for slapd are configured to your liking. The suffix and all directory paths need to be configured and valid for all this to work. You'll also need to define your list of indexes.

You specify your indexes using the following format:

```
index {<attrlist> | default} [pres,eq,approx,sub,none]
```

The following is an example:

```
index cn,sn,uid pres,eq,approx,sub
index objectClass eq
```

This creates presence, equality, approximate, and substring indexes for the cn, sn, and uid attributes and an equality index for the objectClass attribute. Not all index types are available with all attribute types. An example of usage is as follows:

```
$ slapindex -b dc=Your,dc=Company
```

This will reindex your directory, with a base DN of dc=Your,dc=Company using the default slapd.conf configuration file on your server.

Once you've created the base configurations for your system, you can use the slapadd program to import LDIF entries into your directory. An example of its usage is as follows:

```
$ slapadd -v -b dc=Your,dc=Company -f slapd2.conf -l file.ldif
```

This will add the contents of file.ldif to your directory with a base DN of dc=Your,dc=Company in verbose mode (-v) while reading the alternate configuration file slapd2.conf.

To view (or *cat*, which is taken from the Unix command) your directory in database order, you can use the slapcat program. This outputs the contents of your database into an LDIF file suitable for importing with slapadd. An example of its usage is as follows:

```
$ slapcat -l output.ldif -b dc=Your,dc=Company
```

This will output, to output.ldif, the contents of your directory with the base DN of dc=Your,dc=Company.

▓**Note** The following sections explain the slapadd and slapcat commands in more detail.

Using LDAP Search Filters

Tools allow you to communicate with a directory, but the real power lies in the search filters that you'll be using to retrieve data from your OpenLDAP directory. RFC 1960, *A String Representation of LDAP Search Filters,* first defined the network representation of a search filter transmitted to an LDAP server. It defined a human-readable format that represented the string filters you have available.

Listing 4-2 shows an LDAP search filter.

Listing 4-2. *LDAP Search Filter*

```
Filter::= CHOICE {
    And [0] SET OF Filter,
    Or [1] SET OF Filter,
    Not [2] Filter,
    EqualityMatch [3] AttributeValueAssertion,
    Substrings [4] SubstringFilter,
    GreatOrEqual [5] AttributeValueAssertion,
    LessOrEqual [6] AttributeValueAssertion,
    Present [7] AttributeType,
    ApproxMatch [8] AttributeValueAssertion,
}

SubstringFilter ::= SEQUENCE {
 type AttributeType,
 SEQUENCE OF CHOICE {
  initial [0] LDAPString,
  any [1] LDAPString,
  final [2] LDAPString
 }
}

AttributeValueAssertion ::= SEQUENCE {
 attributeType    AttributeType,
 attributeValue   AttributeValue
}

AttributeType ::= LDAPString
AttributeValue ::= OCTET STRING
LDAPString ::= OCTET STRING
```

LDAPString in Listing 4-2 is limited to the IA5 character set. AttributeType is a string representation of the attribute type name and is defined in [1]. AttributeValue OCTET STRING has the form defined in [2]. Filter is encoded for transmission over a network using the Basic Encoding Rules (BERs) defined in [3], with simplifications described in [1].

In December 1997, RFC 2254, also named *A String Representation of LDAP Search Filters,* replaced RFC 1960 and made modifications to the basic format to include support for LDAP 3's extended match filters. You should understand both in order to facilitate communication with both LDAP 2 and LDAP 3 client-server combinations.

Listing 4-3 shows a string representation of LDAP search filters.

Listing 4-3. *String Representation of LDAP Search Filters*

```
Filter ::= CHOICE {
And [0] SET OF Filter,
or [1] SET OF Filter,
not [2] Filter,
equalityMatch [3] AttributeValueAssertion,
substring [4] SubstringFilter,
greaterOrEqual [5] AttributeValueAssertion,
lessOrEqual [6] AttributeValueAssertion,
present [7] AttributeDescription,
approxMatch [8] AttributeValueAssertion,
extensibleMatch [9] MatchingRuleAssertion
}

SubstringFilter ::= SEQUENCE {
Type AttributeDescription,
SEQUENCE OF CHOICE {
 Initial [0] LDAPString,
 Any [1] LDAPString,
 Final [2] LDAPString
 }
}

AttributeValueAssertion ::= SEQUENCE {
AttributeDesc AttributeDescription,
AttributeValue AttributeValue
}

MatchingRuleAssertion ::= SEQUENCE {
MatchingRule [1] MatchingRuleID OPTIONAL,
Type [2] AttributeDescription OPTIONAL,
MatchValue [3] AssertionValue,
DnAttributes [4] BOOLEAN DEFAULT FALSE
}

AttributeDescription ::= LDAPString
AttributeValue ::= OCTET STRING
MatchingRuleID ::= LDAPString
AssertionValue ::= OCTET STRING
LDAPString ::= OCTET STRING
```

LDAPString in Listing 4-3 is limited to the UTF-8 encoding of the ISO 10646 character set [4]. AttributeDescription is a string representation of the attribute description and is defined in [1]. AttributeValue and AssertionValue OCTET STRING have the form defined in [2]. Filter is encoded for transmission over a network using the BERs defined in [3], with simplifications described in [1].

The grammar shown in Listing 4-4 uses the string representation of an LDAP search filter. It uses a prefix format to denote value, which I'll demonstrate in later examples.

Listing 4-4. *String Representation of an LDAP Search Filter*

```
<filter> ::= '(' <filtercomp> ')'
<filtercomp> ::= <and> | <or> | <not> | <item>
<and> ::= '&' <filterlist>
<or> ::= '|' <filterlist>
<not> ::= '!' <filter>
<filterlist> ::= <filter> | <filter> <filterlist>
<item> ::= <simple> | <present> | <substring>
<simple> ::= <attr> <filtertype> <value>
<filtertype> ::= <equal> | <approx> | <greater> | <less>
<equal> ::= '='
<approx> ::= '~='
<greater> ::= '>='
<less> ::= '<='
<present> ::= <attr> '=*'
<substring> ::= <attr> '=' <initial> <any> <final>
<initial> ::= NULL | <value>
<any> ::= '*' <starval>
<starval> ::= NULL | <value> '*' <starval>
<final> ::= NULL | <value>
```

In Listing 4-4, <attr> is a string representing an AttributeType and has the format defined in [1]. <value> is a string representing an AttributeValue, or part of one, and has the form defined in [2]. If a <value> must contain one of the characters *, (, or), these characters should be escaped by preceding them with the backslash (\) character. Note that although both the <substring> and <present> productions can produce the attr=* construct, this construct is used only to denote a presence filter.

While it's always good to understand the defined set of standards as they apply to search filters, real-world examples demonstrate their usage in a friendlier way (see Table 4-3).

Table 4-3. *Search Filter Examples*

Goal of Search	Search Filter	Explanation
GivenName is Tom	givenname=Tom	This is a simple search where an attribute value is on the left and a search string is on the right.
GivenName is Tom W	(givenname="Tom W")	Parentheses and quotes are recommended to differentiate this from the command-line parameters.
GivenName is Tom W *and* Objectclass is YourCompanyPerson	(&(givenname="Tom W") (Objectclass=YourCompanyPerson))	This is prefixed by an ampersand (&) to show that you want both sets of criteria to be met.

Using OpenLDAP Utilities

OpenLDAP provides you with a robust set of tools you can use to read, modify, destroy, and utilize data stored within the directory. A firm grasp of all the tools and parameters is necessary to become an expert in OpenLDAP and the overall world of LDAP. All the OpenLDAP utilities are, in some way or another, direct interfaces to the standard libraries calls given to you. The utilities (and other components of OpenLDAP, such as configuration files) you'll be working with will be divided into the standard man page sections (see Table 4-4).

Table 4-4. *Man Page Sections*

Man Page Section	Explanation	Examples
1	General commands, tools, and utilities.	ldapcompare, ldapmodify, ldapdelete, ldapadd, ldapmodrdn, ldappasswd, ldapsearch, ldapwhoami, ud
2	System services and error numbers.	No information relevant to OpenLDAP
3	User-level library functions.	ldap_delete, ldap_add, ldap_search, ldap_abandon. Refer to the programming-related chapters of this book.
4	Device drivers, protocols, and network interfaces.	No information relevant to OpenLDAP
5	File formats used or read by various programs.	LDIF format, slapd.conf, ldap.conf, .ldaprc, ud.conf, slapd.replog, slapd.access
6	Games and demos.	No information relevant to OpenLDAP
7	Miscellaneous useful information pages.	No information relevant to OpenLDAP
8	System maintenance and operation commands.	slapcat, mail500, slapadd, slapd, slapindex, slapdpasswd, slurpd
9	This system contains information about the interfaces and subroutines in the kernel.	No information relevant to OpenLDAP

Whenever a number in parentheses follows a component of OpenLDAP, it refers to the particular man page section to which it refers. This is useful because the same name may be used for a configuration file and a utility. That is, login (1) may refer to the login command, and login (5) may refer to a configuration file by the same name. These numbers will help differentiate the terms. Each of these sections can also have subsections, as shown in Table 4-5.

Table 4-5. *Man Page Subsections*

Man Page Section	Explanation
C	Daemons and related tools that interface with daemons
P	Perl utilities
PM	Perl modules
M	Ncurses, terminal components
X	X Window system programs or system libraries
Menu	Ncurses, SVR4-compatible screen menus
Ncurses	Ncurses terminal screen painting
Curses	Curses terminal screen painting
Form	Curses, SVR4-compatible screen forms
Nas	Network audio system libraries
Readline	GNU readline prompt routines
Emacs20	Emacs system commands
Emacs21	Emacs system commands
Vga	Svgalib components
Snmp	Net-SNMP libraries
Tcl	TCL libraries
TclX	Extended TCL libraries
Tcsh	Tcsh shell components
Gcc	GNU C compiler library components
SSL	SSL libraries and components

ldapmodify (1) and ldapadd (1)

The ldapmodify (1) and ldapadd (1) programs are interfaces to the ldap_modify (3) and ldap_add (3) library calls. The following is a synopsis of their command-line options:

```
ldapmodify [-a]  [-c]  [-S file] [-n] [-v] [-k] [-K] [-M[M]]
[-d debuglevel] [-D binddn]  [-W]  [-w passwd]
[-y passwdfile]  [-H ldapuri] [-h ldaphost]
[-p ldapport] [-P 2|3] [-O security-properties]
[ I] [ Q] [ U authcid]
[-R realm] [-x] [-X authzid] [-Y mech] [-Z[Z]] [-F][-f file]

ldapadd [-c] [-S file] [-n]  [-v]  [-k] [-K]  [-M[M]]
[-d debuglevel] [-D binddn]  [-W]  [-w passwd]
[-y passwdfile] [-h ldaphost] [-p ldap-port]  [-P 2|3]  [-O security-properties]
 [-I]   [-Q]   [-U authcid] [-R
realm] [-x] [-X authzid] [-Y mech] [-Z[Z]][-F] [-f file]
```

The ldapadd (1) program is a hard link to the ldapmodify (1) tool. When ldapadd (1) is invoked, the -a (add new entry) flag is turned on automatically. The specific command-line options for these utilities are as follows:

-a: Add new entries. This sets the default changetype to add (changetype: add). The default for ldapmodify is modify (changetype: modify). If invoked as ldapadd, this flag is set.

-c: Continuous operation mode. Errors are reported, but ldapmodify will continue with modifications. The default is to exit after reporting an error. Imagine the scenario where you want to make 10,000 modifications to your directory. For whatever reason, your operation fails after 8,000. So 8,000 commands have completed successfully, but you have 2,000 left to go. Instead of attempting to figure out where the program left off, you can run the 10,000 operations again in continuous mode and ignore the first 2,000 errors, which will most likely complain that the modification you're trying to make has already been done.

-S *file*: Add or change records that were skipped because of an error are written to *file*, and the error message returned by the server is added as a comment.

-n: Show what would be done but don't actually modify the entries. This option is useful for debugging in conjunction with the -v flag.

-v: Use verbose mode, with many diagnostics written to STDOUT.

-k: Use Kerberos IV authentication instead of simple authentication. You must compile with Kerberos support for this option to have any effect.

-K: Same as -k but does only step 1 of the Kerberos IV bind.

-F: Force application of all changes regardless of the contents of the input lines that begin with replica:. (By default, replica: lines are compared against the LDAP server host and port in use to decide if a replog record should actually be applied.)

-M[M]: Enable the Manage DSA-IT control. -MM makes control critical.

-d *debuglevel*: Set the LDAP debugging level to the number specified here. The ldapmodify tool must be compiled with LDAP_DEBUG defined for this option to have any effect.

-f *file*: Read the entry modification information from *file* instead of from STDIN.

-x: Use simple authentication instead of Simple Authentication and Security Layer (SASL).

-D *binddn*: Use the DN *binddn* to bind to the LDAP directory.

-W: Prompt for simple authentication. This is used instead of specifying the password on the command line. This is useful when you're performing operations at a higher security level than the people who are looking over your shoulder.

-w *password*: Use *password* as the password for simple authentication.

-y *passwdfile*: Use the complete contents of *passwdfile* as the password for simple authentication.

-H ldapuri: Specify uniform resource indicators (URIs) referring to the LDAP server(s).

-h ldaphost: Specify an alternative host on which the LDAP server is running. This is primarily used to perform LDAP operations against remote LDAP servers. The default host that's being used to perform the command against is local. This option has been deprecated in favor of -H.

-p ldapport: Specify an alternate Transmission Control Protocol (TCP) port where the LDAP server is listening. This option has been deprecated in favor of -H.

-p 2|3: Specify the LDAP version to use.

-O security-properties: Specify SASL security properties.

-I: Enable SASL Interactive mode. Always prompt. The default is to prompt only as needed.

-Q: Enable SASL Quiet mode. Never prompt.

-U authcid: Specify the authentication ID for the SASL bind. The form of the ID depends on the actual SASL mechanism used.

-R realm: Specify the realm of the authentication ID for the SASL bind. The form of the realm depends on the actual SASL mechanism used.

-X authzid: Specify the requested authorization ID for the SASL bind. authzid must be one of the following formats: dn:_distinguished name_ or u:_username_.

-Y mech: Specify the SASL mechanism to be used for authentication. If it isn't specified, the program will choose the best mechanism the server understands.

-Z[Z]: Issue StartTLS extended operation. If you use -ZZ, the command will require the operation to be successful.

The standard input, whether STDIN is used (which is the default mode of operation) or a file with the -f parameter is used (which is always recommended), you'll be using the standard LDIF format to perform commands against the server. In other words, ldapmodify will serve as one of the primary interfaces you have to your directory. I've already discussed various operations of the LDIF format, so it'd be redundant to go into much detail here. I'll cover the generic file file.ldif to illustrate examples of the ldapmodify utility.

ldapsearch (1)

The ldapsearch (1) utility is an interface to the ldap_search (3) library call. The following is a synopsis of the available command-line options:

```
ldapsearch  [-n]  [-u]  [-v]  [-k]  [-K]  [-t]  [-A] [-L[L[L]]] [-M[M]]
[-d debuglevel]
[-f file] [-D binddn] [-W] [-w passwd]  [-y passwdfile] [-H ldapuri]
[-h ldaphost]   [-p ldapport]  [-P 2|3] [-b searchbase] [-s base|one|sub]
[-a never|always|search|find] [-l timelimit] [-z sizelimit]
[-O security-properties]
[-I]   [-Q]   [-U authcid] [-R realm] [-x] [-X authzid] [-Y mech]
[-Z[Z]] filter [attrs...]
```

This utility opens a connection to an LDAP server and performs the searches that you specify on the command line. It has the following options:

-n: Show what would be done but don't actually perform the search. This is useful for debugging in conjunction with -v.

-u: Include the User Friend Name form of the DN in the output.

-v: Run in verbose mode, with many diagnostics written to STDOUT.

-V: Print version information (-VV only).

-k: Use Kerberos IV authentication instead of simple authentication.

-K: Same as -k but does only step 1 of the Kerberos IV bind.

-t: Write retrieved values to a set of temporary files. This is useful for dealing with non-ASCII values such as jpegPhoto or audio files.

-A: Retrieve attributes only (no values). This is useful when you just want to see if an attribute is present in an entry and aren't interested in the specific values.

-L: Search results are displayed in LDIF format. A single -L restricts the output to LDIF 1. A second -L disabled comments. A third -L disables printing of the LDIF version. The default is to use an extended version of LDIF.

-M[M]: Enable the Manage DSA-IT control. -MM makes control critical.

-S attribute: Sort the entries returned based on attribute.

-d debuglevel: Set the LDAP debugging level to debuglevel. The ldapsearch binary must be compiled with LDAP_DEBUG defined for this option to have any effect.

-f file: Read a series of lines from file, performing one LDAP search for each line. In this case, the filter given on the command line is treated as a pattern where the first occurrence of %s is replaced with a line from file. If file is a single - character, then the lines are read from STDIN.

-F prefix: This is the uniform resource locator (URL) prefix for files.

-x: Use simple authentication instead of SASL.

-D binddn: Use the DN binddn to bind to the LDAP directory.

-W: Prompt for simple authentication. This is used instead of specifying the password on the command line.

-w password: Use password as the password for simple authentication.

-y passwdfile: Use the complete contents of passwdfile as the password for simple authentication.

-H ldapuri: Specify URI(s) referring to the LDAP server(s).

-h *ldaphost*: Specify an alternate host on which the LDAP server is running. This option has been deprecated in favor of -H. Keep in mind that other versions of ldapsearch may not support this option, so familiarity with both methods is a must.

-p *ldapport*: Specify an alternate TCP port on which the LDAP server is listening. This also has been deprecated in favor of the -H ldapuri format.

-b *searchbase*: Use *searchbase* as the starting point for the search instead of the default. This is a useful option in a directory environment that isn't flat.

-s base | one | sub: Specify the scope of the search to be one of base, one, or sub to specify a base object, one-level, or subtree search. The default is sub.

-a never | always | search | find: Specify how alias dereferencing is done. Should be one of never, always, search, or find to specify that aliases are never dereferenced, are dereferenced when searching, or are dereferenced only when locating the base object for the search. The default is to never dereference aliases.

-P 2|3: Specify the LDAP version to use.

-l *timelimit*: Wait at most *timelimit* seconds for a search to complete. A *timelimit* of 0 removes the ldap.conf limit. A server may impose a maximum time limit that only the root user can override.

-z *sizelimit*: Retrieve at most *sizelimit* entries for a search. A sizelimit of 0 removes the ldap.conf limit. A server may impose a maximum size limit that only the root user can override.

-O security-properties: Specify SASL security properties.

-I: Enable SASL Interactive mode. Always prompt. The default is to prompt only as needed.

-Q: Enable SASL Quiet mode. Never prompt.

-U authcid: Specify the authentication ID for the SASL bind. The form of the ID depends on the actual SASL mechanism used.

-R realm: Specify the realm of authentication ID for the SASL bind. The form of the realm depends on the actual SASL mechanism used.

-X authzid: Specify the proxy authorization for the SASL bind. authzid must be one of the following formats: dn:_distinguished name_ or u:_username_.

-Y mech: Specify the SASL mechanism to be used for authentication. If it isn't specified, the program will choose the best mechanism that's known by the server.

-Z[Z]: Issue StartTLS extended operation. If you use -ZZ, the command will require the operation to be successful.

During your initial setup and usage, and especially while you're experimenting and familiarizing yourself with an LDAP environment, you'll be working with clear text and basic authentication methods that don't utilize some of the advanced security features of OpenLDAP. Unlike

other LDAP deployments, which often look at security as an afterthought, the default configurations for all your clients will look for a secure infrastructure for communication. That is, upon
issuing a simple command to search for uid=91358, you'll be prompted for SASL authentication
passwords, like so:

```
$ ldapsearch -h ldap -p 389 -b dc=Your,dc=Company uid=91358
SASL/DIGEST-MD5 authentication started
Please enter your password:
```

The examples I'll use to demonstrate the usage of some of these utilities will have -x
added to their command lines to disable SASL authentication, like so:

```
$ ldapsearch -h ldap -p 389 -x -b dc=Your,dc=Company uid=91358
```

Depending on your actual configurations, you may get something like this:

```
# extended LDIF
#
# LDAPv3
# base <dc=Your,dc=Company> with scope sub
# filter: uid=91358
# requesting: ALL
#


# 91358, People,YourCompany.com
```

The data will be followed by the actual contents of your directory, but the comments
serve as header information for each of your requests—and to help you understand what your
actual request meant to the LDAP server. In the previous example, you can see that the "base"
chosen was dc=Your,dc=Company; the scope, which I didn't specify, was set to sub, and the filter
chosen was uid=91358. Because I didn't specify attributes (at the end of the command line) to
return, the entire contents of the entry or entries that satisfied the filter were returned, like so:

```
$ ldapsearch -h ldap -p 389 -x -b dc=Your,dc=Company uid=91358 dn uid
```

Adding the trailing data of dn uid to the end of the example request would return only the
dn and uid of the entries being sent back to the client.

ldapdelete (1)

The ldapdelete (1) utility is an interface to the ldap_delete (3) library call. The following is
a synopsis of the available command-line options:

```
ldapdelete  [-n]  [-v] [-k] [-K] [-c] [-M[M]] [-d debuglevel] [-f file]
[-D binddn] [-W] [-w passwd] [-y passwdfile] [-H ldapuri] [-h ldaphost]
[-P 2|3] [-p ldapport] [-O security-properties] [-U authcid] [-R realm]
[-x] [-I] [-Q] [-X authzid] [-Y mech] [-Z[Z]] [dn]...
```

This utility opens a connection to an LDAP server, binds, and deletes one or more entries.
The following list defines the command-line options for this utility:

-r: Delete records recursively.

-n: Show what would be done but don't actually delete entries. This is useful for debugging in conjunction with -v.

-v: Use verbose mode, with many diagnostics written to STDOUT.

-V: Print version information (-VV only).

-k: Use Kerberos IV authentication instead of simple authentication.

-K: Same as -k but does only step 1 of the Kerberos IV bind.

-c: Continuous operation mode. Errors are reported, but the utility will continue with deletions. The default is to exit after reporting an error.

-M[M]: Enable the Manage DSA-IT control. -MM makes control critical.

-d debuglevel: Set the LDAP debugging level to debuglevel. The utility must be compiled with LDAP_DEBUG defined for this option to have any effect.

-f file: Read a series of DNs from a file, one per line, performing an LDAP delete for each.

-x: Use simple authentication instead of SASL.

-D binddn: Use the DN binddn to bind to the LDAP directory.

-W: Prompt for simple authentication. This is used instead of specifying a password on the command line.

-w password: Use password as the password for simple authentication.

-y passwdfile: Use complete contents of passwdfile as the password for simple authentication.

-H ldapuri: Specify URI(s) referring to the LDAP server(s).

-h ldaphost: Specify an alternate host on which the LDAP server is running. Deprecated in favor of -H.

-p ldapport: Specify an alternate TCP port where the LDAP server is listening. Deprecated in favor of -H.

-P 2|3: Specify LDAP version to use.

-r: Do a recursive delete. If the DN specified isn't a leaf, its children, and all their children, are deleted down the tree. No verification is done, so if you add this switch, ldapdelete will happily delete large portions of your tree. A typical scenario of where this will be used is in a system where you have a large system with multiple branches. You'd search for values you need deleted but are nested extremely deep in the system. Instead of generating a list of DNs to delete, this would do it for you.

-O security-properties: Specify SASL security properties.

-I: Enable SASL Interactive mode. Always prompt. The default is to prompt only as needed.

-Q: Enable SASL Quiet mode. Never prompt.

-U authcid: Specify the authentication ID for the SASL bind. The form of the ID depends on the actual SASL mechanism used.

-R realm: Specify the realm of authentication ID for the SASL bind. The form of the realm depends on the actual SASL mechanism used.

-X authzid: Specify the proxy authorization for the SASL bind. authzid must be one of the following formats: dn:_distinguished name_ or u:_username_.

-Y mech: Specify the SASL mechanism to be used for authentication. If it isn't specified, the program will choose the best mechanism that's known by the server.

-Z[Z]: Issue StartTLS extended operation. If you use -ZZ, the command will require the operation to be successful.

The ldapdelete tool is similar to ldapmodify or ldapadd in that it takes input in LDIF to be processed against the server. The command-line options for ldapdelete should be familiar when looking at the other LDAP tool sets. When using ldapmodify, you need to specify a changetype operation for each dn that's being modified. Using ldapdelete assumes that the changetype operation is delete (or you're using the wrong tool!) and lets you skip this step.

On the command line, your operation may exist as such:

```
$ ldapdelete -x -h krakow -p 389 -c -v
```

A successful operation would return some basic initialization information and allow input via STDIN, like so:

```
ldap_initialize( ldap://krakow:389 )
```

If you want to use an LDIF file as input, you'd use the following:

```
$ ldapdelete -x -h krakow -p 389 -c -v -f file.ldif
```

The LDIF file would contain a list of the full DNs for all the users you'd like to delete. The trick here is that if you perform an LDIF search to obtain a list of users (or objects) that need to be deleted, they're prefixed by information that isn't necessarily instantly compatible with the ldapdelete utility. For example, assume you want to delete a DN in your directory with a relative distinguished name (RDN) of uid=test_user1. The return from the search would yield you the following:

```
dn: uid=test_user1,ou=Special Users,dc=Your,dc=Company
```

Adding changetype: delete would make the following a valid statement for the ldapmodify utility:

```
dn: uid=test_user1,ou=Special Users,dc=Your,dc=Company
changetype: delete
```

However, the ldapdelete tool would require you cut off the initial dn: in front of the full DN of the object you want to delete in order for it to be accepted as input. Performing the delete while including the dn: would yield the following:

```
dn: uid=test_user1,ou=Special Users,dc=Your,dc=Company
deleting entry "dn: uid=test_user1,ou=Special Users,dc=Your,dc=Company"
Delete Result: No such object (32)
Matched DN: ou=special users,dc=Your,dc=Company
```

This is because when the server splits the information, it happens from reverse, using a comma (,) as the standard delimiter. See Table 4-6 for the objects that are found and known by the server.

Table 4-6. *Matching Logic for* ldapdelete

Order	Object	Explanation
1	dc=com	Part of the base DN but existing as its own entity within the directory.
2	dc=YourCompany	Part of the base DN and, technically, a child of dc=com. However, objects found here would be combined and known as dc=Your,dc=Company.
3	ou=Special Users	The branch of the tree that this account exists within. In this case, the organizationalUnit is Special Users.
4	dn: uid=test_user1	In this case, your goal is to find and parse uid=test_user1. However, because a dn: was added to the beginning of this entry, this is the equivalent of performing a search for (dn: uid=test_user1). This will not yield any results and, instead, should be replaced with uid=test_user1.

The end result of all of this is having the LDIF file you're using contain the following:

```
uid=test_user1,ou=Special Users,dc=Your,dc=Company
```

Unfortunately, because all the operations you're working with here don't specify any authentication information (bind DN, credentials, and so forth), you're connecting as an anonymous user and don't have any specific access rights, by default, to the directory. Running the ldapdelete tool with your desired input will yield the following result:

```
uid=test_user1,ou=Special Users,dc=Your,dc=Company
deleting entry "uid=test_user1,ou=Special Users,dc=Your,dc=Company"
Delete Result: Insufficient access (50)
Additional info: Insufficient 'delete' privilege to
delete the entry 'uid=test_user1,
ou=Special Users,dc=Your,dc=Company'.
```

The solution would be to specify credentials on the command line (such as using a special account that has access rights to the directory that will allow you to complete this operation).

ldapmodrdn (1)

The ldapmodrdn (1) utility is an interface to the ldap_modrdn2 (3) library call. The following is a synopsis of available command-line options:

```
ldapmodrdn  [-r]  [-n]  [-v]  [-k]  [-K]  [-c]  [-M[M]]  [-d debuglevel]
[-D binddn]
[-W]  [-w passwd]  [-y passwdfile]  [-H ldapuri]  [-h ldaphost]  [-p ldapport]
[-P 2|3]  [-O security-properties]  [-I]  [-Q]  [-U authcid  [-R realm]  [-x]
[-X authzid]  [-Y mech]  [-Z[Z]][-s][-V][-f file]  [dn rdn]
```

This utility opens a connection to an LDAP server, binds, and modifies the RDN of a given entry or set of entries. The following list defines the command-line options for this utility:

-r: Remove old RDN values from the entry. The default is to keep old values. If old values are kept, this is just like making a copy of the entry.

-s: newsup: This is a new superior entry.

-n: Show what would be done but don't actually change entries. This option is useful for debugging in conjunction with -v.

-v: Use verbose mode, with many diagnostics written to STDOUT.

-k: Use Kerberos IV authentication instead of simple authentication. This is assuming you already have a valid ticket-granting ticket. This utility must be compiled with Kerberos support for this option to have effect.

-K: This is the same as -k but does only step 1 of the Kerberos IV bind. This is useful when connecting to a slapd and no x500dsa.hostname principal is registered with your Kerberos domain controller.

-c: Continuous operation mode. Errors are reported, but ldapmodrdn will continue with modifications. The default is to exist after reporting an error.

-n: Show what would be done but don't actually modify the entries. This option is useful for debugging in conjunction with the -v flag.

-v: Use verbose mode, with many diagnostics written to STDOUT.

-V: Print version information (-VV only).

-k: Use Kerberos IV authentication instead of simple authentication. You must compile with Kerberos support for this option to have any effect.

-K: Same as -k but does only step 1 of the Kerberos IV bind.

-F: Force application of all changes regardless of the contents of the input lines that begin with replica: (by default, replica: lines are compared against the LDAP server host and port in use to decide if a replog record should actually be applied).

-M[M]: Enable the Manage DSA-IT control. -MM makes control critical.

-d debuglevel: Set the LDAP debugging level to the number specified here. The ldapmodify tool must be compiled with LDAP_DEBUG defined for this option to have any effect.

-f file: Read the entry modification information from file instead of from STDIN.

-x: Use simple authentication instead of SASL.

-D *binddn*: Use the DN *binddn* to bind to the LDAP directory.

-W: Prompt for simple authentication. This is used instead of specifying the password on the command line. This is useful when you're performing operations at a higher security level than the people who are looking over your shoulder.

-w *password*: Use *password* as the password for simple authentication.

-y *passwdfile*: Use the complete contents of *passwdfile* as the password for simple authentication.

-H ldapuri: Specify URI(s) referring to the LDAP server(s).

-h ldaphost: Specify an alternative host on which the LDAP server is running. This is primarily used to perform LDAP operations against remote LDAP servers. The default host that's being used to perform the command against is local. This option has been deprecated in favor of -H.

-p ldapport: Specify an alternate TCP port where the LDAP server is listening. This option has been deprecated in favor of -H.

-p 2|3: Specify the LDAP protocol version to use.

-O security-properties: Specify SASL security properties.

-I: Enable SASL Interactive mode. Always prompt. The default is to prompt only as needed.

-Q: Enable SASL Quiet mode. Never prompt.

-U authcid: Specify the authentication ID for the SASL bind. The form of the ID depends on the actual SASL mechanism used.

-R realm: Specify the realm of the authentication ID for the SASL bind. The form of the realm depends on the actual SASL mechanism used.

-X authzid: Specify the requested authorization ID for the SASL bind. *authzid* must be one of the following formats: dn:_distinguished name_ or u:_username_.

-Y mech: Specify the SASL mechanism to be used for authentication. If it's not specified, the program will choose the best mechanism the server understands.

-Z[Z]: Issue StartTLS extended operation. If you use -ZZ, the command will require the operation to be successful.

slapcat (8C)

The slapcat utility generates LDIF output based on the contents of a slapd database. It selects the given database determined by the default number or suffix and writes the corresponding LDIF to STDOUT or a file specified on the command line. The LDIF generated by this tool is suitable for use with slapadd (8). As the entries are in database order, not superior first order, they can't be loaded with ldapadd (8) without being reordered. That is, in order to create an entry within ou=People, ou=People first needs to exist. If it doesn't exist, then a violation exists.

The following is a synopsis of the available command-line options:

```
/usr/local/sbin/slapcat [-v] [-c] [-d level] [-b suffix | -n dbnum]
[-f slapd.conf] [-l ldif-file]
```

The following list defines the command-line options for this utility:

- -v: Enable verbose mode.

- -c : Enable continue (ignore errors) mode.

- -d level: Enable debugging messages as defined by the specified level.

- -b suffix: Use the specified suffix to determine for which database to generate output. You can't use the -b option in conjunction with the -n option.

- -n dbnum: Generate output for the dbnum-th database listed in the configuration file. You can't use the -n option in conjunction with the -b option.

- -f slapd.conf: Specify an alternative slapd.conf file.

- -l ldif-file: Write LDIF to the specified file instead of STDOUT.

Your directory should be stopped when utilizing this tool.

slapadd (8C)

The slapadd utility adds entries, in LDIF, to an LDAP directory. It opens the database specified on the command line and adds entries corresponding to the specified LDIF file to the database directly. As slapadd is designed to accept LDIF in database order, as produced by slapcat, it doesn't verify that superior entries exist before adding an entry, doesn't perform all user and system schema checks, and doesn't maintain operational attributes (such as createTimeStamp and modifiersName).

The following is a synopsis of available command-line options:

```
/usr/local/sbin/slapadd [-v]  [-c]  [-u]  [-d  level]  [-b suffix] [-n dbnum]
 [-f slapd.conf] [-l ldif-file]
```

The following list defines the command-line options for this utility:

- -v: Enable verbose mode.

- -c : Enable continue (ignore errors) mode.

- -u : Enable dry run mode. This won't write to the database.

- -d level: Enable debugging messages as defined by the specified level.

- -b suffix: Use the specified suffix to determine for which database to generate output. You can't use the -b option in conjunction with the -n option.

- -n dbnum: Generate output for the dbnum-th database listed in the configuration file. You can't use the -n option in conjunction with the -b option.

- -f slapd.conf: Specify an alternative slapd.conf file.

- -l ldif-file: Read LDIF from the specified file instead of STDIN.

Your directory should be stopped when utilizing this tool.

slapindex (8C)

The slapindex utility regenerates directory indexes based on the current contents of your directory. It opens the database specified on the command line and updates all indexes for this particular directory.

The following is a synopsis of the available command-line options:

```
/usr/local/sbin/slapindex [-v] [-c] [-d level] [-b suffix | n dbnum]
 [-f slapd.conf]
```

The following list defines the command-line options for this utility:

- -v: Enable verbose mode.

- -c : Enable continue (ignore errors) mode.

- -d level: Enable debugging messages as defined by the specified level.

- -b suffix: Use the specified suffix to determine for which database to generate output. You can't use the -b option in conjunction with the -n option.

- -n dbnum: Generate output for the dbnum-th database listed in the configuration file. You can't use the -n option in conjunction with the -b option.

- -f slapd.conf: Specify an alternative slapd.conf file.

Your directory should be stopped when utilizing this tool.

Summary

After reading this chapter, you'll be able to install a basic OpenLDAP directory, and you'll have a working knowledge of some of the basic tools that have been provided for you. For many OpenLDAP installations you may encounter in the field, this is about as far as the basic administrator cares to go. In the next chapters, you'll be able to utilize your new knowledge and expand your directory to fit your custom environment.

CHAPTER 5

■■■

Implementing OpenLDAP

The default installation of OpenLDAP will work on almost any host. However, the defaults may make it difficult, in the future, to appropriately scale your system. Spending an extra few hours fully planning a system deployment will easily make up for having to reconfigure a badly installed host once you're in production mode. So it's highly recommended that you appropriately scale the host from the beginning.

For starters, you should know the approximate size of your initial deployment in terms of distinguished names (DNs). I recommend storing each entry in your directory as a single DN and not working with a model that requires a relationship between multiple DNs to represent data that may better be represented in a single object. For example, you can have the primary relative distinguished name (RDN) be uid=Tjackiewicz with a pointer, within the object, to cn=Account 1 or bad, number=9305. This model requires relationships, and you end up with a dynamic number of objects in your directory. That is, you have a single user ID (uid) for Tom Jackiewicz with all relevant data stored under that particular DN, and it remains a single entry whether this person has 5 accounts or 50 accounts. Other models would create a new DN for each of the necessary accounts, which would require you to have 6 DNs if there are 5 accounts (1 primary DN and 5 additional) or 51 DNs if there are 50 accounts (1 primary DN and 50 additional). This creates a problem for appropriately scaling and integrating applications, as the greatest amount of overhead is necessary when manipulating separate objects in the system, not just attribute names and values.

How Much RAM Do You Need?

The amount of random access memory (RAM) that systems require can vary. Realize that base requirements for a system really don't take much RAM into account. Sure, software may require 32 megabytes (MB) of RAM to install and run, but just how useful would that system be? What if you require additional indexes, or what if multiple applications are connected to it? You should answer the following questions to determine how much RAM is necessary:

- How many entries, such as individual DNs, do you have in your system?

- How many attributes do you have indexed in your environment?

- How many applications will be accessing your environment, and how many new sets of data will each of these requirements need?

Starting with the first question, a good measurement of the number of entries starts with the total user base of your existing applications. Many factors will come into play that may make this more complicated. For example, many applications, such as those used by your human resources (HR) department, often keep records of active and inactive employees. While your company many have only 10,000 active employees, the total number of records may exceed 100,000! To have your system be a good replacement or complement to existing systems, it may need to maintain all records. External-facing applications may also have records of all your vendors and customers. These could be the same size or even larger than your active employee population. Take these factors into account during your planning.

Each application has different requirements and will require a specific set of indexes depending on the data that's being searched. A phone directory alone may require that information pertaining to the department, clearance, variations of your name, and other identity information is searchable (for equality and presence) and even substring searchable. This will create a significant load on the system and increase the amount of memory that you'll require. Other applications, such as a mail server, may require only that the mail server, mail path, and e-mail address is searchable. Each application will have different requirements as you continue investigating your needs. A good integration will show that many of the attributes you've already indexed are the only ones required for a specific integration.

You can actually count the physical index files for your installation. But this assumes you already have a directory running. When this data isn't available, you must use estimates based on the size of the directory entry and how many attributes will be indexed. Envision the scenario where you have 500,000 entries in your directory and require seven indexes. You can estimate the dbcachesize and cachesize components of your system as follows:

```
Dbcachesize: Index file size * Number of indexes
Cachesize: Size per entry * Number of entries
```

You can then add the results of these operations to estimate the amount of RAM necessary for your application. Always plan for future growth, and estimate how new applications integrated within your environment will use existing indexes or request new ones.

In the fictional scenario, you may end up with the following:

```
Dbcachesize: 50 * 7 =  210MB of RAM
Cachesize: 5k * 500,000 =  2500MB of RAM
```

The final result would be 2710MB of RAM plus the overhead of the other applications and the operating system.

Obviously, the different types of threading libraries, the types of central processing units (CPUs), and the way the internals of the operating system work will yield different results. These tips are merely a baseline that you can use to evaluate system configurations and to verify whether a given host may be a candidate for a Lightweight Directory Access Protocol (LDAP) server.

How Much Disk Space Do You Need?

While the CPU and RAM capabilities of your system usually take the highest priorities, you must also look into other system configurations that, in today's fast-paced information technology environment, may be available to you. New technologies will always be emerging; if you choose to use new technologies within your company, you'll find that this will impact your server configuration decisions. With RAM being a replacement for physical disks in many system configurations, basic physical disk requirements (which were once the cornerstone of system configuration) are often overlooked. The overall performance of a given application is often bottlenecked or hindered by the speed at which data can be retrieved from storage. Don't be caught in the group that asks how much capacity a system needs to deliver. Rather, become part of the group that asks what the appropriate response time of a system configuration should be. With standard disk configurations nearly 100 gigabytes (GB), it's all too common for systems to be configured with a pair of disks, minimizing the physical number of heads available.

You should use a Redundant Array of Independent Disks (RAID) configuration whenever possible. RAID is the concept of using multiple disks acting as one. Although many new configurations exist today, the original definition of RAID had levels from 0 to 5, with a total of six configurations. Each has its strength and weaknesses but serves the common goal of increasing data redundancy and performance.

RAID 0, or standard striping, is a fast and simple configuration that takes two disks and just concatenates them to form a single disk. Unfortunately, RAID 0 is subject to the failure of one of the disks. RAID 1 is simply the mirroring of information on one disk across to another. In this configuration, data is given extra redundancy. RAID 10 (0+1 or 1+0) is a combination of mirroring and striping disks. RAID 2 protects storage using different functions and isn't as common. RAID 3 protects data using a parity scheme. RAID 4 gives you an extra parity disk. Network Appliance made this common, as the company uses it across its systems. RAID 5 enables you to have better random access of information but decreases write performance. RAID 6 is similar to RAID 5 but provides even worse write overhead. You should research the type of RAID configuration necessary for your organization.

Taking into account standard system configuration practices, it's a good idea to have separate partitions or physical disks for different types of data being stored within your system. Because a disk relies on physical heads to appropriately function, it's beneficial to layer disks across multiple controllers and have different physically separated filesystems located physically apart.

Table 5-1 shows the types of information you'll be dealing with in an LDAP configuration.

Table 5-1. *LDAP Configurations*

Type of Data	Storage Requirements
Operating system	The standard operating system installation should be installed separately from any of your application instances.
Operating system logs	The logs related to the running of the base operating system should be stored on a separate disk.
Application binaries	While not requiring specific input/output (I/O) configurations, it's advised that the installation instance and the data be separated. This also enables future movement of information during standard archiving methods.
Application logs	Application logs, though not often recommended in production environments, should be kept separate from the rest of your information.
Application data	Application data—that is, the database and indexes themselves—should be kept on a separate disk for maximum I/O throughput.

When provisioning hosts, the response time of your disks is often overlooked in favor of the physical amount of space. While many advancements in disk technology have been made, you're still dealing with physical heads, platters, and spindles that are limited. Space will always be an issue, but resist the urge to ask for 72GB of disk space, which may be provided to you as a single hard drive, and instead ask for 72GB of usable disk space with 8 millisecond (ms) maximum throughput on your system.

Considering Security in Your Implementation

To make up for the overall insecurity of Transmission Control Protocol/Internet Protocol (TCP/IP), new layers of security have been added to common protocols to decrease the chances of many types of security violations. To function securely, LDAP relies on many security functions. Methods of security in an LDAP environment include various types of client authentications, client authorization by means of access control, data integrity protection, resource limitation, and server-based authentication and authorization functions.

You may be working with multiple types of LDAP instances.

- A read-only directory containing no sensitive data that's accessible to anyone; TCP connection hijacking or IP spoofing isn't a problem. This directory requires no security functions except administrative service limits.

- A read-only directory containing no sensitive data where read access is granted based on identity; TCP connection hijacking isn't currently a problem. This scenario requires a secure authentication function.

- A read-only directory containing no sensitive data where the client needs to ensure that the directory data is authenticated by the server and not modified while being returned from the server.

- A read-write directory, containing no sensitive data, where read access is available to anyone, but write access requires authorization. This scenario requires a secure authentication function.

- A directory containing sensitive information requiring session confidentiality and secure authentication.

Authentication

Authentication credentials are the information that's provided by one party (the user) to another (the server) to show the identity of the user. Authentication is the process of generating, transmitting, and verifying these credentials and the associated identity. Authentication information is supplied by the "bind" operation. A client initiates a connection, or *binds* to the system, and provides the server with the appropriate authentication information.

Anonymous: When a client initiates a connection to the server but doesn't offer credentials, an anonymous session is created. An anonymous session is also created when a bind operation hasn't been completed successfully. An LDAP client may also force anonymous authentication by using a zero-length string with the simple authentication choice.

Password-based or simple authentication: Simple authentication is established with a client sends an identity (the bind DN) and a simple password during the initiation of a connection. This type of authentication is typically not suitable for an environment that has access to outside networks.

Certificate-based authentication: LDAP also supports authentication using a client-side certificate.

The bind operation is defined as follows:

```
BindRequest ::= [APPLICATION 0] SEQUENCE {
 version INTEGER (1 .. 127 ),
 name LDAPDN,
 authentication AuthenticationChoice
}

AuthenticationChoice ::= CHOICE {
 simple [0] OCTET STRING,
 -- 1 and 2 reserved
 sasl [3] SaslCredentials
}

SaslCredentials ::= SEQUENCE {
 mechanism LDAPString,
 credentials OCTET STRING OPERATION
}
```

In this request, version is a version number indicating the version of the protocol to be used during this session, name is the name of the directory object that the client is binding as, and authentication is information used to authenticate the bind DN.

Upon receipt of the request, the server will authenticate the requesting client. The server will then return a bind response indicating the status of the request. For some authentication mechanisms, it may be necessary for the client to invoke the request multiple times. This depends on the security requirements of the implementation and the mechanisms used. The authenticated identity of a session may change during the life of the session with version 3 of LDAP.

SASL

As defined by RFC 2222, Simple Authentication and Security Layer (SASL) is a method for adding authentication support to connection-based protocols. A security layer between a client and a server is negotiated during protocol initiation. If a server supports the SASL mechanism, it initiates an authentication protocol exchange. This consists of a series of server challenges and client responses that are specific to the request mechanism. The challenges and responses are defined by the mechanisms as binary tokens of arbitrary length. The protocol's profile then specifies how these binary tokens are encoded for transfer over the established connection. After receiving the authentication command or any client response, a server may issue a challenge, indicate failure, or indicate completion. The protocol's profile specifies how the server indicates which it's doing. After receiving a challenge, a client may issue a response or abort the exchange. The protocol's profile specifies how the client indicates which it's doing.

During the authentication protocol exchange, the mechanism performs authentication, transmits an authorization identity (a user ID) from the client to the server, and negotiates the use of a mechanism-specific security layer. If the use of a security layer is agreed upon, then the mechanism must also define or negotiate the maximum cipher-text buffer size that each side is able to receive.

If use of a security layer is negotiated, the layer is applied to all subsequent data sent over a connection. The security layer takes effect immediately following the last response of the authentication exchange for data sent by the client and the completion indication for data sent by the server. Once the security layer is in effect, the security layer processes the protocol stream.

You can implement SASL support in OpenLDAP using Cyrus SASL. You can obtain more information on the Cyrus SASL project at http://asg.web.cmu.edu/sasl/. The libraries are available via File Transfer Protocol (FTP) at ftp://ftp.andrew.cmu.edu/pub/cyrus-mail/. Upon retrieving the package, you'll want to install and link them against your Sleepycat DB libraries before running the configuration scripts for installation.

Set CPPFLAGS and LDFLAGS to point to the appropriate locations for your environment, like so:

```
$ env CPPFLAGS="-I/usr/local/BerkeleyDB.4.2/include" \
LDFLAGS="-L/usr/local/BerkeleyDB.4.2/lib" ./configure
```

After setting these parameters, you can follow them with the standard installation instructions for the base build of the system. You'll need to create the SASL user database using the saslpasswd2 command. This command takes the following options:

```
saslpasswd [-p] [-d] [-c] [-n] [-f file] [-u domain] [-a appname] userid
```

The server administrator uses this command to set a user's SASL password for server programs and SASL mechanisms that use the standard libsasl database of user secrets. Its options are as follows:

-p: This sets pipe mode. saslpasswd will neither prompt for the password nor verify that it was entered correctly. This is the default when STDIN isn't a terminal.

-c: This creates an entry for the user if the user doesn't already exist. This is mutually exclusive with the -d (delete user) flag.

-d: This deletes the entry for the user. This is mutually exclusive with the -c (create user) flag.

-n: This doesn't set the plain-text userPassword attribute for the user.

-u domain: This is the domain. In other words, this is the user realm.

-f file: Use file for sasldb.

-a appname: Use appname as application name.

The following command sets the administrative password:

```
$ saslpasswd2 -c admin
```

The previous parameter (admin) refers to the uid of the account; thus, the profile in LDAP Interchange Format (LDIF) may look like the following:

```
dn: uid=admin, ou=People, dc=Your,dc=Company
objectClass: Top
objectClass: Person
objectClass: Organizationalperson
objectClass: Inetorgperson
uid: admin
userPassword: password
```

Upon being asked for a password, enter the same password you specified for the administrative account within your LDAP system. Upon completion of this, you can set the sasl-regexp directive within the slapd.conf file.

```
sasl-regexp uid=<username>,cn=<realm>,cn=<mech>,cn=auth
```

For example:

```
sasl-regexp uid=(.*),cn=ldaphost,cn=DIGEST-MD5, \
cn=auth uid=$1,ou=People,dc=Your,dc=Company
```

This username is taken from SASL and inserted into the LDAP search string in the place of $1. Yours is typically your Fully Qualified Domain Name (FQDN).

Upon restarting slapd, you can test to see if your configuration worked by running an ldapsearch command, like so:

```
$ ldapsearch -U admin@realm -b dc=Your,dc=Comapny objectclass=*
```

You'll see the following output:

```
SASL/DIGEST-MD5 authentication started
```

Now enter your password, like so:

```
SASL username: admin@realm
SASL SSF: 128
SASL installing layers
```

This will be followed by the results of the filter you specified during the LDAP search. I'll discuss security methods and other integrations with SASL in more detail in subsequent sections.

SASL Proxy Authorization

SASL allows authenticated users to perform operations as other users. This feature is known as *proxy authorization* and occurs after the user has obtained an authentication DN. The server will then make a decision about whether to allow the authorization to occur. If it's allowed, the user's LDAP connection is switched to have a binding DN derived from the authorization identity, and the LDAP session proceeds with the access of the new authorization DN.

This sort of service is useful when one entity needs to act on the behalf of many other users. For example, you could create role accounts for specific tasks that you have to perform changes as someone else. This gives you the ability to become a user during a help desk call to perform extra debugging that's beyond the user's knowledge.

Once slapd has the authorization DN, the actual approval process begins. You'll need to add saslAuthzTo and saslAuthzFrom as attributes within your user profile information in LDAP to allow basic SASL authentication. Both can be multivalued. The saslAuthzTo attribute is a source rule, and it's placed into the entry associated with the authentication DN to tell what authorization DNs the authenticated DN is allowed to assume. The second attribute is a destination rule, and it's placed into the entry associated with the requested authorization DN to tell which authenticated DNs may assume it.

The choice of which authorization policy attributes to use is up to the administrator. Source rules are checked first in the person's authentication DN entry, and if none of the saslAuthzTo rules specify that the authorization is permitted, the saslAuthzFrom rules in the authorization DN entry are then checked. If neither case specifies that the request be honored, the request is denied. Since the default behavior is to deny authorization requests, rules specify only that a request be allowed; no rules tell what authorizations to deny.

Take a look at the following LDAP entry:

```
dn: cn=Helpdesk,dc=Your,dc=Company
saslAuthzTo: ldap:///dc=your,dc=company??sub?(objectclass=Person)
```

Any user who authenticated as cn=Helpdesk,dc=Your,dc=Company could authorize any other LDAP entry under the search base dc=Your,dc=Company that has an objectClass of Person. Be careful when assigning this information, as it's extremely powerful and easy to abuse. You may want to limit the scope of this attribute as follows:

```
saslAuthzTo: uid=.*,dc=Your,dc=Company
```

Shared-Secret Mechanisms

Cyrus SASL supports several shared-secret mechanisms. To do this, it needs access to the plain-text password (unlike mechanisms that pass plain-text passwords over the wire, where the server can store a hashed version of the password).

Secret passwords are normally stored in Cyrus SASL's own sasldb database, but if OpenLDAP software has been compiled with Cyrus SASL 2.1, then it's possible to store the secrets in the LDAP database itself. With Cyrus SASL 1.5, secrets may be stored only in the sasldb database. In either case it's important to apply file access controls and LDAP access controls to prevent exposing the passwords. To use secrets stored in the LDAP directory, place plain-text passwords in the userPassword attribute. It will be necessary to add password-hash {CLEARTEXT} to your slapd.conf file to make sure that passwords changed through LDAP are stored in plain text. Wherever the passwords are stored, a mapping will be needed from SASL authentication IDs to regular DNs. The DIGEST-MD5 mechanism produces authentication IDs of the form uid=<username>,cn=<realm>,cn=digest-md5,cn=auth.

You specify the SASL mechanism you want to use with -Y on the command line. To utilize DIGEST-MD5, you use ldapsearch -Y DIGEST-MD5 followed by the rest of your command-line parameters.

The authentication mechanism in the slapd server will use SASL library calls to obtain the authenticated user's username, based on whatever underlying authentication mechanism was used. This username is in the namespace of the authentication mechanism, not in the LDAP namespace. As stated previously, that username is reformatted into an authentication request DN of the following form:

```
uid=<username>,cn=<realm>,cn=<mechanism>,cn=auth
```

You shouldn't add LDAP entries of this form to your LDAP database. Chances are you have an LDAP entry for each of the people who will be authenticating to LDAP, laid out in your directory tree, and the tree doesn't start at cn=auth. But if your site has a clear mapping between the username and an LDAP entry for the person, you'll be able to configure your LDAP server to automatically map an authentication request DN to the user's authentication DN. It isn't required that the authentication request DN or the user's authentication DN resulting from the mapping refers to an entry held in the directory. However, you'll need to tell the slapd server how to map an authentication request DN to a user's authentication DN. You do this by adding one or more sasl-regexp directives to the slapd.conf file. This directive takes two arguments, like so:

```
sasl-regexp    <search pattern>    <replacement pattern>
```

The authentication request DN is compared to the search pattern using regular expressions. If it sees multiple sasl-regexp directives, only the first whose search pattern matches the authentication identity is used. The string that's output from the replacement pattern should be the authentication DN of the user in a legitimate LDAP DN format.

The search pattern can contain any of the regular expression characters listed in regexec (3C). The main characters of note are a dot (.), an asterisk (*), and the open and close parentheses ((and)). Essentially, the dot matches any character, the asterisk allows zero or more repeats of the immediately preceding character or pattern, and terms in parentheses are remembered for the replacement pattern. The replacement pattern will produce the final authentication DN of the user. Anything from the authentication request DN that matched a string in parentheses in the search pattern is stored in the variable $1. That variable $1 can appear in the replacement pattern and will be replaced by the string from the authentication request DN. If there were multiple sets of parentheses in the search pattern, the variables $2, $3, and so on, are used.

For example, suppose the user's authentication identity is written as the DN string uid=tjackiewicz,cn=yourcompany.com,cn=DIGEST-MD5,cn=auth and the entry in LDAP is uid=tjackiewicz,ou=People,dc=Your,dc=Company. You'd write the sasl-regexp to create this match as follows:

```
sasl-regexp
uid=(.*),cn=yourcompany.com,cn=DIGEST-MD5,cn=auth
uid=$1,ou=People,dc=Your,dc=Company
```

Some sites may have people's DNs spread to multiple areas of the LDAP tree, such as if an ou=accounting tree and an ou=engineering tree had people interspersed between them. Or there may not be enough information in the authentication identity to isolate the DN, such as if the previous person's LDAP entry looked like this:

```
dn: cn=tom jackiewicz,ou=person,dc=Your,dc=Company
objectclass: Person
cn: tom jackiewicz
uid: tjackiewicz
```

In this case, the information in the authentication identity can be used only to search for the user's DN, not derive it directly. For both of these situations, and others, the replacement pattern in the sasl-regexp directives will need to produce an LDAP uniform resource locator (URL), described in the next section.

When you don't have enough information in the authentication identity to derive a person's authentication DN directly, the sasl-regexp directives in the slapd.conf (5) file will need to produce an LDAP URL. You can then use this URL to perform an internal search of the LDAP database to find the person's authentication DN.

An LDAP URL, similar to other URLs, has the following form:

```
ldap://<host>/<base>?<attrs>?<scope>?<filter>
```

This contains all the elements necessary to perform an LDAP search: the name of the server <host>, the LDAP DN search base <base>, the LDAP attributes to retrieve <attrs>, the search scope <scope> (which is one of the three options base, one, or sub), and an LDAP search filter <filter>. Since the search is for an LDAP DN within the current server, the <host> portion should be empty. The <attrs> field is also ignored since only the DN is of concern. These two elements are left in the format of the URL to maintain the clarity of what information goes where in the string.

Suppose that the person in the previous example did in fact have an authentication username of adamson and that information was kept in the attribute uid in their LDAP entry. The sasl-regexp directive may be written as follows:

```
sasl-regexp
uid=(.*),cn=example.com,cn=kerberos_v4,cn=auth
ldap:///ou=person,dc=example,dc=com??sub?(uid=$1)
```

This will initiate an internal search of the LDAP database inside the slapd server. If the search returns exactly one entry, it's accepted as being the DN of the user. If more than one entry is returned, or if zero entries are returned, the authentication fails, and the user's connection is left bound as the authentication request DN.

Note that if the search scope <scope> in the URL is base, then the only LDAP entry that will be returned is the search base DN <base>, so the actual search of the database is skipped. This is equivalent to setting the replacement pattern in the directive to a DN directly, as in the previous section.

The attributes that are used in the search filter <filter> in the URL should be indexed to allow faster searching. If they aren't, the authentication step alone can take uncomfortably long periods, and users may assume the server is down.

A more complex site may have several realms in use, each mapping to a different subtree in the directory. These can be handled with statements of the following form:

```
# Match Engineering realm
    sasl-regexp
        uid=(.*),cn=engineering.example.com,cn=digest-md5,cn=auth
        ldap:///dc=eng,dc=example,dc=com??sub?(&(uid=$1)(objectClass=person))

  # Match Accounting realm
    sasl-regexp
        uid=(.*),cn=accounting.example.com,cn=digest-md5,cn=auth
        ldap:///dc=accounting,dc=example,dc=com??sub? \
(&(uid=$1)(objectClass=person))
```

```
      # Default realm is customers.example.com
    sasl-regexp
        uid=(.*),cn=digest-md5,cn=auth
        ldap:///dc=customers,dc=example,dc=com??sub? \
(&(uid=$1)(objectClass=person))
```

X.509 Certificates

A *public key certificate* is a digitally signed statement from one entity, saying that the public key (and some other information) of another entity has some specific value. You can see the most visible implementations of X.509 certificates when using your Web browser. However, in back-end systems, certificates are often utilized for other tasks, such as server-to-server validation. In a client-to-multiserver environment, you can use certificates at almost every level of interaction. You can use X.509 certificates as an external source of authentication information within SASL.

Transport Layer Security

OpenLDAP clients and servers are capable of using the Transport Layer Security (TLS) framework to provide integrity and confidentiality protection. TLS uses X.509 certificates for client and server identification. TLS, according to the Internet Engineering Task Force (IETF), is the successor protocol to SSL. In fact, original versions of TLS (version 1) were nearly identical to SSL (version 3). The goal of TLS is to serve as a transport layer protocol that provides the ability to establish an end-to-end secure channel of communication. Confidentiality, integrity, and key exchange are required components for a transport layer protocol to be successful. A clear definition of this type of protocol will include requirements for keys, encryption, and supported authentication mechanisms. Because this is only in the transport layer, TLS runs on top of TCP.

TLS, as implemented within LDAP, is specified in RFC 2830, *Lightweight Directory Access Protocol (v3): Extension for Transport Layer Security*. It's specified that a client may perform a StartTLS operation by specifying an ExtendedRequest (which is part of the LDAP v3 specification) containing the object identifier (OID) for the StartTLS operation (1.3.6.1.4.1.1466.20037). An LDAP ExtendedRequest is defined as follows:

```
ExtendedRequest::= [APPLICATION 23] SEQUENCE {
 RequestName [0] LDAPOID,
 RequestValue [1] OCTET STRING OPTIONAL
}
```

The RequestValue field is kept empty during the StartTLS request. When a StartTLS extended request is made, the server must send a positive response for communication to be established.

```
ExtendedResponse::= [APPLICATION 24] SEQUENCE {
 COMPONENTS OF LDAPResult,
 ResponseName [10] LDAPOID OPTIONAL,
 Response [11] OCTET STRING OPTIONAL
}
```

The StartTLS extended response must contain a responseName field that will correspond with the responseName field during the extended request. The resulting code from the communication initialization can be either "success," which means the server is willing and able to negotiate TLS, or another response that can then be used to either try again or completely abort the request. The available result codes are as follows:

- `OperationsError`: Operation sequencing is incorrect; for example, TLS is already established.

- `ProtocolError`: TLS isn't supported, or an incorrect structure exists.

- `Referral`: This particular server doesn't support TLS, but the one given in the referral may.

- `Unavailable`: This indicates a significant error with TLS or an unavailable server.

The goals of using the TLS protocol with LDAP are to ensure connection confidentiality and integrity and to optionally provide for authentication. TLS expressly provides these capabilities. All security gained via using the StartTLS operation is actually gained from using TLS itself. The StartTLS operation, on its own, doesn't provide any additional security. TLS is just one of the tools provided and incorporated into LDAP that serves as a building block for a security system. That is, the incorporation of multiple security procedures and protocols as an all-encompassing package is necessary for running a secure LDAP environment.

Access Control

An *access control policy* is a set of rules defining the protection of resources, generally in terms of the capabilities of persons or other entities accessing those resources. A common expression of an access control policy is an access control list. Security objects and mechanisms enable the expression of access control policies and their enforcement. Attributes within your LDAP system store this information. A request, when a server is processing it, may be associated with a wide variety of security-related factors. The server uses these factors to determine whether and how to process the request. These are called access control factors (ACFs). They may include source IP address, encryption strength, type of operation being requested, time of day, and a variety of others. Some factors may be specific to the request itself, and others may be environmental. Access control policies are expressed in terms of ACFs, such as "a request having the ACFs I,j,k can perform operation Y on resource Z." Currently no standard exists for access control information in LDAP, which has always been a major cause of concern.

Kerberos

Kerberos is a network authentication protocol. It's designed to provide strong authentication for client-server applications by using secret key cryptography. MIT created Kerberos as a solution to network security problems. The Kerberos protocol uses strong cryptography so that a client can prove its identity to a server (and vice versa) across an insecure network connection. After a client and server have used Kerberos to prove their identities, all incoming and outgoing communication is encrypted to assure privacy and data integrity. Kerberos is a good solution to network security problems and provides tools of authentication and strong cryptography over the network to help secure information across your infrastructure. The Generic Security Services Application Programming Interface (GSSAPI) mechanism with SASL is used to support Kerberos V. GSSAPI is discussed in great detail in RFC 2743 and RFC 1964.

To use the GSSAPI mechanism with slapd, you must create a service key with a principal for LDAP service within the realm for the host on which the service runs. You'll need to specify sasl-realm in your slapd.conf file if the LDAP server host's FQDN isn't the same as the name of your realm. You can modify the option sasl-secprops to constrain the mechanisms that SASL will accept. If you run slapd on ldap.yourcompany.com and your realm is YOURCOMPANY.COM, you need to create a service key with the following principal:

ldap/ldap.yourcompany.com@YOURCOMPANY.COM

This key will need to exist in the keytab file in /etc/krb5.keytab or wherever your implementation has set it. To use the GSSAPI mechanism to authenticate to the directory, the user obtains a ticket-granting ticket (TGT) prior to running the LDAP client. When using OpenLDAP client tools, the user may mandate the use of the GSSAPI mechanism by specifying -Y GSSAPI as a command option.

OpenLDAP associates a nonmapped authentication request DN of the following form:

uid=<primary[/instance]>,cn=<realm>,cn=gssapi,cn=auth

A user with the Kerberos principal tom@YOURCOMPANY.COM would have the associated DN of uid=tom,cn=yourcompany.com,cn=gssapi,cn=auth.

Understanding Replication

Centralized storage of data doesn't necessarily mean a centralized server. The ability to distribute information across multiple servers is key to a redundant environment. Replication is the mechanism used to copy information from one directory to a series of others. The mechanism is also used to keep this information in sync across all LDAP systems.

With replication, you're able to more easily achieve fault tolerance, better performance, and localized management of information across multiple nodes.

You need to understand multiple concepts related to replication.

Master: The master server is the authoritative source of your LDAP information. It's the server that ultimately controls writes to your directory and pushes data across to other systems.

Slave or consumer: A slave or consumer is a host that provides read access to directory data. When a write operation needs to be processed, the request is forwarded to the master using a referral.

Replica hub: A hub may serve as a buffer between a master and a slave. A hub accepts replication information from the original source of data (master) and quickly pushes it to all the slave servers. Typically, because of the excess overhead, a replica hub isn't configured to accept client reads.

Most modern LDAP deployments (where LDAP is used as it should be, not just a localized storage area for local configuration files), it's necessary to support some level of replication. Often the decisions on how to create your replicated environment are made based on similar criteria used to create your directory information tree (see Table 5-2).

Table 5-2. *Decisions About Server Layout*

Input	Output	Explanation
Single organization, small office	Replication for performance and redundancy Master, some consumers	In a small environment without logical "nodes," it may be a good idea to have information replicated to allow for higher availability of information.
Single organization, multiple offices	Replication for performance and redundancy Master, replica head(s), some consumers	The more consumers you need to support, the more replica heads may be necessary to support this functionality.

OpenLDAP utilizes slurpd to handle replication. This daemon runs in parallel with the slapd instance on the master server and utilizes standard LDIF statements and LDAP to propagate changes. The slurpd process utilizes a changelog to keep track of what changes take place on the master server. Based on information contained in this log, slurpd generates LDIF statements and propagates them to the rest of the hosts within the replication model.

changelog/Replication Log

The changelog contains LDIF records showing what has changed on the system since the log was generated. That is, each time any change to your data is made, that change is stored as a transaction record within your changelog. This acts as a "journal" that can be used to rebuild systems from a certain date or to maintain changes across systems that contain a large number of records. Imagine a host with 100,000 records. If synchronization needs to occur from one host to another, either the entire directory can be viewed and the changes can be generated and processed, or the changelog can be viewed and only the 1,000 changes that occurred since the last synchronization can be processed.

The slurpd process uses the changelog fully. In future integration projects, you'll see that meta-directory systems and other applications will also use this. However, realize that the changelog, if enabled on more than a single host, decreases system performance and is inconsistent. If Host A is on change 10 and Host B is on change 14, any system that relies on the changelog to update its own records won't be able to differentiate between the changes. This makes it necessary to rely on a single host with a single changelog for the appropriate consistency.

When slapd is configured to generate a changelog, this file contains LDIF records of changes. It also contains the relevant replication sites and a time stamp. Operational attributes (such as the modifier's name and various time stamps) will also be stored. Using previous examples, imagine the following scenario:

```
dn: uid=tjackiewicz,ou=People,dc=Your, dc=Company
objectclass: top
objectclass: inetorgperson
cn: Tom Jackiewicz
sn: Jackiewicz
uid: Tjackiewicz
```

If you wanted to change the CN from Tom Jackiewicz to Thomas Jackiewicz, you'd generate an LDIF statement to perform the operation.

```
dn: uid=tjackiewicz,ou=People,dc=Your, dc=Company
changetype: modify
replace: cn
cn: Thomas Jackiewicz
```

The changelog will also contain a similar statement but may include operational attributes as well—things you don't necessarily have to use. Multiple replica lines can, and will, exist in your environment if you have more than just a single master and single consumer.

```
replica: LDAPConsumer.YourCompany.com:389
time: 0403030334
dn: uid=tjackiewicz,ou=People,dc=Your, dc=Company
changetype: modify
replace: cn
cn: Thomas Jackiewicz
-
replace: modifiersName
modifiersName: cn=Directory Manager
-
replace: modifyTimestamp
modifyTimestamp: 20040204030303342
```

The other items were also stored in the changelog, but the standard statement, in LDIF, showing the modification that was made, was included. Almost everything in LDAP can be broken down into LDIF, which is the most common denominator you're using. To elaborate, the record begins with one or more lines, indicating the replicas to which the change is to be propagated.

```
replica: <hostname[:portnumber]>
```

The time the change took place is given, as the number of seconds since Jan. 1, 1970, with an optional decimal extension to ensure uniqueness.

```
time: <integer[.integer]>
```

The DN of the entry being modified is then provided, along with the changetype information.

```
dn: <distinguishedname>
changetype: <[modify|add|delete|modrdn]>
add: <attributetype>
<attributetype>: <value1>
<attributetype>: <value2>

...
-
```

The terms *changelog* and *replication log* will be used interchangeably, as they represent the same function—the ability to log changes on an LDAP host as they occur. Different implementations of LDAP use a variety of different formats and terms for this.

slurpd

In summary, slurpd is the process used to propagate changes from the master directory to others in the hierarchy. When slurpd sees a change, it locks the changelog, makes its own copy, releases the lock, and forks a copy of itself for each downwind system to which it needs to push information.

The options for startup and configuration are as follows:

-d debug-level: Turns on debugging as defined by debug-level. If this option is specified, even with a zero argument, slurpd will not fork or disassociate from the invoking terminal. Some general operation and status messages are printed for any value of debug-level, which is taken as a bit string, with each bit corresponding to a different kind of debugging information. The debug levels that can be used here are consistent with slapd.

-f slapd-config-file: Specifies the slapd configuration file to use.

-r slapd-replog-file: Specifies the name of the slapd replication log file or the changelog. Normally, the name of the changelog is read from the slapd configuration file. This file should be located in a readable directory.

-o: Specifies to run in "one-shot" mode. Normally, slurpd processes the changelog file and then watches for more entries to be appended. In one-shot mode, slurpd processes an existing changelog and then stops.

-t temp-dir: This is the temporary directory that's used to store the local locked copy of the changelog.

-k srvtab-file: Specifies the location of the Kerberos srvtab file that contains keys for the replica slapd instances. This option overrides the srvtab argument to the replica directive in the slapd configuration file.

The first step in replication requires the configuration of a master and slapd instance. To make an existing slapd instance into a replication master, configuration changes are necessary to the slapd.conf configuration file.

On the master, add a replica directive for each replica. The binddn= parameter should match the updatedn option in the corresponding slave. Add a replogfile directive that specifies the location of the replication log (or changelog).

On the slave, make sure your base configurations are the same as your master. It's not wise to attempt to have different base DNs and schemas across multiple hosts that are, in a sense, acting as a single entity. In a master-to-consumer configuration, it isn't necessary to include the previous master changes on the slave (that is, no replica directive and no replogfile). You'll need to include the updatedn line and make sure it's consistent with the master. The DN given should match the DN given in the binddn= parameter of the corresponding replica= directive in the master slapd.conf file. The updatedn shouldn't be the same as the rootdn of the slave database.

The master configuration modifications may look like the following:

```
replica host=Consumer.YourCompany.Com:389
    binddn="cn=Replication Manager"
    bindmethod=simple credentials=password
    replogfile /var/lib/openldap/replication.log
```

Another more standard and current method of specifying the host information is as follows:

```
replica uri=ldap://Consumer.YourCompany.Com:389
    binddn="cn=Replication Manager"
    bindmethod=simple credentials=password
    replogfile /var/lib/openldap/replication.log
```

In these configurations, for the consumer Consumer.YourCompany.Com, which is an LDAP server running on port 389 on this particular host, I'll connect as cn=Directory Manager using the password of password and propagate changes stored in the replogfile location.

The same operation, using a more secure method, LDAPS, on port 636 is as follows:

```
replica uri=ldaps://Consumer.YourCompany.Com:636
    binddn="cn=Replication Manager"
    bindmethod=simple credentials=password
    replogfile /var/lib/openldap/replication.log
```

The configurations on the individual consumers may exist as follows:

```
updatedn "cn=Replication Manager"
```

Ensure that the DN you give has the appropriate permissions to update the directory.

updateref

To ensure that the slave starts functioning with an exact copy of the master data, the master server needs to be stopped, and the database needs to be appropriately synchronized. During this synchronization process, it's necessary to put the master in read-only mode. This way, changes made during this process are rejected.

You have multiple methods of performing the synchronization. However, to be safe and to breed good habits, you should use the slapcat program to output the master directory into LDIF format. Using LDIF instead of directly copying database files (as is often suggested and documented) avoids any potential incompatibilities between different server configurations.

Importing Databases

I'm working with the assumption that you already have a database you want to import and create replication agreements in. (If you don't currently have a set of data you're working with, it isn't necessary to read this section.) You have many ways of accessing and retrieving data in a usable format such as LDIF. However, you need to be aware of some main differences between the methods that are available to you (see Table 5-3).

Table 5-3. *Local vs. Remote LDAP Utilities*

Utility	Scope	Pro/Con
slapcat	Local server with physical access to the directory.	Pro: Takes into account all directory- and database-level information that wouldn't be available when accessing via other methods. Con: Need local directory access, privileges. Proprietary application.
ldapsearch	Local or remote server. No special access, beyond access to the directory via the LDAP protocol, is required.	Pro: Can be used across multiple directories, LDAP protocol versions, vendors, and implementations. Con: Operational attributes and internal data may not be retrievable, thus this can't always be relied upon to completely build a mirror directory.

All LDAP implementations require some method of conversion from an existing directory (stored in a number of database files) to LDIF format suitable for creating a clone. This is necessary because of the types of data that may exist in a directory, including standard user and informational records, internal metadata, and various operators used to control information processing. Much of the "other" data isn't necessarily accessible using standard tools (or APIs) to access the information. For example, the entry of uid=tjackiewicz,ou=People,dc=Your, dc=Company may be made up of five attributes and object classes at first glance. However, internal attributes (such as entrydn, uniqueid, and others that may be used by meta-directories and other systems) may be hidden from standard view. Additionally, the specific order of information in the record (which shouldn't matter for most purposes) may also need to be maintained. For this reason, the ability to export data as it actually exists needs to be available.

slapcat

OpenLDAP provides slapcat for this functionality. The utility is used to generate LDIF output based on the contents of the slapd database itself. Instead of communicating with standard APIs to the LDAP server itself, it opens the specific database files stored locally and generates LDIF output based on their contents. Because the entries processed are in database order, not superior first order, they can't be loaded with standard LDAP utilities. That is, because the database may have uid=X,ou=A,ou=B,ou=C,dc=Your,dc=Company in the database first, before all its dependencies, only the slapadd program can be used to add it. This entry (RDN of uid=X) depends on the existence of all its parents (ou=A, ou=B, and so on), but within the database files themselves, they may be defined after the actual entry.

The syntax for slapcat is as follows:

```
slapcat [-v] [-c] [-d level] [-b suffix] [-n dbnum]
[-f slapd.conf] [-l ldif-file]
```

The options are as follows:

- -v: Enables verbose mode.

- -c: Enables continue (ignore errors) mode.

- -d level: Enables debugging messages as defined by the specified debug level. This debug level is compatible with those for the slapd server.

- -b suffix: Uses the specified suffix to determine for which database to generate output. You can't use this option in conjunction with the -n option.

- -n dbnum: Generates output for the dbnum-th database listed in the configuration file. You can't use the -n option in conjunction with the -b option.

- -f slapd.conf: Specifies an alternative configuration file.

- -l ldif-file: Writes LDIF to the specified file instead of STDOUT.

You must ensure that slapd isn't running during this process to ensure consistency of the database being read.

Testing

Upon completion of the replication tasks, you must restart the master directory server. Perform a basic change in your system (in other words, modify an entry) to see that the corresponding changelog is being modified.

Now you can start the slurpd process. Upon startup, slurpd should immediately connect to the consumer LDAP server and propagate your change. When a change is propagated and slurpd receives an error, it writes the reason for the error and the replication record to a reject file. The reject file is located in the same directory as the replication log. It maintains the same name but is appended with .rej. In these examples, if the directive replogfile is set to the value of /var/lib/openldap/replication.log, the resulting file would be /var/lib/openldap/replication.log.rej. The format of the rejection list is similar to the replication log itself. Had the previous example been a rejection, it would look like this:

```
ERROR: error message
replica: LDAPConsumer.YourCompany.com:389
time: 0403030334
dn: uid=tjackiewicz,ou=People,dc=Your, dc=Company
changetype: modify
replace: cn
cn: Thomas Jackiewicz
-
replace: modifiersName
modifiersName: cn=Directory Manager
-
replace: modifyTimestamp
modifyTimestamp: 20040204030303347
```

A sample rejection log entry follows:

```
ERROR: No such attribute
```

It's possible to use slurpd to process a rejection log with its one-shot mode. In normal operation, slurpd watches for more replication records to be appended to the replication log file. In one-shot mode, by contrast, slurpd processes a single log file and exits. slurpd ignores ERROR lines at the beginning of replication log entries, so it's not necessary to edit them out before feeding it the rejection log.

To use one-shot mode, specify the name of the rejection log on the command line as the argument to the -r flag and specify one-shot mode with the -o flag. For example, to process the rejection log file /usr/local/var/openldap/replog.slave.YourCompany.com:389 and exit, use the following command:

```
slurpd -r /usr/tmp/replog.slave.YourCompany.com:389 -o
```

Understanding Referrals

Referrals are one way to extend the scope of your directory beyond a single server and, if you so desire, add it to a global network linked much like DNS. The concept of referrals is inherited from X.500. You can approach the concept of referrals in two ways, described next.

DNS Resource Records for Service Location

The first is to look at them like root server lists in DNS, in that each server has a superior server that ultimately is authoritative for providing lists (or referrals) to other servers in order to create a global directory hierarchy. This is implemented in DNS resource records for service locations, as defined by RFC 2782. Most existing LDAP implementations don't support the location of directory services using DNS SRV resource records. However, most services support generation of referrals to superior servers.

Using these records in DNS is akin to mail servers discovering and utilizing mail exchange (MX) hosts or a client looking at a global directory to request information. If an LDAP client adhering to RFC 2782 standards wants to discover an LDAP server that supports TCP and provides LDAP services for YourCompany.com, it would look up the following:

```
_ldap._tcp.YourCompany.com
```

The format for the SRV RR is as follows:

```
_Service._Proto.Name TTL Class SRV Priority Weight Port Target
```

The options are as follows:

Service: This is the symbolic name for the desired service with an underscore prepended so that it isn't confused with typical DNS information.

Proto: This is the symbolic name of the desired protocol. Currently, _TCP and _UDP would be the best candidates for inclusion here.

Name: This is the domain to which this resource record refers.

TTL: This is the RFC 1035-compliant time to live, or the expiration.

Class: This is the RFC 1035-compliant class. SRV records occur in the IN Class.

Priority: This is the priority of this target host. A client must attempt to contact the target host with the lowest-numbered priority it can reach. Target hosts with the same priority should be tried in an order defined by the weight field.

Weight: This is a server selection mechanism. The weight field specifies a relative weight for entries with the same priority. Large weights should be given a proportionately higher probability of being selected.

Port: This is the port on this target host that's used for this service. LDAP will use port 389 for standard communications and 636 for secure communications.

Target: This is the domain name of the target host. There must be one or more address records for this name, and it must not be an alias. A target of "." indicates that the service isn't available at this particular domain.

The overall goal of using these resource records in your DNS tables is to provide clients with a way to retrieve well-known services (WKS) without the need of being preconfigured. The original problem statement may have been an Internet service provider requiring a list of configuration options including MAIL, POP3, IMAP4, NNTP, and other services. Resource records publishing names of these services in a standard way would solve many of the issues surrounding the maintenance of lists.

Global referrals are a complement to this type of configuration. The root service locates services associated with a given fully qualified domain name by querying DNS for the LDAP SRV resource records. For the domain YourCompany.Com, the service would issue an SRV query for _ldap._tcp.YourCompany.Com, as explained previously. A successful query will return one or more resource records of the following form:

```
ldap.tcp.YourCompany.Com.  IN SRV 0 0 389 ldap.YourCompany.Com.
```

For each record that is returned, an LDAP URL is constructed. From this example record, the URL would be as follows:

```
ldap://ldap.YourCompany.Com:389/
```

These URLs are then returned in the referral. The referral is then used to forward information to various servers configured among the network of LDAP servers to which your host belongs.

Localized Scope

The other, which is more local and not part of a global directory goal, allows LDAP to look at different trees for different sets of information. This is based on the assumption that some directories are just too large to be stored within a single entity. In this case, parts of the tree are stored on alternate hosts. Pointers (or referrals) from the local server's DN for a particular tree hold the referral showing the alternate location on another server.

The referral is used in a way similar to a symbolic link in your filesystem. It allows the linking of directories from certain parts of the tree. For example, in a simple directory information tree (DIT) structure that has your company split across ou boundaries of the United States and China (ou=USA and ou=CHINA), a referral from the directory located in the United States may have a referral to the directory in China, thus allowing independent control of information.

```
dn: ref="ldap://CHINAHOST/ou=CHINA,dc=Your,dc=Company"
objectclass: referral
```

This would result in any search that traverses this particular tree to establish communication with a new directory on a new host. LDAP clients will need to be aware of referrals and appropriately follow them. When fully implemented (and when control over the client adherence to standards is under your control), this will allow you to master and distribute information across multiple hosts.

Understanding the Installation Structure

Upon successfully installing the software, perusing the standard file hierarchy of the distribution will give you greater insight into the system configurations. The file hierarchy can be divided into multiple sections, each which will be discussed.

Base system configurations exist, as in standard Unix systems, in an /etc directory structure. However, OpenLDAP, as in other open-source software initiatives, uses /usr/local/etc. To make configurations easier, I'll stick with the base system configurations whenever possible. If this isn't possible, I'll note it to maintain consistency throughout. The default installation of OpenLDAP doesn't run, thus forcing you to actually configure it. You may notice that other software packages you've configured in the past let you start the system without any specific configurations and embedded default messages somewhere in the host. This isn't the case here. You'll need to uncomment the system configurations and change them in order for the system to even start appropriately.

ldap.conf

The configuration file ldap.conf is the first place you'll be making configurations for your system. The basic file looks like this:

```
#
# LDAP Defaults
#
# See ldap.conf(5) for details
# This file should be world readable.
#BASE    dc=OpenLDAP, dc=Org

#HOST    ldap.openldap.org

#HOST    ldap.openldap.org ldap-master.openldap.org:666
#PORT    389

#SIZELIMIT      12

#TIMELIMIT      15

#DEREF          never
```

This configuration file is used to set systemwide defaults for LDAP clients. Realize that many of the initial configurations you'll be making may seem redundant, because you'll not only be creating configurations for your server but also the default configurations for all your clients. Setting default client configurations will allow you to use a standard set of LDAP tools without needing to specify all the command-line arguments for each query. While these are global system configurations, the same file can exist as ldaprc or .ldaprc in an individual home directory to override these defaults. This is useful for developers who may need to access multiple LDAP servers for information, not just yours.

The following sections describe the configuration options.

Systemwide Configurations

The following are the systemwide configuration options:

BASE <basedn>: This specifies the default base DN to use when performing LDAP operations.

HOST <name[:port] ...>: This specifies the name or names or LDAP servers that should be accessed by default. The server name can be specified as a host, a FQDN, or an IP address. Additional ports can be specified after the hostname. The default port used is 389.

PORT <port>: This specifies the default port used when connecting to LDAP servers.

SIZELIMIT <integer>: This specifies a size limit to use when performing searches. Some directories can be thousands or millions of objects in size. This is a client-enforced limit that will ensure that the results of a specific query don't exceed a specific size. A limit of 0 specifies an unlimited number of acceptable results.

TIMELIMIT <integer>: This specifies a time limit to use when performing searches. A setting of 0 specifies an unlimited time.

DEREF <when>: This specifies how alias dereferencing is done when performing a search. The <when> can be specified as never, in which aliases are never dereferenced; searching, where aliases are dereferenced in subordinates of the base object; finding, where aliases are dereferenced when locating the base object of the search; or always, where aliases are dereferenced in both searching and locating the base object of the search.

User-Only Configurations

The following is the user-only configuration option:

- BINDDN <dn>: This specifies the default bind DN to use when performing LDAP operations. The bind DN must be specified as a DN.

SASL Options

If OpenLDAP is built with SASL support, more options are available for client configurations.

SASL_MECH <mechanism>: Specifies the SASL mechanism to use. This is a user-only option.

SASL_REALM <realm>: Specifies the SASL realm. User-only.

SASL_AUTHCID <authcid>: Specifies the authentication identity. User-only.

SASL_AUTHZID <authcid>: Specifies the proxy authentication identity. User-only.

SASL_SECPROPS <properties>: Specifies Cyrus SASL security properties. The <properties> can be specified as a comma-separated list of the following:

- None (without any other properties) causes the properties defaults (noanonymous,noplain) to be cleared.

- Noplain disables mechanisms susceptible to simple passive attacks.

- Noactive disables mechanisms susceptible to active attacks.

- Nodict disables mechanisms susceptible to passive dictionary attacks.

- Noanonymous disables mechanisms that support anonymous login.

- Forwardsec requires forward secrecy between sessions.

- Passcred requires mechanisms that pass client credentials (and allows mechanisms that can pass credentials to do so).

Minssf=<factor>: Specifies the minimum acceptable SECURITY STRENGTH FACTOR as an integer approximating the effective key lengths used for encryption. The setting 0 implies no protection; 1 implies integrity protection only; 56 allows DES or other weak ciphers; 112 allows triple DES and other strong ciphers; and 128 allows RC4, Blowfish, and other modern strong ciphers. The default is 0.

Maxssf=<factor>: Specifies the maximum acceptable SSF as an integer. See MINSSF.

Maxbufsize=<factor>: Specifies the maximum security layer receiving buffer size allowed. 0 disables this feature.

slapd.conf

This file contains configuration information for the slapd daemon and other system tools you'll be potentially using. This file consists of a series of global configuration options that apply to slapd as a whole (including all back ends).

```
#
# See slapd.conf(5) for details on configuration options.
# This file should NOT be world readable.
#

include        /usr/local/etc/openldap/slapd.at.conf
include        /usr/local/etc/openldap/slapd.oc.conf
schemacheck    off
#referral      ldap://root.openldap.org/
pidfile        /usr/local/var/slapd.pid
argsfile       /usr/local/var/slapd.args


#######################################################################
# ldbm database definitions
#######################################################################
```

```
database        ldbm
suffix          "dc=my-domain, dc=com"
#suffix         "o=My Organization Name, c=US"
rootdn          "cn=Manager, dc=my-domain, dc=com"
#rootdn         "cn=Manager, o=My Organization Name, c=US"
# cleartext passwords, especially for the rootdn, should
# be avoid.  See slapd.conf(5) for details.
rootpw          secret
# database directory
# this directory MUST exist prior to running slapd AND
# should only be accessable by the slapd/tools  Mode 700 recommended.
directory       /usr/local/var/openldap-ldbm
```

This file contains a significant amount of configuration options that will dictate how your OpenLDAP server operates. The important options that need to be configured before your server is functional are database, suffix, rootdn, rootpw, and the paths pointing to other files. Make sure these options are all configured to your liking.

The more in-depth configuration options for this file are as follows:

Access to <what> [by <who> <access> <control>]+: Grants access to a set of entries and/or attributes by one or more requestors.

Allow <features>: Specifies a set of features (separated by whitespace) to allow. These include the following:

- Bind_v2 allows acceptance of LDAPv2 bind requests.

- Bind_anon_cred allows anonymous bind when credentials aren't empty.

- Bind_anon_dn allows unauthenticated (anonymous) bind when credentials aren't empty.

- Update_anon allows unauthenticated update operations to be processed.

Argsfile <filename>: The absolute name of a file that will hold the slapd server's command-line options.

Attributeoptions [option-name] ...: Attribute options, such as tags related to languages and prefixes, are defined here.

Attributetype (<oid> [NAME <name>] [OBSOLETE] [DESC <description>] [SUP <oid>] [EQUALITY <oid>] [ORDERING <oid>] [SUBSTR <oid>] [SYNTAX <oidlen>] [SINGLE-VALUE] [COLLECTIVE] [NO-USER-MODIFICATION] [USAGE <attributeUsage>]): Specifies an attribute type using LDAPv3 syntax as defined in RFC 2252.

Concurrency <integer>: Specifies the desired level of concurrency.

Conn_max_pending <integer>: Specifies the maximum number of pending requests for an anonymous session. If requests are submitted faster than the server can process them, they will be queued up to this limit. If the limit is exceeded, the session is closed.

Conn_max_pending_auth <integer>: Specifies the maximum number of pending requests for an authenticated session.

Defaultsearchbase <dn>: Specifies a default search base to use when client submits a nonbase search request with an empty base DN.

Disallow <features>: Specifies a set of features to disallow. These include the following:

- Bind_anon disables acceptance of anonymous bind.

- Bind_simple disables simple authentication.

- Bind_krbv4 disables Kerberos V4 authentication.

- Tls_2_anon disables StartTLS from forcing session to anonymous status.

- Tls_authc disables StartTLS if authenticated.

Gentlehup {on | off }: A SIGHUP (kill -HUP): Causes only a gentle shutdown attempt. slapd will stop listening for new connections but won't close the connection for active (already established) clients. Future write operations will return unwilling to perform. slapd terminates when all clients have closed their connections. This can be useful if you want to terminate the server and start a new slapd server with another database without disruption.

Idletimeout <integer>: Specifies the number of seconds to wait before forcibly closing an idle client connection.

Include <filename>: Reads additional configuration information from the given file before continuing with the next line of the current file.

Limits <who> <limit> [<limit> [...]]: Specifies time and size limits based on whom initiated an operation. This is useful when special users (such as those for use by applications and not connected to real people) are necessary for your system.

Loglevel <integer>: Specifies the level at which debugging statements and operation statistics should be syslogged. This is useful for various levels of debugging that may be required during the initial configuration (and error validation) within your environment. For a production environment, the level should be set to as low as possible to not degrade performance on your system. The log levels are additive, meaning that the desired level of logging, which can include any or all of the levels below, need to be added together to obtain the desired level. For example, in order to log debug packet handling (2), and packets sent and received (16), your log level would be set to 18. The available levels are as follows:

- 1 means trace function calls.

- 2 means debug packet handing.

- 4 means heavy trace debugging.

- 8 means connection management.

- 16 means print packets sent and received.

- 32 means search filtering processing.

- 64 means configuration file processing.

- 128 means access control list processing.

- 256 means stats log connections/operations/results.

- 512 means stats log entries sent.

- 1024 means print communication with shell back ends.

- 2048 means entry parsing.

`Moduleload <filename>`: Specifies the name of a dynamically loadable module to load. The filename may be an absolute path name or a simple filename. Nonabsolute filenames are searched for in the directories specified by the `modulepath` option. This option requires that `slapd` be compiled with `-enable-modules`.

`Modulepath <pathspec>`: Specifies a list of directories to search for loadable modules. Typically the path is a colon-separated path, but this depends on the operating system.

`Objectclass ( <oid> [NAME <name>] [DESC <description>] [OBSOLETE] [SUP <oids>] [{ABSTRACT | STRUCTURAL | AUXILIARY }] [MUST <oids>] [MAY <oids>]`: Specifies an object class using the LDAPv3 syntax defined in RFC 2252. Object classes are structural by default.

`Objectidentifier <name> { <oid> | <name>[:<suffix>] }`: Defines a string name that equates to the given OID. The string can be used in place of the numeric OID in object class and attribute definitions. This is typically used when an OID prefix has not been defined for your organization and temporary values need to be used. For example, with the object class of `YourCompanyPerson`, you can use `YourCompanyPerson-oid` for the OID string.

`Password-hash <hash>`: The option sets the hash to be used when generating user passwords, stored in `userPassword`, during the processing of LDAP password modify extended operations (RFC 3052). The `<hash>` must be one of {SSHA}, {SHA}, {SMD5}, {MD5}, {CRYPT}, or {CLEARTEXT}. {SHA} uses the SHA-1 algorithm, and {SSHA} uses a seed. {MD5} and {SMD5} use the MD5 algorithm, the latter with a seed. {CRYPT} uses `crypt` (3). {CLEARTEXT} indicates that the password should be added to `userPassword` as clear text. This should be a significant source of discussion within your company when integrating with legacy applications that utilize LDAP as a synchronization source because some old applications may not be able to appropriately utilize certain ciphers.

`Password-crypt-salt-format <format>`: Specifies the format of the salt passed to `crypt` (3) when generating {CRYPT} passwords.

`Pidfile <filename>`: The absolute name of a file that will hold the `slapd` server's process ID (PID).

`Referral <URL>`: Specifies the referral to pass back when `slapd` can't find a local database to handle a request.

`Require <conditions>`: Specifies a set of conditions to require. The directive must be specified globally or per database. The options are as follows:

- Bind requires a bind operation prior to the directory operations.

- LDAPv3 requires a session to be using LDAP version 3.

- Authc requires authentication prior to the directory operations.

- SASL requires SASL authentication prior to the directory operations.

- None can be used to require no conditions.

Reverse-lookup on | off: Toggles client name lookups.

RootDSE <file>: Specifies the name of an LDIF file containing user-defined attributes for the root DSE. These attributes are returned in addition to the attributes normally produced by slapd.

Sasl-authz-policy <policy>: Specifies which rules to use for SASL proxy authorization. Proxy authorization allows a client to authenticate to the server using one user's credentials while specifying a different identity to use for authorization and access control evaluation.

Sasl-host <fqdn>: Specifies the FQDN used for SASL processing.

Sasl-realm <realm>: Specifies a SASL realm.

Sasl-regexp <match> <replace>: Used by the SASL authorization mechanism to convert a SASL authentication username to an LDAP DN. When an authorization request is received, the SASL username, realm, and mechanism are taken and complied into a SASL name in the following form: Uid=<username>[,cn=<realm>],cn=<mechanism>,cn=auth. This SASL name is then compared against the match regular expression, and if the match is successful, the SASL name is replaced with the replace string. If wildcard strings exist in the match regular expression that are enclosed in parentheses—for example, uid=(.*),cn=.*—then regular expression rules for pattern matching apply.

Sasl-secprops <properties>: Specifies Cyrus SASL security properties.

Schemadn <dn>: Specifies the DN for the subschema subentry that controls the entries on this server. The default is cn=Subschema.

Security <factors>: Specifies a set of factors to require. An integer value is associated with each factor and is roughly equivalent to the encryption key length to require (in other words, 112 for 3DES and 128 for Blowfish). The directive may be specified globally or per database.

Ssf=<n>: Specifies the overall security strength factor.

Transport=<n>: Specifies the transport security strength factor.

TLS=<n>: Specifies the TLS security strength factor.

SASL=<n>: Specifies the SASL security strength factor.

Update_ssf=<n>: Specifies the overall security strength factor to require for directory updates.

Update_transport=<n>: Specifies the transport security strength factor to require for directory updates.

Update_tls=<n>: Specifies the TLS security strength factor to require for directory updates.

Update_sasl=<n>: Specifies the security strength factor to require for directory updates.

Simple_bind=<n>: Specifies the security strength factor required for simple username/password authentication.

Sizelimit {<integer>|unlimited}, sizelimit size[.{soft|hard|unchecked}]=<integer> [...]: Specifies the maximum number of entries to return from a search operation. The default size limit is 500.

Sockbuf_max_incoming <integer>: Specifies the maximum incoming LDAP PDU size for anonymous sessions.

Sockbuf_max_incoming_auth <integer>: Specifies the maximum incoming LDAP PDU size for authenticated sessions.

slapd.at.conf

This file contains attribute syntax definitions for your directory; in other words, it contains the data types that can be stored in each attribute. The default value for an attribute is cis; thus, you don't necessarily need to include attributes of that type in this file. You need to modify this file during your implementation of LDAP as you define and document the schema your company will be using. By default, the file looks like this:

```
attribute       homephone                          tel
attribute       mobiletelephonenumber     mobile   tel
attribute       aliasedObjectName                  dn
```

slapd.oc.conf

This file includes object class definitions for your directory. The object class definitions state which attributes are required and which are optional within your directory. You need to modify this file during your implementation of LDAP as you define and document the schema your company will be using. By default, this file looks like this:

```
objectclass person

requires
                objectClass,
                sn,
                cn
```

```
allows
        description,
        seeAlso,
        telephoneNumber,
        userPassword
```

Summary

After reading this chapter, you should understand the base system configurations in your OpenLDAP directory and some of the configurations you can utilize to create a secure environment.

CHAPTER 6

■ ■ ■

Scripting and Programming LDAP

The power of any system lies in your ability to use it. While this is a generic statement, you can probably agree that systems that provide little to no capability to directly communicate with their data, structures, or configurations serve you poorly. Storing data in a system that provides limited tools, besides a graphical user interface (GUI), to retrieve this information—or one that uses proprietary and undocumented data format—isn't as extensible as tools that give you access to well-documented internal information.

This isn't the case with Lightweight Directory Access Protocol (LDAP), as many methods are available for searching, storing, manipulating, and utilizing the data stored within the directory. You'll never have a shortage of ways of accomplishing the same task using which-ever method you're familiar with using.

For many people, the simplest and most straightforward method of using the directory may be the extensive set of command-line utilities available to you. The standard operations you'll need are available to you using `ldapsearch` and `ldapmodify`. You can utilize the power of these utilities within shell scripts, Perl scripts, or any number of other scripting utilities. It's good to familiarize yourself with these tools to make your directory your own.

Utilizing Command-Line Tools

Not everyone is a programmer. Not every task requires a well-written program. Many times you'll have a base set of tools available to you and realize that you don't need to bother with anything else. In these scenarios, you're able to combine the best set of tools available to you with a script. *Scripting* is the process of grouping together a set of commands that are often repeated. You can use multiple tools that can be used for scripting, the most common of which are `perl` or standard shell commands.

You must first familiarize yourself with the command-line utilities you'll be using for your scripting. I'll discuss more specific command-line options in other chapters, but here I'll review some of the basic commands you'll need to use. The most common commands you'll be utiliz-ing for scripting are `ldapsearch` and `ldapmodify`. You can use the command-line option `-h` to specify the hostname you're connecting to, `-p` to specify the port, `-D` to specify the simple bind credentials, `-w` to specify your password, and `-f` to accept input from a file. You use the `-c` flag to continually process data even if one of the operations fails. For more verbose output, you can use -v. This information is written to STDERR, and your scripts can parse the output and generate events based on it.

The differences between scripting and programming are often subtle and debatable. For your purposes, I'll show how to script a process that relies on external commands and isn't self-contained. That is, scripting involves running perl operations that depend on system() calls, not internal operations. An example of this is relying on @output = `ldapsearch $hostname`; instead of @output = ldapsearch_s(parameters);. If you want to perform the same operation across a number of hosts, it's a good idea to script this operation rather than typing it multiple times.

For example, you may want to process LDAP Interchange Format (LDIF) files based on the class of host. In an environment with many machines, it'd be frustrating to keep repeating the same commands while replacing one or two parameters in each. In the beginning, you have to execute the set of commands shown in Listing 6-1.

Listing 6-1. *Repetitive Tasks*

```
$ /usr/local/bin/ldapmodify -h host1 -p 389 \
 -D "cn=directory manager" \
 -w password -v -c -a -f file1.ldif
$ /usr/local/bin/ldapmodify -h host1 -p 389 \
 -D "cn=directory manager" \
 -w password -v -c -a -f file2.ldif
$ /usr/local/bin/ldapmodify -h host1 -p 389 \
 -D "cn=directory manager" \
 -w password -v -c -a -f file3.ldif
$ /usr/local/bin/ldapmodify -h host1 -p 389 \
 -D "cn=directory manager" \
 -w password -v -c -a -f file4.ldif
$ /usr/local/bin/ldapmodify -h host1 -p 389 \
 -D "cn=directory manager" \
 -w password -v -c -a -f file5.ldif
$ /usr/local/bin/ldapmodify -h host1 -p 389 \
 -D "cn=directory manager" \
 -w password -v -c -a -f file6.ldif
$ /usr/local/bin/ldapmodify -h host2 -p 389 \
 -D "cn=directory manager" \
 -w password -v -c -a -f file1.ldif
$ /usr/local/bin/ldapmodify -h host2 -p 389 \
 -D "cn=directory manager" \
 -w password -v -c -a -f file2.ldif
$ /usr/local/bin/ldapmodify -h host2 -p 389
 -D "cn=directory manager" \
 -w password -v -c -a -f file3.ldif
$ /usr/local/bin/ldapmodify -h host2 -p 389 \
 -D "cn=directory manager" \
 -w password -v -c -a -f file4.ldif
$ /usr/local/bin/ldapmodify -h host2 -p 389 \
 -D "cn=directory manager" \
 -w password -v -c -a -f file5.ldif
```

```
$ /usr/local/bin/ldapmodify -h host2 -p 389 \
 -D "cn=directory manager" \
 -w password -v -c -a -f file6.ldif
...
```

The goal of the commands is to update a series of hosts (in this case, host1 and host2) with a series of LDIF files (file1.ldif through file6.ldif). Which host receives which files has a set of logic associated with it. Master hosts get one set of files, and consumers get another. Obviously, having to retype the commands is frustrating at the least. Therefore, you should script operations such as these. You should set parameters that often change as variables within the script (see Listing 6-2).

Listing 6-2. *Repetitive Tasks Scripted*

```
#!/bin/bash

### Paths and passwords
LDIFDIR='/home/tom/global'
BINDDN='cn=directory manager'
BINDPW='password'
LDAPMODIFY='/usr/local/bin/ldapmodify'

### Some defaults
TYPE=replica
VERBOSE=
QUIET=
HOSTS=



### Print out usage info
Usage() {
  echo "Usage: 'basename $0' [ -t master|replica ] [ -v|-q ] <hostname[:port]> [
hostname[:port]] ..."
}

### Parse out command-line args
while true ; do
  if getopts t:vhq arg ; then
    case $arg in
      t) TYPE="$OPTARG" ;;
      v) VERBOSE="yes" ;;
      q) QUIET="yes" ;;
      h) Usage ; exit 0 ;;
      *) Usage ; exit 1 ;;
    esac
```

```
        else
          if [ "$arg" = "?" ] ; then
            shift $(($OPTIND - 1))
            HOSTS="$*"
          fi
          break
        fi
done

if [ -n "$QUIET" -a -n "$VERBOSE" ] ; then
  Usage
  exit 1
fi

if [ -z "$HOSTS" ] ; then                           ### Nothing to do :(
  Usage
  exit 1
fi

### Which files do we want to use?
FILES="\
      file1.ldif \
      file2.ldif \
      file3.ldif \
      file4.ldif \
      file5.ldif \
      file6.ldif \
    "

### These are contingent upon the type of system being installed.
case $TYPE in
  master)
    FILES="$FILES \
      fileMASTER.ldif \
    "
  ;;
  replica)
    FILES="$FILES \
      fileREPLICA.ldif \
    "
  ;;
  *)
    Usage
    exit 1
  ;;
esac
```

```
for HOST in $HOSTS ; do
  PORT=389
  if echo $HOST | grep ':' >& /dev/null ; then
    PORT=${HOST/*:}
    HOST=${HOST/:*}
  fi
  [ "$QUIET" ] || echo "Server Name: $HOST (port: $PORT)"
  for FILE in $FILES ; do
    [ "$QUIET" ] || echo "$LDAPMODIFY" -h $HOST -p $PORT -D \
 "$BINDDN" -w "$BINDP W" -v -c -a -f "$LDIFDIR/$FILE"
    [ "$VERBOSE" ] && "$LDAPMODIFY" -h $HOST -p $PORT -D \
 "$BINDDN" -w "$BINDPW" -v -c -a -f "$LDIFDIR/$FILE"
[ "$VERBOSE" ] && "$LDAPMODIFY" -h $HOST -p $PORT -D \
"$BINDDN" -w "$BINDPW" -v -c -a -f "$LDIFDIR/$FILE"
    [ "$VERBOSE" ] || "$LDAPMODIFY" -h $HOST -p $PORT -D \
"$BINDDN" -w "$BINDPW" -c -a -f "$LDIFDIR/$FILE" >& /dev/null
  done
done
```

The script is basic but gives you the ability to perform multiple (and different) operations based on set criteria. Scripting such as this is extremely useful and reduces the amount of error that's introduced by having to retype commands. Running the script in Listing 6-2 without any command-line options yields the following results:

```
$ ./update.sh
Usage: update.sh [ -t master|replica ] [ -v|-q ] <hostname[:port]>
[hostname[:port]] ...
```

You can use this script to create a replica instance of a directory with the appropriate files but run it as follows:

```
$ ./update.sh -t replica ldaphost
Server Name: ldaphost (port: 389)
...
```

Additionally, you could also script modifying the LDAP data, which would be a useful tool. Let's say you have a basic problem with data in your LDAP server and want to change all users with cn=Tom to cn=TommyBoy. Going through the data manually or going through an administrative interface is time-consuming and opens up the system to manual errors. Scripting something such as this would be easy using pcrl or other scripting tools.

First, you need to find the users with the information you seek.

```
$ ldapsearch -h ldaphost -p 389 -b dc=Your,dc=Company cn=Tom
```

Either this can be outputted to a file with > FILE.IN or can be throw into an array as follows:

```
@OUTPUT = `ldapsearch -h ldaphost -p 389 -b dc=Your,dc=Company cn=Tom`;
```

Second, to view the contents of this data, you may want to do this:

```
for $line(@OUTPUT) {
  print $line;
}
```

The contents of $line will be the distinguished name (DN) of the users found as a result of the previous command, as follows:

```
dn: uid=tjackiewicz,ou=People,dc=Your,dc=Company
dn: uid=tsurapruik,ou=People,dc=Your,dc=Company
dc: uid=tdogg,ou=People,dc=Your,dc=Company
```

You could, for each $line of output, generate the following LDIF commands:

```
$line
changetype: modify
replace: cn
cn: TommyBoy
```

Although not a complicated procedure, the ability to manipulate data within a script gives you flexibility over controlling information and quickly solving problems.

LDAP Controls

The LDAP v3 protocol allows clients and servers to use a new mechanism, known as a *control*, for extending LDAP operations. A control is a way to specify additional information as part of a request and response. For example, a client can send a control to a server as part of a request to indicate that a server should sort the search results before sending the results back to the client. Servers are also given the ability to send a control back to a client during the authentication process, which lets the client know that a password is about to expire.

A control specifies the unique object identifier (OID), as defined by the creator of this control, an indication of whether the control is critical to the operation, and optional data related to the control (for example, for the server-side sorting control, the attributes used for sorting search results). This LDAP control mechanism serves as a secondary array of information that can be used by the client to perform additional actions based on its contents.

The OID identifies the control. If you plan to use a control, you need to make sure that the server supports the control. When your client includes a control in a request for an LDAP operation, the server may respond in one of the following ways.

If the server supports this control and if the control is appropriate to the operation, the server should use the control when performing the operation. If the client marks a control as critical but the server doesn't support it, a result code indicating an error should be returned. The error you'll see most often is LDAP_UNAVAILABLE_CRITICAL_EXTENSION. If a control is marked as not critical and the server doesn't support the operation, the server should ignore the control and perform the operation—completely ignoring the control. Servers also have the ability to send controls back to clients.

The following data structure represents a control:

```
typedef struct ldapcontrol {
    char                        *ldctl_oid;
    struct berval               ldctl_value;
    char                        ldctl_iscritical;
}
LDAPControl, *PLDAPControl;
```

In this structure, `idctl_oid` specifies the OID of the control, `idctl_value` contains a structure containing data associated with this control, and `idctl_iscritical` specifies whether the control is critical to the operation. (`LDAP_OPT_ON` indicates that the control is critical, and `LDAP_OPT_OFF` indicates that the control isn't critical.)

To include a control in a request, call one of the LDAP v3 application programming interface (API) functions (functions with names ending in `_ext` and `_ext_s`). These functions allow you to pass in an array of server controls and an array of client controls. I'll discuss these in more details in subsequent sections. You can also include controls in a request by specifying the array of controls in the `LDAP_OPT_SERVER_CONTROLS` option. However, these controls will be sent to the server with every request. If the control is specific to a certain type of operation, you should use the `_ext` and `_ext_s` functions instead.

When you're done working with a control or with an array of controls, you should free them from memory. Failure to do so may result in the reuse of these controls by subsequent calls to the LDAP API functions that may not need them.

Table 6-1 lists some of the OIDs for server controls.

Table 6-1. *Server Control OIDs*

OID	Defined Name in `ldap.h`	Description of Control
2.16.840.1.113730.3.4.3	LDAP_CONTROL_PRESISTENTSEARCH	Persistent search control
2.16.830.1.11.3730.3.4.4	LDAP_CONTROL_PWDEXPIRED	Password expired control
2.16.830.1.11.3730.3.4.5	LDAP_CONTROL_PWEXPIRING	Password expiring control
1.2.840.11355.6.1.4.473	LDAP_CONTROL_SORTREQUEST	Server-side sorting control

According to the LDAP v3 protocol specification, servers should list any controls that they support in the `supportedControl` attribute in the root DSA-Specific Entry (DSE). DSA is an X.500 term that refers to an LDAP server, or *directory systems agent.* The root DSE is the topmost entry within your LDAP directory. Listing 6-3 shows a simple command-line program that searches for the root DSE and prints the values of the `supportedControl` attribute.

Listing 6-3. *Print Value of* `supportedControl`

```
#include "ldap.h"
static char *usage = "Usage: listctrl -h <hostname> -p <portnumber>\n";
```

```c
/* Associate OIDs of known controls with descriptions. */
struct oid2desc {
    char    *oid;
    char    *desc;
};
static struct oid2desc oidmap[] = {
    {LDAP_CONTROL_MANAGEDSAIT,          "Manage DSA IT control"},
    {LDAP_CONTROL_SORTREQUEST,          "Server-side sorting control"},
    {LDAP_CONTROL_PERSISTENTSEARCH,     "Persistent search control"},
    {LDAP_CONTROL_VLVREQUEST,           "Virtual list view control"},
    {LDAP_CONTROL_PWEXPIRED,            "Password expired control"},
    {LDAP_CONTROL_PWEXPIRING,           "Password expiration warning control"},
    { NULL, NULL }
};
int
main( int argc, char **argv )
{
    LDAP        *ld;
    LDAPMessage    *result, *e;
    char        *hostname = NULL;
    char        **vals;
    char        *attrs[2];
    int         i, j, c, portnumber = LDAP_PORT, rc;
    LDAPControl    **serverctrls = NULL, **clntctrls = NULL;
    /* Parse the command line arguments. */
    while ( ( c = getopt( argc, argv, "h:p:" ) ) != -1 ) {
        switch ( c ) {
        case 'h':
            hostname = strdup( optarg );
            break;
        case 'p':
            portnumber = atoi( optarg );
            break;
        default:
            printf( "Unsupported option: %c\n", c );
            printf( usage );
            exit( 1 );
        }
    }
    /* By default, connect to ldaphost at port 389. */
    if ( hostname == NULL || hostname[0] == NULL ) {
        hostname = "ldaphost";
    }
    /* Initialize the connection. */
    if ( (ld = ldap_init( hostname, portnumber )) == NULL ) {
        perror( "ldap_init" );
        return( 1 );
    }
```

```
/* Set automatic referral processing off. */
if ( ldap_set_option( ld, LDAP_OPT_REFERRALS, LDAP_OPT_OFF )
  != LDAP_SUCCESS ) {
    ldap_perror( ld, "ldap_set_option" );
    return( 1 );
}
/* Search for the root DSE and retrieve only the
   supportedControl attribute. */
attrs[ 0 ] = "supportedControl";
attrs[ 1 ] = NULL;
rc = ldap_search_ext_s( ld, "", LDAP_SCOPE_BASE, "(objectclass=*)",
  attrs, 0, serverctrls, clntctrls, NULL, NULL, &result );
/* Check the search results. */
switch( rc ) {
/* If successful, the root DSE was found. */
case LDAP_SUCCESS:
    break;
/* If the root DSE was not found, the server does not comply
   with the LDAP v3 protocol. */
case LDAP_PARTIAL_RESULTS:
case LDAP_NO_SUCH_OBJECT:
case LDAP_OPERATIONS_ERROR:
case LDAP_PROTOCOL_ERROR:
    printf( "LDAP server %s:%d returned result code %d (%s).\n"
    "This server does not support the LDAP v3 protocol.\n",
    hostname, portnumber, rc, ldap_err2string( rc ) );
    return( 1 );
    break;
/* If any other value is returned, an error must have occurred. */
default:
    ldap_perror( ld, "ldap_search_ext_s" );
    return( 1 );
    break;
}
/* Get the root DSE from the results.
   Since there is only one root DSE, there
   should be only one entry in the results. */
e = ldap_first_entry( ld, result );
/* Get and print the values of the supportedControl attribute. */
if (e != NULL &&
    (vals = ldap_get_values(ld, e, "supportedControl")) != NULL ) {
    printf( "\nControls Supported by %s:%d\n", hostname, portnumber );
    printf( "=================================================\n" );
    for ( i = 0; vals[i] != NULL; i++ ) {
        printf( "%s\n", vals[i] );
        for ( j = 0; oidmap[j].oid != NULL; j++ ) {
            if ( !strcmp( vals[i], oidmap[j].oid )) {
                printf( "\t%s\n", oidmap[j].desc );
```

```
        }
      }
    }
    /* Free the values allocated by ldap_get_values(). */
    ldap_value_free( vals );
    printf( "\n" );
  }
  /* Free memory allocated by ldap_search_ext_s(). */
  ldap_msgfree( result );
  ldap_unbind( ld );
  return( 0 );
}
```

Upon successfully running this script, you'll see the following output:

```
Controls Supported by ldaphost:389
```

This would then be followed by a list of the controls that are supported by the particular server to which you're connecting.

The LDAP_CONTROL_PRESISTENTSEARCH control is one of the most powerful controls you'll be using. A *persistent* search is an ongoing search operation that allows your LDAP client to get notification of changes to the directory. This is often a better alternative for meta-directories (for example) than using changelog databases. To use persistent searching for change notification, you create a "persistent search" control that specifies the types of changes you want to track. You include the control in a search request. If an entry in the directory is changed, the server determines if the entry matches the search criteria in your request and if the change is the type of change you're tracking. If both of these are true, the server sends the entry to your client. The definition for this control could be as follows:

```
int ldap_create_persistentsearch_control( LDAP *ld, int changetypes,
    int changesonly, int return_echg_ctls, char ctl_iscritical,
    LDAPControl **ctrlp );
```

You can specify the following information:

changetypes specifies the type of change you want to track. You can specify any of the following (or any combination of the following using a bitwise OR operator):

- LDAP_CHANGETYPE_ADD indicates you want to track added entries.

- LDAP_CHANGETYPE_DELETE indicates you want to track deleted entries.

- LDAP_CHANGETYPE_MODIFY indicates you want to track modified entries.

- LDAP_CHANGETYPE_MODDN indicates you want to track renamed entries.

- LDAP_CHANGETYPE_ANY indicates you want to track all changes to entries.

`changesonly` indicates whether you want the server to return all entries that initially matched the search criteria (zero to return all entries and nonzero to return only the entries that change).

`return_echg_ctls` indicates whether you want entry change notification controls included with every modified entry returned by the server (nonzero to return entry change notification controls).

LDAP API

LDAP provides access to a powerful API based on the Internet Engineers Task Force (IETF) C LDAP API draft specification. Both synchronous communication and asynchronous communication are available to best use any familiar method of access. Refer to http://www.mozilla.org/ directory/ietf-docs/draft-ietf-ldapext-ldap-c-api-05.txt for complete specifications and additional information.

The basic interaction is as follows: A session handle is created using an initialization call—`ldap_init` (3) or `ldap_initialize` (3). To follow standards and compatibility across a number of LDAP-compliant systems, `ldap_init` (3) is the preferred method of use. This call performs an LDAP bind and is the equivalent of providing host and port information using any of the standard command-line utilities. Keep in mind that this is simply establishing communication with the LDAP server by establishing communication as LDAP over Transmission Control Protocol (TCP), LDAP over LDAP, or LDAP over IPC (Unix domain sockets). The connection is raw and established but not yet usable. The API, unlike the command-line utilities, requires multiple calls to be made in order to establish a usable level of communication with the server. The calls you have available can be performed in synchronous or asynchronous modes. The default for calls is asynchronous, but adding `_s` to the end of the call will allow you to perform synchronous commands against the system.

The next call during the base establishment of communication is `ldap_bind` (3) (or `ldap_simple_bind`, `ldap_sasl_bind` (3), or the synchronous equivalents, depending on your requirements), in which authentication information for the session is provided. This is like providing the BINDDN and BINDPW parameters in the command-line utilities.

Before doing any work within your available session, you need to construct the parameters for the LDAP operation to be performed. For example, you need to set up the core of the function that you want to run, such as a search operation. Once you've gathered your requirements and made them ready, you have an LDAP connection available to you with which you can perform all the standard (and even more creative) functions against the server. These options will be discussed in more detail later in this chapter. Results returned from these routines are interpreted by calling the LDAP parsing routines, such as `ldap_parse_result` (3). Errors can be interpreted by calling `ldap_err2string` (3). Results and errors are returned in an opaque structure called LDAPMessage. Routines are provided to parse this structure and to step through entries and attributes returned. Routines are also provided to interpret errors.

The result includes a result code (such as LDAP_SUCCESS, which means all is well) and may include other error-related information. For some operations, a number of entries will also be returned.

The communication is halted by calling `ldap_unbind_ext` (3). That is, once you've performed the desired operations, you've received the results you need, and you have no need to keep an LDAP session active, you're done.

Synchronous vs. Asynchronous

LDAP is completely asynchronous in that multiple operations can be done at the same time. Like any modern protocol, the results can be sent in one order, and the results can be retrieved in another. Each function call is originated with a value and returned with the same. This is used to keep track of which particular thread is associated with the origin.

After an asynchronous operation is initiated, the application must follow up the function calls in order to appropriately parse the results. In synchronous operations, because a single set of input and output data is available, this isn't necessary.

Using the synchronous LDAP operation functions has the disadvantage that the application will block (or wait) until the server completes the request, and it returns all entries and the final result to the application at once. On some systems, you won't be taking advantage of the full power of the server capacity by relying on this method. However, for simple operations, it may be worth the performance degradation for the time saved developing the application.

With synchronous operations, even though multiple operations can be initiated on separate threads, the thread safety support will serialize these requests at the client, prohibiting them from being initiated to the server. To ensure that the operations are initiated to the server, you should use asynchronous operations when running in an environment where multiple client program threads may be making calls to the LDAP programming interface.

Various SDKs

You can find the University of Michigan's LDAP server code (on which everything today is originally based), a C-language software development kit (SDK), and other links to documentation and LDAP mailing lists at http://www.umich.edu/~dirsvcs/ldap/.

You can find IBM's C and Java SDKs at http://www.ibm.com/java.

Downloading the Netscape C SDK

The Netscape Directory SDK gives developers the complete set of software libraries, command-line utilities, sample code, and documentation needed to build applications that access networked directory data using LDAP v2 or v3 (RFC 2251, an Internet standard). This is the authoritative set of APIs that are globally used as the base for any LDAP development. The Netscape C SDK is available at http://developer.netscape.com/tech/directory/downloads.html. It includes a complete set of software libraries, command-line utilities, sample code, and documentation needed for your applications that need to access LDAP v3. The following information on utilizing CVS comes from the Mozilla site; you can find general updates to the procedures at http://www.mozilla.org.

Anyone can check out the sources via Concurrent Versions System (CVS), but only certain people have the ability to check in via CVS. I'll concentrate on giving you the ability to check out the latest source code.

To check out the sources, you need to be running CVS 1.10, or later, and have your $CVS-ROOT set to the following:

```
:pserver:anonymous@cvs-mirror.mozilla.org:/cvsroot
```

The password for user anonymous is anonymous.

You also need GNU make (also referred to interchangeably as *make* or *gmake*) for this to be functional appropriately. Using your Unix host (Solaris, Linux, or any system with GNU-based utilities), the following commands will let you check out code:

```
$ setenv CVSROOT :pserver:anonymous@cvs-mirror.mozilla.org:/cvsroot
$ cvs login
(Logging in to anonymous@cvs-mirror.mozilla.org)
CVS password: anonymous
$ cvs checkout mozilla/client.mk
U mozilla/client.mk
$ cd mozilla
$ make -f client.mk checkout
```

This automates a CVS checkout process that's prone to change.

You need to run cvs login only once. It will remember anonymous's password in your $HOME/.cvspass file.

The -z3 parameter causes the files (and diffs) to be compressed while in transit. This is almost always the right thing to do; you should probably just put cvs -z3 in your $HOME/.cvsrc file to make it the default on all CVS commands.

▓Note -z9 offers a logarithmic improvement in compression at an exponential cost in central processing unit (CPU) time. Therefore, I recommend -z3, which seems to be optimal in most cases.

In a Windows environment, you need CVS version 1.10 or newer. To use CVS under Windows, you must have unpacked the source from the .tar file, not from a .zip. The .zip file format doesn't store dates with enough accuracy for CVS, so updating source unpacked from a .zip with CVS takes a really long time because the CVS client must send most files to the server to determine if they've changed.

The checkout procedure is similar to that for Unix.

```
C:\> set CVSROOT=:pserver:anonymous@cvs-mirror.mozilla.org:/cvsroot
C:\> set HOME=\TEMP
C:\> cvs login
(Logging in to anonymous@cvs-mirror.mozilla.org)
CVS password: anonymous
C:\> cvs checkout mozilla/client.mk
U mozilla/client.mk
C:\> cd mozilla
C:\> make -f client.mk pull_all
```

This automates a CVS checkout process that's prone to change.

If the -z3 parameter doesn't work, you don't have CVS and/or gzip installed correctly. Your life will be much easier if you correct this, rather than omitting that parameter.

You also need to have the HOME environment variable set to a sensible directory, or CVS will complain.

You can also use the CVS client to obtain the source code using the following command:

```
$ cvs co -P DirectorySDKSourceC
```

Pull the code for libraries that LDAP C SDK needs using the following commands:

```
$ cvs co -r NSPR_4_2_2_RELEASE mozilla/nsprpub
$ cvs co -r NSS_3_7_7_RTM mozilla/security/coreconf mozilla/security/nss
$ cvs co -r DBM_1_61_RTM mozilla/dbm mozilla/security/dbm
```

Build Netscape Portable Runtime (NSPR) and Network Security Services (NSS) (if not using binary releases of those components) by executing these commands:

```
$ cd mozilla/security/nss
$ gmake nss_build_all
```

Build the LDAP C SDK (libraries and tools), like so:

```
$ cd mozilla/directory/c-sdk
$ ./configure --with-nss
$ gmake
```

If your build is successful, the LDAP C SDK libraries, command-line tools, and header files will be placed under mozilla/dist/<OSNAME>.OBJ/.

■**Note** You can build without Secure Sockets Layer (SSL) support by skipping the NSS-related build steps and omitting the --with-nss on the configure command. You'll still need a binary copy of NSPR, or you'll need to build NSPR from source.

API Calls

You'll be using many calls to the server during your work. Although the following API is still supported, its use is deprecated. Using the newer replacement APIs (which are also discussed in this chapter) is strongly encouraged.

ldap_init (3) and ldap_initialize (3): These initialize the LDAP library without opening a connection to the server. The TCP connection itself isn't opened until it's needed by some additional LDAP operation.

ldap_result (3): This waits for the result from an asynchronous operation. This processes the results of each individual LDAP call. These are sorted by a message ID.

ldap_abandon (3): This abandons (aborts) an asynchronous operation.

ldap_add (3) and ldap_add_s (3): These add an entry to the directory.

ldap_bind (3) and ldap_bind_s (3): These bind to the directory. These are deprecated in favor of ldap_simple_bind and ldap_simple_bind_s.

ldap_simple_bind (3) and ldap_simple_bind_s: These bind to the directory using simple authentication.

ldap_unbind (3) and ldap_unbind_s (3): These unbind from the LDAP server and close the connection.

ldap_memfree (3): This disposes of memory allocated by the LDAP routines being used.

ldap_compare (3) and ldap_compare_s (3): These compare directory entries.

ldap_delete (3) and ldap_delete_s (3): These delete a directory entry.

ldap_perror (3): This prints an LDAP error indication to STDERR (standard error).

Ld_errono (3): This indicates an LDAP error.

ldap_result2error (3): This extracts LDAP error indication from LDAP result.

ldap_Errlist (3): This lists LDAP errors and their meanings.

ldap_err2string (3): This converts LDAP error indication to a string.

ldap_first_attribute (3): This returns the first attribute name in an entry.

ldap_next_attribute (3): This returns the next attribute name in an entry.

ldap_first_Entry (3): This returns the first entry in a chain of search results.

ldap_next_entry (3): This returns the next entry in a chain of search results.

ldap_get_dn (3): This extracts the DN from an entry.

ldap_explode_dn (3): This converts a DN into its component parts.

ldap explode rdn (3): This converts a relative DN (RDN) into its component parts.

ldap_get_values (3): This returns an attribute's values.

ldap_get_values_len (3): This returns an attribute's values with lengths.

ldap_value_free (3): This frees allocation memory by ldap_get_values (3).

ldap_value_free_len (3): This frees memory allocated by ldap_get_values_len (3).

ldap_count_values (3): This returns the number of values.

ldap_count_values_len (3): This returns the number of values.

ldap_modify (3) and ldap_modify_s (3): These modify a directory entry.

ldap_mods_free (3): This frees an array of pointers to mod structures used by ldap_modify (3).

ldap_modrdn2 (3) and ldap_modrdn2_s (3): These modify the RDN of an entry. These are deprecated in favor of ldap_rename.

ldap_msgfree (3): This frees the results allocated by ldap_result (3).

ldap_msgtype (3): This returns the message type of a message from ldap_result (3).

ldap_msgid (3): This returns the message ID of a message from ldap_result (3).

ldap_search (3) and ldap_search_s (3): These search the directory.

ldap_search_st (3): This searches the directory utilizing a client-side timeout.

`ldap_is_ldap_url` (3): This checks a URL string to see if it's an LDAP URL.

`ldap_url_parse` (3): This breaks up an LDAP URL string into its components.

`ldap_sort_entries` (3): This sorts a list of search results.

`ldap_sort_values` (3): This sorts a list of attribute values.

`ldap_sort_strcasecmp` (3): This compares a case-insensitive string.

Obtaining the LDAP Perl API

Perl is fast becoming the premier language for system administrators, scripters, and application programmers. Its ease of use and combination of scripts and programming make it a powerful tool that can be utilized to create a number of applications. The Perl API for LDAP provides a simple way to facilitate communications with your LDAP server. Many APIs are available. PerLDAP is written and maintained by a small group of LDAP fanatics: Leif Hedstrom, Michelle Hedstrom, Kevin McCarthy, and Clayton Donley. The primary Web site for information, maintenance, and information regarding PerLDAP is `http://www.perldap.org`. This API is a subset of the formal LDAP version 2 API (referenced in RFC 1823) along with extra functions added by Software.com to enable you to build provisioning scripts, billing reports, and other such tools. PerLDAP is an open-source development project and was the result of a joint effort between Netscape and Clayton Donley, an open-source developer. PerLDAP currently provides basic functions to allow Perl users to access and manipulate directories easily. Based on developer feedback and involvement, PerLDAP will continue to evolve in order to include additional functionality in future releases.

PerLDAP (also known as Perl-LDAP) consists of two main components to write LDAP clients: an interface to the C SDK API and a set of object-oriented Perl classes. The API interface is almost 100 percent compatible with Netscape's C SDK, but it's harder to use than the object-oriented layer. The object-oriented interface is meant to be an easier way to write most common LDAP clients. PerLDAP is a set of modules written in Perl and C that will allow developers to leverage their existing Perl knowledge to easily write and manage LDAP-enabled directory applications. PerLDAP makes it easy to search, add, delete, and update directory entries. For example, Perl developers can easily build Web applications to access information stored in a directory or create directory synchronization tools that function between different directories.

The source is available via both CVS and File Transfer Protocol (FTP). Building this package is fairly straightforward but requires some knowledge about using compilers and compiler tools on your system. If you're uncomfortable using these tools, I recommend you get one of the prebuilt binary distributions instead. To build the module, you'll need the following:

- Perl, version 5.003 or later. I definitely recommend you to use v5.004 or later.

- An ANSI-C compiler (for example, `gcc-2.x` or Visual C++ 5.0).

- The LDAP client libraries and include files (for example, the SDK from Netscape Communications).

See the README file for information on retrieving binaries. You can download (or check out via CVS) the Directory SDK source; see `http://www.mozilla.org/directory/` for further information.

This package uses the normal Perl 5 MakeMaker installation system. To generate a Makefile appropriate for your platform, run perl on the provided Makefile.PL script, like so:

```
$ perl Makefile.PL
```

You may have to use the command perl5 or perl-5.004, depending on how you installed perl-5. The script will now ask you a few questions to find the necessary library and include files. A typical configuration session is as follows:

```
$ perl5 Makefile.PL
```

The important question is where your LDAP SDK is installed; in the previous example the base directory is /opt/ldapsdk3. This directory should have two subdirectories, named lib and include. If you installed the SDK in the standard /usr hierarchy, use the default value as provided by the install script. Assuming you get no errors or warning, proceed with the build and install, like so:

```
$ make
$ make install
```

Binary distributions are available via FTP from ftp://ftp.perldap.org/pub/perldap/Binaries. You can navigate branches under this subdirectory to find the appropriate version. Binary distributions exist for almost every system. You can even obtain RPMs and packages for Solaris here. The Linux RPM package is at ftp://ftp.perldap.org/Binaries/perldap-rh16.i386.rpm. Install it using the following command:

```
$ rpm -i perldap-rhl6.i386.rpm
```

The Solaris package is at ftp://ftp.perldap.org/pub/perldap/Binaries/perldap-solaris2-sparc.pkg.gz. Install it using the following command:

```
$ gzip -d perldap-solaris2-sparc.pkg.gz
$ pkgadd -d perldap-solaris2-sparc.pkg
```

Windows versions are available on the site as well.

Using the LDAP Perl API

The Perl functions you'll be dealing with are directly associated with the functions available in the Netscape C SDK, as there's a reliance on this API for the Perl libraries to function. The LDAP Perl API is split between error-processing functions, connection-management functions, functions that perform operations on entries, access control, and memory management.

Error Processing

You can use the ldap_err2string(rc) function for error processing. It returns an error associated with an LDAP error code. The input taken is denoted as rc, which is any return code from an LDAP API function call.

```
my $rc = ldap_xxx(..); # any ldap call
my $errstr = ldap_err2string($rc);
print "Error was: $errstr";
```

Connection Management Functions

You can use the following functions for managing client connections to an LDAP server.

ldap_open(host, port)

This opens a connection to an LDAP server on a specific host and port. It returns a connection handle (an LDAP* pointer). Its parameters are as follows:

- host: The name of the network host where the LDAP directory resides

- port: The port the server is listening on (the default is 389)

The following code shows a basic example of using this function:

```
$ldap_host = "ldaphost";
($LOGIN,$PASSWORD)=('root','');
my $ld=ldap_open($ldap_host, 389);
```

ldap_simple_ bind_s(ld, login, password)

This function authenticates a user to the directory and returns an LDAP status code. Its parameters are as follows:

- ld: Connection handle returned by ldap_open

- login: String containing the login name

- password: String containing the password

The following code shows a basic example of using this function:

```
my $rc = ldap_simple_bind_s($ld,$LOGIN,$PASSWORD);
```

ldap_unbind(ld)

This function disconnects and unbinds from the LDAP server and returns an LDAP status code. Its parameter is as follows:

- ld: Connection handle returned by ldap_open

The following code shows a basic example of using this function:

```
$rc = ldap_unbind($ld);
```

Functions That Perform Operations on Entries

The following functions perform operations on entries in the LDAP database.

ldap_add_s(ld, dn, data)

This function adds an entry to the LDAP directory and returns an LDAP status code. Its parameters are as follows:

- ld: Connection handle returned by ldap_open

- dn: DN of the entry to be added.

- data: Hash containing attribute names and values to be added

The following code shows a basic example of using this function:

```
# add a country
$country="myowncountry";
$country_dn="c=$country";
$country_data={
'objectclass'=>['country'],
'c'=>['USA', 'US', 'America'],
'telephonenumber'=>['1'],
};
($dn,$data)=($country_dn,$country_data);
$rc = ldap_add_s($ld,$dn,$data);

# add an organization in that country
$org_dn="o='SwampLand Ltd.', $country_dn";
$org_data={
'objectclass'=>['top', 'organization'],
'o'=>['SwampLand Ltd.', 'SLD'],
'telephonenumber'=>['(408)555-5555'],
};
$rc = ldap_add_s($ld,$org_dn,$org_data);>
```

ldap_modify_s(ln,dn, data)

This function modifies one or more attributes on an entry and returns an LDAP status code. Its parameters are as follows:

- ld: Connection handle returned by ldap_open

- dn: DN of the entry to be modified

- data: Hash containing attribute names and values to be modified

The following code shows a basic example of using this function:

```
$new_country_data={
# Notice 'r' for REPLACE
'telephonenumber' => {'r' => [123]},
};
$rc = ldap_modify_s($ld,$dn,$new_country_data);
```

ldap_delete_s(ld, dn)

This function deletes an entry from the LDAP directory and returns an LDAP status code. Its parameters are as follows:

- ld: Connection handle returned by ldap_open

- dn: DN of the entry to be deleted

The following code shows a basic example of using this function:

```
$rc = ldap_delete_s($ld,$country_dn);
```

ldap_modrdn_s(ld, dn, newrdn)

This function modifies the relative distinguished name (RDN) of an entry in the database and returns an LDAP status code. (This function can move the entry to a new location in the database.) Its parameters are as follows:

- ld: Connection handle returned by ldap_open

- dn: DN of the entry to be modified

- newrdn: New RDN for the entry

The following code shows a basic example of using this function:

```
$new_c="c=IownFrance";
$rc = ldap_modrdn_s($ld,$country_dn,$new_cn,0);
```

ldap_rename_s(ld, dn, newrdn, newbase, deleteold)

This function renames an entry in the LDAP directory and returns an LDAP status code. Its parameters are as follows:

- ld: Connection handle returned by ldap_open

- dn: DN of the entry to be renamed

- newrdn: New RDN for the entry

- newbase: New base DN under which the entry is to be added

- deleteold: 0 means don't delete the old entry, and 1 means delete the old entry

The following code shows a basic example of using this function:

```
$new_c1="c=anewcountry";
$rc = ldap_rename_s($ld,$dn,$new_c1,$org_dn,0)');
```

ldap_search_s(ld, dn, scope, filter, attrs, attrsonly, result)

This function searches the LDAP directory and returns an LDAP status code. Its parameters are as follows:

- ld: Connection handle returned by ldap_open

- dn: DN of the entry from which the search is to start

- scope: Search scope (LDAP_SCOPE, LDAP_SCOPE_ONELEVEL, LDAP_SCOPE_SUBTREE)

- filter: LDAP search filter

- attrsonly: 0 = Return attributes and values; 1 = Return attribute names only

- result: Opaque pointer containing search results; used in later LDAP calls

The following code shows a basic example of using this function:

```
$start_from=$org_dn;
$filter="(objectclass=*)";
$attrs=[];
$result;
$rc = ldap_search_s( \
 $ld,$start_from,LDAP_SCOPE_ONELEVEL,$filter,$attrs,0,$result)
```

ldap_count_entries(ld, result)

This returns a count of the number of entries returned by the last search operation. The resulting count is an integer value. Its parameters are as follows:

- ld: Connection handle returned by ldap_open

- result: Opaque pointer returned by a previous call to ldap_search_s

For example:

```
$count=ldap_count_entries($ld,$result);
print "\$count=$count\n";
```

ldap_get_all_entries(ld, result)

This returns an array containing all entries found in the last search operation. The result of this operation is an LDAP status code. Its parameters are as follows:

- ld: Connection handle returned by ldap_open

- result: Opaque pointer returned by a previous call to ldap_search_s

For example:

```
%record = %{ldap_get_all_entries($ld,$result)};
my @dns = (sort keys %record);
print $#dns+1 . " entries returned.\n";

%r=%{ldap_get_all_entries($ld, $result)};
print "Entries are:";
for $n (sort keys %r) {
 print "<$n>\n";
 for $v (sort keys %{$r{$n}}) {
  print ":\t$v\n";
 }
}
```

Access Control Information Function

Access control information (ACI) exists as a set of rules within the directory. Each rule specifies permissions for a set of users accessing a targeted set of LDAP entries. Within a rule, permissions may apply to every attribute, to attributes within a particular object class, or to a single attribute.

ldap_apply_aci_rule_s creates or modifies an ACI rule. It sets the permissions for the users identified by bindDn, accessing the entries identified by targDn, objclass, attr, and realm. If a rule already exists for the specified bindDn, bindType, targDn, objclass, attr, and realm, the permissions are adjusted accordingly. If, after adjustment, all permissions are set to DEFAULT, the rule is removed.

The parameters using this call include the following:

- ld: Connection handle returned by ldap_open.

- bindDn: DN of the binding entry. You may specify LDAP_DIT_ROOT or LDAP_ACI_SELF here.

- bindType: Type of bind DN (such as subtree or group).

- targDn: DN of the target entry. You may specify LDAP_DIT_ROOT here.

- objclass: Optional object class name. If this isn't set, this must be null.

- attr: Optional attribute name. If this isn't set, this must be null.

- realm: Scope of the entry named by targDn or its children.

- perms: A summation of allowed permission values (for example, LDAP_ACI_ALLOW_READ).

An example of this structure is as follows:

```
int ldap_apply_aci_rule_s(
LDAP * ld,
const char * bindDn,
const LDAPBindType bindType,
```

```
const char * targDn,
const char * objclass,
const char * attr,
const LDAPRealm realm,
const LDAPPerms perms);
```

Memory Management Function

ldap_msgfree(result) frees memory associated with a result returned by ldap_search_s
and returns an LDAP status code. result is an opaque pointer returned by a previous call
to ldap_search_s. For example:

```
$rc = ldap_msgfree($result)
```

Mozilla::LDAP::API

The following are the available API methods for Mozilla::LDAP::API.

ldap_abandon(ld,msgid)

This abandons an asynchronous LDAP operation. Its input parameters are as follows:

- ld: LDAP Session Handle

- msgid: Integer

This is its output: status (as an integer). Its availability is V2/V3.
For example:

```
$status = ldap_abandon($ld,$msgid);
```

ldap_abandon_ext(ld,msgid,serverctrls,clientctrls)

This abandons an asynchronous LDAP operation with controls. Its input parameters are as
follows:

- ld: LDAP Session Handle

- msgid: Integer

- serverctrls: LDAP Control List Pointer

- clientctrls: LDAP Control List Pointer

This is its output: status (as an integer). Its availability is V3.
For example:

```
$status = ldap_abandon_ext($ld,$msgid,$serverctrls,$clientctrls);
```

ldap_add(ld,dn,attrs)

This asynchronously adds an LDAP entry. Its input parameters are as follows:

- ld: LDAP Session Handle

- dn: String

- attrs: LDAP Add/Modify Hash

This is its output: status (as an integer). Its availability is V2/V3.
For example:

```
$status = ldap_add($ld,$dn,$attrs);
```

ldap_add_ext(ld,dn,attrs,serverctrls,clientctrls,msgidp)

This asynchronously adds an LDAP entry with controls. Its input parameters are as follows:

- ld: LDAP Session Handle

- dn: String attrs: LDAP Add/Modify Hash

- serverctrls: LDAP Control List Pointer

- clientctrls: LDAP Control List Pointer

- msgidp: Integer

This is its output: status (as an integer) and msgidp (as an integer). Its availability is V2/V3.
For example:

```
$status = ldap_add_ext($ld,$dn,$attrs,$serverctrls,$clientctrls,$msgidp);
```

ldap_add_ext_s(ld,dn,attrs,serverctrls,clientctrls)

This synchronously adds an LDAP entry with controls. Its input parameters are as follows:

- ld: LDAP Session Handle

- dn: String

- attrs: LDAP Add/Modify Hash

- serverctrls: LDAP Control List Pointer

- clientctrls: LDAP Control List Pointer

This is its output: status (as an integer). Its availability is V3.
For example:

```
$status = ldap_add_ext_s($ld,$dn,$attrs,$serverctrls,$clientctrls);
```

ldap_add_s(ld,dn,attrs)

This synchronously adds an LDAP entry. Its input parameters are as follows:

- ld: LDAP Session Handle

- dn: String

- attrs: LDAP Add/Modify Hash

This is its output: status (as an integer). Its availability is V2/V3.
For example:

```
$status = ldap_add_s($ld,$dn,$attrs);
```

ldap_bind(ld,dn,passwd,authmethod)

This asynchronously binds to the LDAP server. Its input parameters are as follows:

- ld: LDAP Session Handle

- dn: String

- passwd: String

- authmethod: Integer

This is its output: status (as an integer). Its availability is V2/V3.
For example:

```
$status = ldap_bind($ld,$dn,$passwd,$authmethod);
```

ldap_bind_s(ld,dn,passwd,authmethod)

This synchronously binds to an LDAP server. Its input parameters are as follows:

- ld: LDAP Session Handle

- dn: String passwd: String

- authmethod: Integer

This is its output: status (as an integer). Its availability is V2/V3.
For example:

```
$status = ldap_bind_s($ld,$dn,$passwd,$authmethod);
```

ldap_controls_free(ctrls)

This frees a list of LDAP controls. Its input parameters are as follows:

- ctrls: LDAP Control List Pointer

This is its output: status: NONE. Its availability is V3.
For example:

```
$status = ldap_controls_free($ctrls);
```

ldap_create_filter(buf,buflen,pattern,prefix,suffix,attr,value,valwords)

This creates an LDAP search filter. Its input parameters are as follows:

- buf: String

- buflen: Integer

- pattern: String

- prefix: String

- suffix: String

- attr: String

- value: String

- valwords: List Reference

This is its output: status (as an integer). Its availability is V2/V3.
For example:

```
$status = ldap_create_filter($buf,$buflen,$pattern,$prefix, \
$suffix,$attr,$value,$valwords);
```

ldap_create_persistentsearch_control(ld,changetypes,changesonly, return_echg_ctrls,ctrl_iscritical,ctrlp)

This creates a persistent search control. Its input parameters are as follows:

- ld: LDAP Session Handle

- changetypes: Integer

- changesonly: Integer

- return_echg_ctrls: Integer

- ctrl iscritical: Integer

- ctrlp: LDAP Control List Pointer

This is its output:

- status (as an integer)
- ctrlp (an LDAP Control List Pointer)

Its availability is V3.
For example:

```
$status = ldap_create_persistentsearch_control($ld,$changetypes, \
$changesonly,$return_echg_ctrls, $ctrl_iscritical,$ctrlp);
```

ldap_delete(ld,dn)

This asynchronously deletes an LDAP entry. Its input parameters are as follows:

- ld: LDAP Session Handle
- dn: String

This is its output: status (as an integer). Its availability is V2/V3.
For example:

```
$status = ldap_delete($ld,$dn);
```

ldap_delete_ext(ld,dn,serverctrls,clientctrls,msgidp)

This synchronously deletes an LDAP entry with controls. Its input parameters are as follows:

- ld: LDAP Session Handle
- dn: String
- serverctrls: LDAP Control List Pointer
- clientctrls: LDAP Control List Pointer
- msgidp: Integer

This is its output:

- status (as an integer)
- msgidp (as an integer)

Its availability is V3.
For example:

```
$status = ldap_delete_ext($ld,$dn,$serverctrls,$clientctrls,$msgidp);
```

ldap_delete_ext_s(ld,dn,serverctrls,clientctrls)

This synchronously deletes an LDAP entry with controls. Its parameters are as follows:

- ld: LDAP Session Handle

- dn: String

- serverctrls: LDAP Control List Pointer

- clientctrls: LDAP Control List Pointer

This is its output: status (as an integer). Its availability is V3.
For example:

```
$status = ldap_delete_ext_s($ld,$dn,$serverctrls,$clientctrls);
```

ldap_delete_s(ld,dn)

This synchronously deletes an LDAP entry. Its input parameters are as follows:

- ld: LDAP Session Handle

- dn: String

This is its output: status (as an integer). Its availability is V2/V3.
For example:

```
$status = ldap_delete_s($ld,$dn);
```

ldap_err2string(err)

This returns the string value of an LDAP error code. Its input parameter is as follows:

- err: Integer

This is its output: status (as a string). Its availability is V2/V3.
For example:

```
$status = ldap_err2string($err);
```

ldap_explode_dn(dn,notypes)

This splits a given DN into its components. Setting notypes to 1 returns the components without their type names. Its input parameters are as follows:

- dn: String

- notypes: Integer

This is its output: status: NONE. Its availability is V2/V3.
For example:

```
$status = ldap_explode_dn($dn,$notypes);
```

ldap_explode_rdn(dn,notypes)

This splits an RDN into its components. Its input parameters are as follows:

- dn: String

- notypes: Integer

This is its output: status: NONE. Its availability is V2/V3.
For example:

```
$status = ldap_explode_rdn($dn,$notypes);
```

ldap_extended_operation(ld,requestoid,requestdata,serverctrls,clientctrls,msgidp)

This performs an asynchronous extended operation. Its input parameters are as follows:

- ld: LDAP Session Handle

- requestoid: String

- requestdata: Binary String

- serverctrls: LDAP Control List Pointer

- clientctrls: LDAP Control List Pointer

- msgidp: Integer

The output is as follows:

- status (as an integer)

- msgidp (as an integer)

Its availability is V3.
For example:

```
$status = ldap_extended_operation($ld,$requestoid,$requestdata,$serverctrls, \
$clientctrls,$msgidp);
```

ldap_extended_operation_s(ld,requestoid,requestdata,serverctrls, clientctrls,retoidp,retdatap)

This performs a synchronous extended operation. Its input parameters are as follows:

- ld: LDAP Session Handle

- requestoid: String

- requestdata: Binary String

- serverctrls: LDAP Control List Pointer

- clientctrls: LDAP Control List Pointer

- retoidp: String

This is its output:

- status: (as an integer)

- retoidp: Return OID

- retdatap: Return Data

Its availability is V3.
For example:

```
$status = ldap_extended_operation_s($ld,$requestoid,$requestdata,$serverctrls, \
$clientctrls,$retoidp,$retdatap);
```

ldap_get_dn(ld,entry)

This returns the DN for an entry. Its input parameters are as follows:

- ld: LDAP Session Handle

- entry: LDAP Message Pointer

This is its output: status (as a string). Its availability is V2/V3.
For example:

```
$status = ldap_get_dn($ld,$entry);
```

ldap_get_entry_controls(ld,entry,serverctrlsp)

This returns the controls for an LDAP entry. Its input parameters are as follows:

- ld: LDAP Session Handle

- entry: LDAP Message Pointer

- serverctrlsp: LDAP Control List Pointer

The following is its output:

- status (as an integer)

- serverctrlsp: LDAP Control List Pointer

Its availability is V3.
For example:

```
$status = ldap_get_entry_controls($ld,$entry,$serverctrlsp);
```

ldap_get_option(ld,option,optdata)

This gets an option for an LDAP session. Its input parameters are as follows:

- ld: LDAP Session Handle

- option: Integer

- optdata: Integer

Its output is as follows:

- status (as an integer)

- optdata: Integer

Its availability is V2/V3.
For example:

```
$status = ldap_get_option($ld,$option,$optdata);
```

ldap_get_values(ld,entry,target)

This gets the values for an LDAP entry and attribute. Its input parameters are as follows:

- ld: LDAP Session Handle

- entry: LDAP Message Pointer

- target: String

This is its output: status: NONE. Its availability is V3.
For example:

```
$status = ldap_get_values($ld,$entry,$target);
```

ldap_get_values_len(ld,entry,target)

This gets the binary values for an LDAP entry and attribute. Its input parameters are as follows:

- ld: LDAP Session Handle

- entry: LDAP Message Pointer

- target: String

This is its output: status: NONE. Its availability is V3.
For example:

```
$status = ldap_get_values_len($ld,$entry,$target);
```

ldap_init(host,port)

This initializes an LDAP session. Its input parameters are as follows:

- host: String

- port: Integer

This is its output: status: LDAP Session Handle. Its availability is V2/V3.
For example:

```
$status = ldap_init($host,$port);
```

ldap_init_getfilter(fname)

This initializes the LDAP filter generation routines to a filename. Its input parameter is as follows:

- fname: Filename String

This is its output: status: LDAP Filter Description Pointer. Its availability is V2/V3.
For example:

```
$status = ldap_init_getfilter($fname);
```

ldap_init_getfilter_buf(buf,buflen)

This initializes the LDAP filter generation routines to a buffer. Its input parameters are as follows:

- buf: String

- buflen: Integer

Its output is status: LDAP Filter Description Pointer. Its availability is V2/V3.
For example:

```
$status = ldap_init_getfilter_buf($buf,$buflen);
```

ldap_is_ldap_url(url)

This returns 1 if an the argument is a valid LDAP URL. Its input parameter is as follows:

- url: String

Its output is status (as an integer). Its availability is V2/V3.
For example:

```
$status = ldap_is_ldap_url($url);
```

ldap_modify(ld,dn,mods)

This asynchronously modifies an LDAP entry. Its input parameters are as follows:

- ld: LDAP Session Handle

- dn: String

- mods: LDAP Add/Modify Hash

Its output is status (as an integer). Its availability is V2/V3.
For example:

```
$status = ldap_modify($ld,$dn,$mods);
```

ldap_modify_ext(ld,dn,mods,serverctrls,clientctrls,msgidp)

This asynchronously modifies an LDAP entry with controls. Its input parameters are as follows:

- ld: LDAP Session Handle

- dn: String

- mods: LDAP Add/Modify Hash

- serverctrls: LDAP Control List Pointer

- clientctrls: LDAP Control List Pointer

- msgidp: Integer

Its output is as follows:

- status (as an integer)

- msgidp (as an integer)

Its availability is V3.
For example:

```
$status = ldap_modify_ext($ld,$dn,$mods,$serverctrls,$clientctrls,$msgidp);
```

ldap_modify_ext_s(ld,dn,mods,serverctrls,clientctrls)

This synchronously modifies an LDAP entry with controls. Its input parameters are as follows:

- ld: LDAP Session Handle

- dn: String

- mods: LDAP Add/Modify Hash

- serverctrls: LDAP Control List Pointer

- clientctrls: LDAP Control List Pointer

Its output is status (as an integer). Its availability is V3.
For example:

```
$status = ldap_modify_ext_s($ld,$dn,$mods,$serverctrls,$clientctrls);
```

ldap_modify_s(ld,dn,mods)

This synchronously modifies an LDAP entry. Its input parameters are as follows:

- ld: LDAP Session Handle

- dn: String

- mods: LDAP Add/Modify Hash

Its output is status (as an integer). Its availability is V2/V3.
For example:

```
$status = ldap_modify_s($ld,$dn,$mods);
```

ldap_modrdn(ld,dn,newrdn)

This asynchronously modifies the RDN of an entry. Its input parameters are as follows:

- ld: LDAP Session Handle

- dn: String newrdn: String

Its output is status (as an integer). Its availability is V2/V3.
For example:

```
$status = ldap_modrdn($ld,$dn,$newrdn);
```

ldap_modrdn_s(ld,dn,newrdn)

This synchronously modifies the RDN of an entry. Its input parameters are as follows:

- ld: LDAP Session Handle

- dn: String

- newrdn: String

Its ouput is status (as an integer). Its availability is V2/V3.
For example:

```
$status = ldap_modrdn_s($ld,$dn,$newrdn);
```

ldap_modrdn2(ld,dn,newrdn,deleteoldrdn)

This asynchronously modifies the RDN of an entry. Its input parameters are as follows:

- ld: LDAP Session Handle
- dn: String
- newrdn: String
- deleteoldrdn: Integer

Its output is status (as an integer). Its availability is V2/V3.
For example:

```
$status = ldap_modrdn2($ld,$dn,$newrdn,$deleteoldrdn);
```

ldap_modrdn2_s(ld,dn,newrdn,deleteoldrdn)

This synchronously modifies the relative distinguished name of an entry. Its input parameters are as follows:

- ld: LDAP Session Handle
- dn: String
- newrdn: String
- deleteoldrdn: Integer

Its output is status (as an integer). Its availability is V2/V3.
For example:

```
$status = ldap_modrdn2_s($ld,$dn,$newrdn,$deleteoldrdn);
```

ldap_next_attribute(ld,entry,ber)

This gets the next attribute for an LDAP entry. Its input parameters are as follows:

- ld: LDAP Session Handle
- entry: LDAP Message Pointer
- ber: Ber Element Pointer

Its output is as follows:

- status: String
- ber: BER Element Pointer

Its availability is V2/V3.
For example:

```
$status = ldap_next_attribute($ld,$entry,$ber);
```

ldap_next_entry(ld,entry)

This gets the next entry in the result chain. Its input parameters are as follows:

- ld: LDAP Session Handle

- entry: LDAP Message Pointer

Its output is status: LDAP Message Pointer. Its availability is V2/V3.
For example:

```
$status = ldap_next_entry($ld,$entry);
```

ldap_parse_sasl_bind_result(ld,res,servercredp,freeit)

This parses the results of an SASL bind operation. Its input parameters are as follows:

- ld: LDAP Session Handle

- res: LDAP Message Pointer

- freeit: Integer

Its output is as follows:

- status (as an integer)

- servercredp

Its availability is V3.
For example:

```
$status = ldap_parse_sasl_bind_result($ld,$res,$servercredp,$freeit);
```

ldap_perror(ld,s)

This prints an LDAP error message. Its input parameters are as follows:

- ld: LDAP Session Handle

- s: String

Its output is status: NONE. Its availability is V2/V3.
For example:

```
$status = ldap_perror($ld,$s);
```

ldap_result(ld,msgid,all,timeout,result)

This gets the result for an asynchronous LDAP operation. Its input parameters are as follows:

- ld: LDAP Session Handle

- msgid: Integer

- `all`: Integer

- `timeout`: Time in Seconds

- `result`: LDAP Message Pointer

Its output is as follows:

- `status` (as an integer)

- `result`: LDAP Message Pointer

Its availability is V2/V3.
For example:

```
$status = ldap_result($ld,$msgid,$all,$timeout,$result);
```

ldap_result2error(ld,r,freeit)

This gets the error number for a given result. Its input parameters are as follows:

- `ld`: LDAP Session Handle

- `r`: LDAP Message Pointer

- `freeit`: Integer

Its output is status (as an integer). Its availability is V2/V3.
For example:

```
$status = ldap_result2error($ld,$r,$freeit);
```

ldap_sasl_bind(ld,dn,mechanism,cred,serverctrls,clientctrls,msgidp)

This asynchronously binds to the LDAP server using a SASL mechanism. Its input parameters are as follows:

- `ld`: LDAP Session Handle

- `dn`: String

- `mechanism`: String

- `cred`: Binary String

- `serverctrls`: LDAP Control List Pointer

- `clientctrls`: LDAP Control List Pointer

- `msgidp`: Integer

Its output is as follows:

- status (as an integer)

- msgidp: Integer

Its availability is V3.
For example:

```
$status = ldap_sasl_bind($ld,$dn,$mechanism,$cred, \
$serverctrls,$clientctrls,$msgidp);
```

ldap_sasl_bind_s(ld,dn,mechanism,cred,serverctrls,clientctrls,servercredp)

This synchronously binds to an LDAP server using a SASL mechanism. Its input parameters are as follows:

- ld: LDAP Session Handle

- dn: String

- mechanism: String

- cred: Binary String

- serverctrls: LDAP Control List Pointer

- clientctrls: LDAP Control List Pointer

Its output is as follows:

- status (as an integer)

- servercredp:

Its availability is V3.
For example:

```
$status = ldap_sasl_bind_s($ld,$dn,$mechanism,$cred, \
$serverctrls,$clientctrls,$servercredp);
```

ldap_search(ld,base,scope,filter,attrs,attrsonly)

This asynchronously searches the LDAP server. Its input parameters are as follows:

- ld: LDAP Session Handle

- base: String

- scope: Integer

- filter: String

- attrs: List Reference

- attrsonly: Integer

Its output is status (as an integer). Its availability is V2/V3.
For example:

```
$status = ldap_search($ld,$base,$scope,$filter,$attrs,$attrsonly);
```

ldap_search_ext(ld,base,scope,filter,attrs,attrsonly,serverctrls,clientctrls, timeoutp,sizelimit,msgidp)

This asynchronously searches the LDAP server with controls. Its input parameters are as follows:

- ld: LDAP Session Handle

- base: String

- scope: Integer

- filter: String

- attrs: List Reference

- attrsonly: Integer

- serverctrls: LDAP Control List Pointer

- clientctrls: LDAP Control List Pointer

- timeoutp: Time in Seconds

- sizelimit: Integer

- msgidp: Integer

Its output is as follows:

- status (as an integer)

- msgidp: Integer

Its availability is V3.
For example:

```
$status = ldap_search_ext($ld,$base,$scope,$filter, \
$attrs,$attrsonly,$serverctrls, \$clientctrls,$timeoutp,$sizelimit,$msgidp);
```

ldap_search_ext_s(ld,base,scope,filter,attrs,attrsonly,serverctrls,clientctrls, timeoutp,sizelimit,res)

This synchronously searches the LDAP server with controls. Its input parameters are as follows:

- ld: LDAP Session Handle

- base: String

- scope: Integer

- `filter`: String

- `attrs`: List Reference

- `attrsonly`: Integer

- `serverctrls`: LDAP Control List Pointer

- `clientctrls`: LDAP Control List Pointer

- `timeoutp`: Time in Seconds

- `sizelimit`: Integer

- `res`: LDAP Message Pointer

Its output is as follows:

- `status` (as an integer)

- `res`: LDAP Message Pointer

Its availability is V3.
For example:

```
$status = ldap_search_ext_s($ld,$base,$scope,$filter,$attrs,$attrsonly,$servrctrls, \
$clientctrls,$timeoutp,$sizelimit,$res);
```

ldap_search_s(ld,base,scope,filter,attrs,attrsonly,res)

This synchronously searches the LDAP server. Its input parameters are as follows:

- `ld`: LDAP Session Handle

- `base`: String

- `scope`: Integer

- `filter`: String

- `attrs`: List Reference

- `attrsonly`: Integer

- `res`: LDAP Message Pointer

Its output is as follows:

- `status` (as an integer)

- `res`: LDAP Message Pointer

Its availability is V2/V3.
For example:

```
$status = ldap_search_s($ld,$base,$scope,$filter,$attrs,$attrsonly,$res);
```

ldap_set_lderrno(ld,e,m,s)

This sets the LDAP error structure. Its input parameters are as follows:

- ld: LDAP Session Handle

- e: Integer

- m: String

- s: String

  Its output is status (as an integer). Its availability is V2/V3.
  For example:

```
$status = ldap_set_lderrno($ld,$e,$m,$s);
```

ldap_set_option(ld,option,optdata)

This sets an LDAP session option. Its input parameters are as follows:

- ld: LDAP Session Handle

- option: Integer

- optdata: Integer

  Its output is status (as an integer). Its availability is V2/V3.
  For example:

```
$status = ldap_set_option($ld,$option,$optdata);
```

ldap_simple_bind(ld,who,passwd)

This asynchronously binds to the LDAP server using simple authentication. Its input parameters are as follows:

- ld: LDAP Session Handle

- who: String

- passwd: String

  Its output is status (as an integer). Its availability is V2/V3.
  For example:

```
$status = ldap_simple_bind($ld,$who,$passwd);
```

ldap_simple_bind_s(ld,who,passwd)

This synchronously binds to the LDAP server using simple authentication. Its input parameters are as follows:

- ld: LDAP Session Handle

- who: String

- passwd: String

Its output is status (as an integer). Its availability is V2/V3.

Listing 6-4 shows how to initialize and LDAP connection and then successfully clean it up.

Listing 6-4. *Initializing/Releasing an LDAP Connection*

```
$status = ldap_simple_bind_s($ld,$who,$passwd);

/* This initializes an LDAP session, followed by cleanup */

#include <stdio.h>
#include <ldap.h>        /* pass -I /path/to/ldap.h in CFLAGS */

/* Optionally, these could also be passed as arguments to our function */
#define MY_LDAP_SERVER   "ldap-server.yourcompany.com"
#define MY_LDAP_PORT     LDAP_PORT

extern LDAP *
my_ldap_init (char *my_DN, char *my_pass)
{
        LDAP    *ldap_handle;
        int     ldap_return;

        /*
        ** Calling ldap_init does not actually cause any communication
        ** between the LDAP client and server, it only creates the LDAP
        ** session handler variable, in this case, pointed to by ldap_handle:
        */
        ldap_handle = ldap_init (MY_LDAP_SERVER, MY_LDAP_PORT);
        if (!ldap_handle) {
                fprintf (stderr,
                        "ldap_init: Couldn't init sessin handle for: %s:%d\n",
                        MY_LDAP_SERVER, MY_LDAP_PORT);
                return NULL;
        }
```

```
/*
** There are two families of LDAP calls, synchronous and asynchronous.
** With synchronous calls the routines block, specifically they will
** wait, until the function has finished.
**
** Note that synchronous calls are called with the same function names
** as their cousins, with the exception that they are given the
** suffix ("_s").
**
** ldap_bind_s(...) are passed four arguments:
**
** ldap_bind_s (LDAP *handle, char *dn, char *password, int auth_type)
**
** Note that if dn and password are passed as NULL, then an anonymous
** (unauthenticated) bind will be attempted. Use the argument
** "LDAP_AUTH_SIMPLE" for simple password based authentication.
*/
ldap_return = ldap_bind_s (ldap_handle, my_DN, my_pass,
        LDAP_AUTH_SIMPLE);

if (ldap_return == LDAP_SUCCESS) {
        /*
        ** A successful bind operation has been established with
        ** the server; you may perform further operations on
        ** ldap_handle.
        */
        return ldap_handle;
}

/*
** This will print an LDAP error associated with the
** handler. */
ldap_perror (ldap_handle, "ldap_bind_s");

/*
** This routine frees all memory allocated by ldap_init() */
ldap_unbind (ldap_handle);
return NULL;

}
```

Listing 6-5 demonstrates how to add users using the C API.

Listing 6-5. *Adding Users*

```
/*
** This code sample adds a brand new DN into the LDAP tree, rooted
** at "ou=People, dc=Your, dc=Company".
*/

#include <stdio.h>
#include <ldap.h>

#define MY_ROOT_DN      "ou=People, dc=Your, dc=Company"

/*
** In this example I am allowing the attributes to be passed
** via a fixed number of arguments. An elaborate way to design
** a serious add function would be to pass an array of attribute/value
** pairs, and dynamically malloc (LDAPMod *) entries based on this.
**
** Also, a new entry would probably require some objectclass entries,
** which this function innocently ignores.
*/
extern char *
my_ldap_insert (char *cn, char *sn, char *mail, char *title)
{
        LDAP            *lh;

        /* Remember that attributes are treated in the API as a list,
        ** even though we are only adding one value per attribute */
        char            *cndata[2], *sndata[2], *maildata[2], *titledata[2];

        /* These each hold a separate attribute field */
        LDAPMod         modcn, modsn, modmail, modtitle;

        /* 4 attributes + NULL */
        LDAPMod         *modadds[5];

        /* We will be building a new DN for this entry */
        char            new_dn[1024];

        /*
        ** Ensure that cn is a set string, and that none of the other
        ** entry attributes are NULL values. Note that we are doing
        ** this before we attempt to bind, in order to attempt to be
        ** somewhat efficient. */
        if (!(cn && *cn && sn && mail && title))
                return NULL;
```

```c
        if (! (lh = my_ldap_init (NULL, NULL)))
                exit (-1);

        /* Create a brand new DN: */
        snprintf (new_dn, sizeof(new_dn) - 1, "cn=%s, %s", cn, MY_ROOT_DN);

        /* This establishes each attribute list: */
        cndata[0] = cn, cndata[1] = NULL;
        sndata[0] = sn, sndata[1] = NULL;
        maildata[0] = mail, maildata[1] = NULL;
        titledata[0] = title, titledata[1] = NULL;

        /* This creates each entry in the (LDAPMod **) list,
        ** One for each attribute: */

        modcn.mod_op = LDAP_MOD_ADD, modcn.mod_type = "cn",
        modcn.mod_values = cndata;

        modsn.mod_op = LDAP_MOD_ADD, modsn.mod_type = "sn",
        modsn.mod_values = sndata;

        modmail.mod_op = LDAP_MOD_ADD, modmail.mod_type = "mail",
        modmail.mod_values = maildata;

        modtitle.mod_op = LDAP_MOD_ADD, modtitle.mod_type = "title",
        modtitle.mod_values = titledata;

        /* Here is where it all comes together */
        modadds[0] = &modcn, modadds[1] = &modsn, modadds[2] = &modmail,
        modadds[3] = &modtitle, modadds[4] = NULL;

        if (ldap_add_s (lh, new_dn, modadds) != LDAP_SUCCESS) {
                ldap_perror (lh, "ldap_add_s");
        } else {
                printf ("New entry added: %s\n", new_dn);
        }

        ldap_unbind (lh);
exit (0);
}
```

Listing 6-6 demonstrates how to delete users using the C API.

Listing 6-6. *Deleting Users*

```c
/* This simply deletes an entry in the LDAP hierarchy. */

#include <stdio.h>
#include <ldap.h>
```

```
extern int
my_ldap_delete (char *cn)
{
        LDAP              *lh;
        char              dn[1024];

        if (!(cn && *cn))
                return -1;

        if (! (lh = my_ldap_init (NULL, NULL)))
                return -1;

        /* DN to delete */
        snprintf (dn, sizeof(dn)-1, "cn=%s, ou=People, dc=Your, dc=Company", cn);
        delval = ldap_delete_s (lh, dn);

        ldap_unbind (lh);
        return (delval == LDAP_SUCCESS) ? 0 : -1;
}
```

Listing 6-7 performs a modrdn operation using the C API.

Listing 6-7. *The* modrdn *Operation*

```
/*
** This code sample renames a DN from:
** DN: "cn=Tom Jackiewicz, ou=People, dc=Your, dc=Company"
**
** To:
** DN: "cn=Tom Pickle, ou=People, dc=Your, dc=Company"
**
*/

#include <stdio.h>
#include <ldap.h>

extern int
tom_ldap_rdn (void)
{
        LDAP            *lh;
        char            *old_dn = "cn=Tom Jackiewicz, ou=People, dc=Your, dc=Company";
        char            *new_dn = "cn=Tom Pickle, ou=People, dc=Your,dc=Company";
        int             rval = 0;
        if (! (lh = my_ldap_init (NULL, NULL)))
                return -1;
```

```
        /*
        ** ldap_modrdn2_s (ldap_handle, char *old_dn, char *new_dn, int delete_old)
        **
        ** If delete_old is TRUE (not zero) then all of the attributes from the
        ** DN will be deleted from the entry.
        */

        if (ldap_modrdn2_s (lh, old_dn, new_dn, 0) != LDAP_SUCCESS) {
                ldap_perror (lh, "ldap_modrdn2_s");
                rval = -1;
        } else {
                printf ("Tom's DN was changed to: %s\n", new_dn);
        }

        ldap_unbind (lh);
return rval;
}
```

Listing 6-8 searches your LDAP system for an e-mail address.

Listing 6-8. *Search for an Address*

```
/* This searches an LDAP directory for e-mail addresses */

#include <stdio.h>
#include <ldap.h>

extern int
my_ldap_search (void)
{
        LDAP            *lh;
        LDAPMessage     *ldap_data,
                        *ldap_walk;
        int             ldap_return;
        char            *attribs[] = {"cn", "mail", "company", "dn"};

        if (! (lh = my_ldap_init (NULL, NULL)))
                return -1;

        /*
        ** ldap_search_s (LDAP *handle, char *base_DN, int scope
        **      char *filter, char *attributes[], LDAPMessage **ldap_data)
        **
        */
        ldap_return = ldap_search_s (lh, "ou=People,dc=Your,dc=Company",
                LDAP_SCOPE_SUBTREE, "(mail=*)", attribs, &ldap_data);
```

```
        if (ldap_return != LDAP_SUCCESS) {
                ldap_perror (lh, "ldap_search_s");
                ldap_unbind (lh);
                return -1;
        }

        /*
        ** ldap_first_entry() and ldap_next_entry() both return NULL
        ** in case of an error (such as no data).  */
        for (ldap_walk = ldap_first_entry (lh, ldap_data);
        ldap_walk; ldap_walk = ldap_next_entry (lh, ldap_walk) {
                char            *DN,
                                *ATTRS;
                BerElement      *BER;

                DN = ldap_get_dn (lh, ldap_walk);
                if (DN) {
                        printf("dn: %s\n", DN);
                        ldap_memfree(DN);
                }

                /*
                ** Print the attributes */
                for (attrs = ldap_first_attribute (lh, ldap_data, &BER);
                attrs; attrs = ldap_next_attribute (lh, ldap_data, BER) {
                        printf("%s\n", attrs);
                        ldap_memfree(attrs);
                }
                putchar('\n');
                if (BER) ber_free (BER, 0);
        }

        ldap_unbind (lh);
        return 0;
}
```

Listing 6-9 shows how to retrieve and sort an entire list of e-mail addresses from your LDAP directory using the C API.

Listing 6-9. *Searching and Sorting Return Data*

```
/* This dumps a sorted list of all e-mail addresses from a domain */

#include <stdio.h>
#include <string.h>
#include <ldap.h>
```

```
extern int
my_ldap_domain_listing (char *domain)
{
        LDAP            *lh;
        LDAPMessage     *ldap_data,
                        *ldap_walk;
        int             ldap_return;
        char            *attribs[] = {"cn", "mail", "company", "dn"};
        char            filter[1024];

        /* Attempt some sanity checking */
        if (!(domain && *domain && rindex(domain, '.')))
                return -1;

        if (! (lh = my_ldap_init (NULL, NULL)))
                return -1;

        snprintf (filter, sizeof(filter)-1,
                "(&(objectclass=person)(mail=*@%s))", domain);

        ldap_return = ldap_search_s (lh, "ou=People,dc=Your,dc=Company",
                LDAP_SCOPE_SUBTREE, filter, attribs, &ldap_data);

        if (ldap_return != LDAP_SUCCESS) {
                ldap_perror (lh, "ldap_search_s");
                ldap_unbind (lh);
                return -1;
        }

        /*
        ** ldap_sort_entries (ldap_handle, LDAPMessage **listp, char *attrib,
        **      int (*compare)(char *s1, char *s2));
        **
        ** ldap_sort_entries uses the function, pointed to by the "compare"
        ** argument to sort all entries (pointed to by listp) on the attribute
        ** field, pointed to by attrib.  Fairly straightforward, quite simple.
        */

        if (ldap_sort_entries (lh, &ldap_data, "mail", strcmp) != LDAP_SUCCESS)
                ldap_perror (lh, "ldap_sort_entries");
                /* No break, ldap_data is still valid even if an error
                ** occurred. */

        /*
        ** ldap_first_entry() and ldap_next_entry() both return NULL
        ** in case of an error (such as no data).  */
```

```
        for (ldap_walk = ldap_first_entry (lh, ldap_data);
     ldap_walk; ldap_walk = ldap_next_entry (lh, ldap_walk) {
            char            *DN,
                            *ATTRS;
            BerElement      *BER;

            DN = ldap_get_dn (lh, ldap_walk);
            if (DN) {
                    printf("dn: %s\n", DN);
                    ldap_memfree(DN);
            }

            /*
            ** Print the attributes */
            for (attrs = ldap_first_attribute (lh, ldap_data, &BER);
            attrs; attrs = ldap_next_attribute (lh, ldap_data, BER) {
                    printf("%s\n", attrs);
                    ldap_memfree(attrs);
            }
            putchar('\n');
            if (BER) ber_free (BER, 0);
    }

    ldap_unbind (lh);
    return 0;
}
```

Listing 6-10 shows how to modify the mail attribute for the DN of cn=Tom Jackiewicz, ou=People, dc=Your, dc=Company using the C API.

Listing 6-10. *Modifying Data*

```
/*
** This code sample updates the DN for:
** DN: "cn=Tom Jackiewicz, ou=People, dc=Your, dc=Company"
**
** It will update the "mail" attribute, replacing it with new data.
**
** Of course this is an over-simplified example; this routine would
** really be useful if the DN (or its componentns) were built by
** supplying it as a parameter, as well as the data being replaced.
**
*/

#include <stdio.h>
#include <ldap.h>
```

```
extern char *
tom_ldap_update (void)
{
        LDAP            *lh;
        LDAPMod         modent,
                        *modptrs[2];
        char            *my_dn =
                        {"cn=Tom Jackiewicz, ou=People, dc=Your, dc=Company",

        /* New e-mail addresses for Tom */
        char            *tomaddrs[] = { "tom@sun4c.net",
                                        "Tom.Jackiewicz@yourcompany.com",
                                        "tom@upt.org",
                                        NULL
        };


        if (! (lh = my_ldap_init (NULL, NULL)))
                return NULL;

        /*
        ** There is one update occurring: */
        modent.mod_op = LDAP_MOD_REPLACE;
        modent.mod_type = "mail";
        modent.mod_values = tomaddrs;

        modptrs[0] = &modent;
        modptrs[0] = NULL;

        /*
        ** ldap_modify_s(ldap_handle, char *dn, LDAPMod **ldap_modlist) :
        **
        ** ldap_modlist is a NULL terminated list of `LDAPMOD *' (pointer to
        ** LDAPMod structure).  The structure contains information pertaining
        ** to the operation type--in this instance, a replace operation,
        ** the attribute effected and a list of the replacement data.
        ** (remember that more than one value can be used for a given
        ** attribute; this is why the API allows for a list of values
        ** given the (char **) parameter):
        **
        ** ldap_modlist[0] -> LDAPMod *mod_ptr -> {
        **                                  mod_op = LDAP_MOD_REPLACE,
        **                                  mod_type = "mail",
        **                                  mod_values = char **data -> {
        **                                          "u@d.com",
        **                                          "u2@d.com",
        **                                          NULL
        **                                  }
```

```
** ldap_modlist[1] -> NULL
**
** }
**
** Since the ldap_modlist is an array of operations, more than one
** operation may appear in the list.
**
** Remember that since we specified that "mail" is being replaced,
** ALL of the values that occured for the mail attribute before
** any call to ldap_modify_s() -- or ldap_modify() are REPLACED
** with the new data, supplied with the mod_values argument.
**
*/

if (ldap_modify_s (lh, my_dn, modptrs) != LDAP_SUCCESS) {
        ldap_perror (lh, "ldap_modify_s");
} else {
        printf ("The update for Tom was successful.\n");
}
ldap_unbind (lh);
return my_dn;
}
```

Performing Operations Against Your OpenLDAP Directory

You'll need to include the following line at the beginning of all your Perl scripts to appropriately specify the API you'll be using:

```
use Net::LDAP qw(:all);
```

The following code binds to your system:

```
$ldap = new Net::LDAP('ldapsearch') || die;
$ldap->bind( version => 3);
```

The following code specifies the connection data:

```
$mesg = $ldap->search ( base => "dc=Your,dc=Company",
filter => "uid=Tom",)
```

You can also add another parameter to return only a subset of the information. The default would be to return all information. For example, you can create the array @attrs containing the attributes you want returned and make another call.

```
@attrs = ("uid","cn");
$mesg = $ldap->search ( base => "dc=Your,dc=Company",
filter => "uid=Tom",
attrs => @attrs")
```

Upon retrieving the appropriate information, you're able to process the information.

```
use Net::LDAP qw(:alforeach $entry ($msg->all_entries) {
  $entry->dump;
}
```

Now you can unbind from the server.

```
$ldap->unbind;
```

Using Java and JNDI

A couple of methods exist for utilizing Java in your LDAP development. The Java Naming and Directory Interface (JNDI) is an API for accessing different kinds of naming and directory services. JNDI isn't specific to a particular naming or directory service; you can use it to access many kinds of systems, including filesystems; distributed objects such as CORBA, Java RMI, and EJB; and directory services such as LDAP, Novell NetWare, and NIS+.

You can also download the Netscape Java API (discussed in earlier in this chapter), which is the Java equivalent of the C API.

I'll demonstrate some of the basic LDAP functionality you can attain via JNDI. RFC 2251–compliant LDAP operations map to specific JNDI methods. The DirContext and LdapContext interfaces provide this mapping. You can find a good tutorial by Michael Yee at http://www.sbfsbo.com/mike/JndiTutorial. JNDI is installed with the Java SDK version 1.3 or better. Visit http://java.sun.com for downloads and additional information. Development with Java is somewhat more intensive than Perl. The scripts are longer and execute much more slowly. If you still want to develop LDAP applications in Java, you'll find the basics in the following list. The examples are modified versions from Mark Wilcox's book, *Implementing LDAP* (Peer Information, 1999), which were subsequently modified by Michael Yee on his Web site.

I've divided basic JNDI programs into three sections: context initialization, binding, and processing. Context initialization and binding rarely change between applications. Context initialization sets the following global variables:

- INITCTX: The name of the service provider. The following comes from Sun, but IBM has a version, too.

  ```
  INITCTX = "com.sun.jndi.ldap.LdapCtxFactory";
  ```

- MY_HOST: Intuitively, this specifies the protocol (LDAP), name of your server, and the port number (389 is default).

  ```
  MY_HOST = "ldap://ldaphost:389";
  ```

- MGR_DN: This is the DN of the LDAP administrator as specified in the rootdn parameter in slapd.conf.

- MGR_PW: This is the administrator's password as specified by the rootpw parameter in slapd.conf.

  ```
  MGR_PW = "secret";
  ```

- MY_SEARCHBASE: This is the root node of your directory as specified in the suffix parameter in slapd.conf.

```
MY_SEARCHBASE = "dc=Your,dc=Company";
```

The binding phase takes these initial variables and sets the environment. The processing phase does all the work and is unique between programs.

I'll include the JNDIAdd2.java program as an example. It adds Napoleon Stabone (a smelly little miniature pinscher) to the example directory.

The key elements for the add process include creating your BasicAttributes objects. A BasicAttributes object named attrs will be loaded into the directory. It contains single-value attributes (cn, sn) and references a list of multivalue attributes (objectclassSet). Notice that this example adds only one cn and one sn attribute (even though LDAP allows more).

```
BasicAttributes attrs = new BasicAttributes();
attrs.put(objclassSet);
attrs.put("ou", "IT");
attrs.put("cn", "Napoleon Stabone");
attrs.put("sn", "Stabone");
attrs.put("telephoneNumber", "1-800-use-LDAP");
attrs.put("l", "Paris");
```

The objclassSet refers to another BasicAttributes object that contains a list of object-Classes including person, organizationalPerson, and inetOrgPerson.

```
BasicAttribute objclassSet = new BasicAttribute("objectclass");
objclassSet.add("person");
objclassSet.add("organizationalPerson");
objclassSet.add("inetOrgPerson");
```

Then you add your BasicAttributes objects to the directory.

```
ctx.createSubcontext(theNewDN, attrs);
```

Listing 6-11 shows the full program, which adds Napoleon Stabone to the IT team. You can see the results by checking via your Netscape Navigator 4.0 or better browser at ldap://ldaphostldaphost/dc=Your,dc=Company?*?sub?(sn=Stabone).

Listing 6-11. *Adding My Dog to Your Infrastructure Using JNDI*

```
//----------------------------------------------------------------
// File:    JNDIAdd2.java
// Desc:    This is a basic add program.
// Compile: javac JNDIAdd2.java
// Use:     java JNDIAdd2
//----------------------------------------------------------------

import java.util.Hashtable;
import java.util.Enumeration;
import javax.naming.*;
import javax.naming.directory.*;
```

```
public class JNDIAdd2
{
   // initial context implementation
   public static String INITCTX = "com.sun.jndi.ldap.LdapCtxFactory";
   public static String MY_HOST = "ldap://ldaphost:389";
   public static String MGR_DN = "cn=Manager,dc=Your,dc=Company";
   public static String MGR_PW = "secret";
   public static String MY_SEARCHBASE = "dc=Your,dc=Company";

   public static void main (String args[])
   {
      try
      {
         //------------------------------------------------------------
         // Binding
         //------------------------------------------------------------

         // Hashtable for environmental information
         Hashtable env = new Hashtable();

         // Specify which class to use for our JNDI Provider
         env.put(Context.INITIAL_CONTEXT_FACTORY, INITCTX);

         // Specify the host and port to use for directory service
         env.put(Context.PROVIDER_URL, MY_HOST);

         // Security Information
         env.put(Context.SECURITY_AUTHENTICATION,"simple");
         env.put(Context.SECURITY_PRINCIPAL, MGR_DN);
         env.put(Context.SECURITY_CREDENTIALS, MGR_PW);

         // Get a reference to a directory context
         DirContext ctx = new InitialDirContext(env);


         //-----------------------------------------------------------
         // Begin the Add process
         //-----------------------------------------------------------

         String theNewDN = "cn=Napoleon Stabone, ou=IT, dc=Your,dc=Company";

         // Multi-valued attributes require their own new BasicAttribute
         // Create the objclassSet to hold all the entry's objectClasses.
         BasicAttribute objclassSet = new BasicAttribute("objectclass");
         objclassSet.add("person");
         objclassSet.add("organizationalPerson");
         objclassSet.add("inetOrgPerson");
```

```
                // Add single and multi-valued attributes to the
                // load variable (attrs).
                BasicAttributes attrs = new BasicAttributes();
                attrs.put(objclassSet);
                attrs.put("ou", "IT");
                attrs.put("cn", "Napoleon Stabone");
                attrs.put("sn", "Stabone");
                attrs.put("telephoneNumber", "1-408-655-4672");
                attrs.put("l", "San Francisco");

                ctx.createSubcontext(theNewDN, attrs);

                //-----------------------------------------------------------
                // End the Add process
                //-----------------------------------------------------------

        } // End try

    catch(Exception e)
    {
        e.printStackTrace();
        System.exit(1);
    }
  }
}
```

The process for modifying records in the directory is as follows:

1. Create a ModificationItem array named mods.

2. Define your modifications and load them into the ModificationItem array specifying the operation: ADD_ATTRIBUTE or REPLACE_ATTRIBUTE (updating the value of an existing attribute).

3. Call the modifyAttributes() function. Notice that the DN of the record you want to modify is the first parameter. It could have (and probably should have) been replaced with a String variable.

Listing 6-12 shows how to modify data within your LDAP system via JNDI calls.

Listing 6-12. *Modifying via JNDI*

```
ctx.modifyAttributes("cn=Susan Surapruik, ou=IT, dc=Your,dc=Company", mods);

//-----------------------------------------------------------
// File:    JNDIMod.java
// Desc:    This is a basic modify program.// Compile: javac JNDIMod.java
// Use:     java JNDIMod
//-----------------------------------------------------------
```

```java
import java.util.Hashtable;
import java.util.Enumeration;
import javax.naming.*;
import javax.naming.directory.*;

public class JNDIMod
{
    // initial context implementation
    public static String INITCTX = "com.sun.jndi.ldap.LdapCtxFactory";
    public static String MY_HOST = "ldap://ldaphost:389";
    public static String MGR_DN = "cn=Manager,dc=Your,dc=Company";
    public static String MGR_PW = "secret";
    public static String MY_SEARCHBASE = "dc=Your,dc=Company";

    public static void main (String args[])
    {
        try
        {
            //------------------------------------------------------------
            // Binding
            //------------------------------------------------------------

            // Hashtable for environmental information
            Hashtable env = new Hashtable();

            // Specify which class to use for our JNDI Provider
            env.put(Context.INITIAL_CONTEXT_FACTORY, INITCTX);

            // Specify the host and port to use for directory service
            env.put(Context.PROVIDER_URL, MY_HOST);

            // Security Information
            env.put(Context.SECURITY_AUTHENTICATION,"simple");
            env.put(Context.SECURITY_PRINCIPAL, MGR_DN);
            env.put(Context.SECURITY_CREDENTIALS, MGR_PW);

            // Get a reference toa directory context
            DirContext ctx = new InitialDirContext(env);


            //------------------------------------------------------------
            // Begin Modify
            //------------------------------------------------------------

            ModificationItem[] mods = new ModificationItem[2];
```

```
                // replace (update) telephone number attribute
                Attribute mod0 = new BasicAttribute("telephoneNumber",
                                                    "123-456-7890");
                // add mobile phone number attribute
                Attribute mod1 = new BasicAttribute("mobile",
                                                    "123-456-1234");

                mods[0] = new ModificationItem(DirContext.REPLACE_ATTRIBUTE, mod0);
                mods[1] = new ModificationItem(DirContext.ADD_ATTRIBUTE, mod1);

             ctx.modifyAttributes("cn=Susan Surapruik, ou=IT, dc=Your,dc=Company", mods);

                //------------------------------------------------------------
                // End Modify
                //------------------------------------------------------------

          } // End try

          catch(Exception e)
          {
             e.printStackTrace();
             System.exit(1);
          }
      }
}
```

Listing 6-13 is like the previous example, but it shows the syntax for removing an attribute from a record.

Listing 6-13. *Modifying an Attribute via JNDI*

```
//------------------------------------------------------------
// File:    JNDIMod2.java
// Desc:    This is a basic delete program.
// Compile: javac JNDIMod2.java
// Use:     java JNDIMod2
//------------------------------------------------------------

import java.util.Hashtable;
import java.util.Enumeration;
import javax.naming.*;
import javax.naming.directory.*;

public class JNDIMod2
{
    // initial context implementation
    public static String INITCTX = "com.sun.jndi.ldap.LdapCtxFactory";
    public static String MY_HOST = "ldap://ldaphost:389";
```

```java
public static String MGR_DN = "cn=Manager,dc=Your,dc=Company";
public static String MGR_PW = "secret";
public static String MY_SEARCHBASE = "dc=Your,dc=Company";

public static void main (String args[])
{
   try
   {
      //-----------------------------------------------------------
      // Binding
      //-----------------------------------------------------------

      // Hashtable for environmental information
      Hashtable env = new Hashtable();

      // Specify which class to use for our JNDI Provider
      env.put(Context.INITIAL_CONTEXT_FACTORY, INITCTX);

      // Specify the host and port to use for directory service
      env.put(Context.PROVIDER_URL, MY_HOST);

      // Security Information
      env.put(Context.SECURITY_AUTHENTICATION,"simple");
      env.put(Context.SECURITY_PRINCIPAL, MGR_DN);
      env.put(Context.SECURITY_CREDENTIALS, MGR_PW);

      // Get a reference toa directory context
      DirContext ctx = new InitialDirContext(env);


      //-----------------------------------------------------------
      // Begin Modify
      //-----------------------------------------------------------

      ModificationItem[] mods = new ModificationItem[2];

      // replace (update) telephone number attribute
      Attribute mod0 = new BasicAttribute("telephoneNumber",
                                     "987-654-3210");
      // delete mobile phone number attribute
      Attribute mod1 = new BasicAttribute("mobile");

      mods[0] = new ModificationItem(DirContext.REPLACE_ATTRIBUTE, mod0);
      mods[1] = new ModificationItem(DirContext.REMOVE_ATTRIBUTE, mod1);

    ctx.modifyAttributes("cn=Susan Surapruik, ou=IT, dc=Your,dc=Company", mods);
```

```
        //------------------------------------------------------------
        // End Modify
        //------------------------------------------------------------

    } // End try

    catch(Exception e)
    {
        e.printStackTrace();
        System.exit(1);
    }
  }
}
```

The deletion process requires very little code. One command will do the trick, as shown in Listing 6-14.

Listing 6-14. *Deleting via JNDI*

```
ctx.destroySubcontext(delDN);
//------------------------------------------------------------
// File:    JNDIDelete.java
// Desc:    This is a basic delete program.
// Compile: javac JNDIDelete.java
// Use:     java JNDIDelete
//------------------------------------------------------------

import java.util.Hashtable;
import java.util.Enumeration;
import javax.naming.*;
import javax.naming.directory.*;

public class JNDIDelete
{
    // initial context implementation
    public static String INITCTX = "com.sun.jndi.ldap.LdapCtxFactory";
    public static String MY_HOST = "ldap://ldaphost:389";
    public static String MGR_DN = "cn=Manager,dc=Your,dc=Company";
    public static String MGR_PW = "secret";
    public static String MY_SEARCHBASE = "dc=Your,dc=Company";


    public static void main (String args[])
    {
        try
        {
            //------------------------------------------------------------
            // Binding
            //------------------------------------------------------------
```

```
        // Hashtable for environmental information
        Hashtable env = new Hashtable();

        // Specify which class to use for our JNDI Provider
        env.put(Context.INITIAL_CONTEXT_FACTORY, INITCTX);

        // Specify the host and port to use for directory service
        env.put(Context.PROVIDER_URL, MY_HOST);

        // Security Information
        env.put(Context.SECURITY_AUTHENTICATION,"simple");
        env.put(Context.SECURITY_PRINCIPAL, MGR_DN);
        env.put(Context.SECURITY_CREDENTIALS, MGR_PW);

        // Get a reference toa directory context
        DirContext ctx = new InitialDirContext(env);


        //-----------------------------------------------------------
        // Begin deletion process
        //-----------------------------------------------------------

        String delDN = "cn=Napoleon Stabone,ou=IT,dc=Your,dc=Company";
        ctx.destroySubcontext(delDN);

        //-----------------------------------------------------------
        // End deletion process
        //-----------------------------------------------------------

    } // End try

    catch(Exception e)
    {
        e.printStackTrace();
        System.exit(1);
    }
  }
}
```

Deleting a record required the least amount of code. Conversely, the search programs required the most.

JNDISearch.java represents the basic search. The MY_FILTER was added to the global variables defined in the context initialization section. You define the search constraints here.

```
public static String INITCTX = "com.sun.jndi.ldap.LdapCtxFactory";
public static String MY_HOST = "ldap://ldaphost:389";
public static String MGR_DN = "cn=Manager,dc=Your,dc=Company";
public static String MGR_PW = "secret";
public static String MY_SEARCHBASE = "dc=Your,dc=Company";
public static String MY_FILTER = "cn=Tom Jackiewicz";
```

The full program appears in Listing 6-15.

Listing 6-15. JNDISearch.java

```java
//-----------------------------------------------------------------
// File:    JNDISearch.java
// Desc:    This is a basic search program.  See MY_FILTER.
//          Includes authenticated search.
// Compile: javac JNDISearch.java
// Use:     java JNDISearch
//-----------------------------------------------------------------

import java.util.Hashtable;
import java.util.Enumeration;
import javax.naming.*;
import javax.naming.directory.*;

public class JNDISearch
{
   // Global Variables
   public static String INITCTX = "com.sun.jndi.ldap.LdapCtxFactory";
   public static String MY_HOST = "ldap://ldaphost:389";
   public static String MGR_DN = "cn=Manager,dc=Your,dc=Company";
   public static String MGR_PW = "secret";
   public static String MY_SEARCHBASE = "dc=Your,dc=Company";
   public static String MY_FILTER = "cn=Tom Jackiewicz";

   public static void main (String args[])
   {
      try
      {
         //----------------------------------------------------------
         // Binding
         //----------------------------------------------------------

         // Hashtable for environmental information
         Hashtable env = new Hashtable();

         // Specify which class to use for our JNDI Provider
         env.put(Context.INITIAL_CONTEXT_FACTORY, INITCTX);

         // Specify the host and port to use for directory service
         env.put(Context.PROVIDER_URL, MY_HOST);

         // Security Information
         env.put(Context.SECURITY_AUTHENTICATION,"simple");
         env.put(Context.SECURITY_PRINCIPAL, MGR_DN);
         env.put(Context.SECURITY_CREDENTIALS, MGR_PW);
```

```java
// Get a reference toa directory context
DirContext ctx = new InitialDirContext(env);


//------------------------------------------------------------
// Search the directory
//------------------------------------------------------------

// Specify the scope of the search
SearchControls constraints = new SearchControls();
constraints.setSearchScope(SearchControls.SUBTREE_SCOPE);

// Perform the actual search
// We give it a searchbase, a filter, and the constraints
// containing the scope of the search
NamingEnumeration results =
        ctx.search(MY_SEARCHBASE, MY_FILTER, constraints);

// Now step through the search results
while ( results != null && results.hasMore() )
{
   SearchResult sr = (SearchResult) results.next();
   String dn = sr.getName();
   System.out.println ("Distinguished Name is " +dn);

   Attributes attrs = sr.getAttributes();

   for (NamingEnumeration ne = attrs.getAll(); ne.hasMoreElements();)
   {
      Attribute attr = (Attribute)ne.next();
      String attrID = attr.getID();

      System.out.println (attrID+":");
      for (Enumeration vals = attr.getAll();vals.hasMoreElements();)
      {
         System.out.println ("\t"+vals.nextElement());
      }
   }

   System.out.println ("\n");
}    // End while loop displaying list of attributes

//------------------------------------------------------------
// End search
//------------------------------------------------------------

} // End try
```

```
      catch(Exception e)
      {
         e.printStackTrace();
         System.exit(1);
      }
   }
}
```

JNDISearch2.java is a more advanced search that lets you specify the search constraints *and* define the attributes you want to display.

```
public static String INITCTX = "com.sun.jndi.ldap.LdapCtxFactory";
public static String MY_HOST = "ldap://ldaphost:389";
public static String MGR_DN = "cn=Manager,dc=Your,dc=Company";
public static String MGR_PW = "secret";
public static String MY_SEARCHBASE = "dc=Your,dc=Company";
public static String MY_FILTER = "cn=Tom Jackiewicz";

// Specify which attributes we are looking for
   public static String MY_ATTRS[] = {"cn", "telephoneNumber", "postalAddress"};
```

This example adds the MY_ATTRS array to the global variable in the context initialization section. The output of this query will display only the cn, telephoneNumber, and postalAddress attributes. Listing 6-16 shows how to search your directory and return only a subset of attributes, not the entire set of information that's available to you.

Listing 6-16. *Searching and Returning Specific Information via JNDI*

```
//---------------------------------------------------------------
// File:    JNDISearch2.java
// Desc:    This search program specifies a list of attributes
//          that should be displayed.
// Compile: javac JNDISearch2.java
// Use:     java JNDISearch2
//---------------------------------------------------------------

import java.util.Hashtable;
import java.util.Enumeration;
import javax.naming.*;
import javax.naming.directory.*;

public class JNDISearch2
{
   // initial context implementation
   public static String INITCTX = "com.sun.jndi.ldap.LdapCtxFactory";
   public static String MY_HOST = "ldap://ldaphost:389";
   public static String MGR_DN = "cn=Manager,dc=Your,dc=Company";
   public static String MGR_PW = "secret";
   public static String MY_SEARCHBASE = "dc=Your,dc=Company";
   public static String MY_FILTER = "cn=Tom Jackiewicz";
```

```java
// Specify which attributes we are looking for
public static String MY_ATTRS[] = {"cn", "telephoneNumber",
                                   "postalAddress"};

public static void main (String args[])
{
   try
   {
      //------------------------------------------------------------
      // Binding
      //------------------------------------------------------------

      // Hashtable for environmental information
      Hashtable env = new Hashtable();

      // Specify which class to use for our JNDI Provider
      env.put(Context.INITIAL_CONTEXT_FACTORY, INITCTX);

      // Specify the host and port to use for directory service
      env.put(Context.PROVIDER_URL, MY_HOST);

      // Security Information
      env.put(Context.SECURITY_AUTHENTICATION,"simple");
      env.put(Context.SECURITY_PRINCIPAL, MGR_DN);
      env.put(Context.SECURITY_CREDENTIALS, MGR_PW);

      // Get a reference toa directory context
      DirContext ctx = new InitialDirContext(env);


      //------------------------------------------------------------
      // Begin search
      //------------------------------------------------------------

      // Specify the scope of the search
      SearchControls constraints = new SearchControls();
      constraints.setSearchScope(SearchControls.SUBTREE_SCOPE);

      // Perform the actual search
      // We give it a searchbase, a filter and the constraints
      // containing the scope of the search
      NamingEnumeration results =
              ctx.search(MY_SEARCHBASE, MY_FILTER, constraints);

      // Now step through the search results
      while ( results != null && results.hasMore() )
      {
         SearchResult sr = (SearchResult) results.next();
         String dn = sr.getName() + ", " + MY_SEARCHBASE;
         System.out.println ("Distinguished Name is " +dn);
```

```java
        // Code for displaying attribute list
        Attributes ar = ctx.getAttributes(dn, MY_ATTRS);

        if (ar == null)        // Has no attributes
        {
           System.out.println("Entry "+ dn );
           System.out.println(" has none of the specified attributes\n");
        }

        else                      // Has some attributes
        {
           // Determine the attributes in this record.
           for (int i=0; i<MY_ATTRS.length; i++)
           {
              Attribute attr = ar.get(MY_ATTRS[i]);
              if (attr != null)
              {
                 System.out.println(MY_ATTRS[i] + ":");

                 // Gather all values for the specified attribute.
                 for ( Enumeration vals=attr.getAll();
                       vals.hasMoreElements(); )
                 {
                    System.out.println ("\t" + vals.nextElement() );
                 }

                 // System.out.println ("\n");
              }
           }
        }
     }
     //-----------------------------------------------------------
     // End search
     //-----------------------------------------------------------


   }                  // end try

 catch(Exception e)
 {
    e.printStackTrace();
    System.exit(1);
 }
 }
}
```

The `javax.name.ldap` API provides support for LDAP v3 extended operations and controls, and it extends JNDI. It extends the `ExtendedRequest` and `ExtendedResponse` interfaces to utilize extended requests and extended results. An application typically doesn't deal directly with these interfaces. Instead, it deals with classes that implement these interfaces.

OASIS Standards

OASIS (which stands for *Organization for the Advancement of Structured Information Standards*) is a not-for-profit international consortium that drives the development, convergence, and adoption of e-business standards. The consortium produces more Web service standards than any other organization; it also produces standards for security, e-business, and standardization efforts in the public sector and for application-specific markets. Founded in 1993, OASIS has more than 3,000 participants representing more than 600 organizations and individual members in 100 countries.

OASIS is distinguished by its transparent governance and operating procedures. Members themselves set the OASIS technical agenda, using a lightweight process expressly designed to promote industry consensus and unite disparate efforts. Completed work is ratified by open ballot. Governance is accountable and unrestricted. Officers of both the OASIS Board of Directors and the Technical Advisory Board are chosen by democratic election to serve two-year terms. Consortium leadership is based on individual merit and isn't tied to financial contribution, corporate standing, or special appointment.

The consortium hosts two of the most widely respected information portals on XML and Web service standards: Cover Pages and XML.org. OASIS member sections include UDDI, CGM Open, LegalXML, and PKI.

OASIS was founded in 1993 under the name SGML Open as a consortium of vendors and users devoted to developing guidelines for interoperability among products that support the Standard Generalized Markup Language (SGML). OASIS changed its name in 1998 to reflect an expanded scope of technical work, including the Extensible Markup Language (XML) and other related standards.

Directory Services Markup Language (DSML)

The following is the specification for the Directory Services Markup Language (DSML). Further information on this emerging technology is available at `http://www.dsmltools.org`. Markup languages, such as HTML and XML, are becoming a popular way to communicate between systems using a known set of parameters. DSML will never be the only way of talking to your directory. It may not even be the most efficient way. Both LDAP and vendor-specific approaches may provide better performance in that area. It may not rack up the most directory transactions per way; Windows-optimized interfaces, driven by Microsoft, could win that honor. However, DSML will provide a common language for working with directories, combining the qualified of vendor independence and accessibility to a wide range of programmers and programs.

Introduction

DSML provides a means for representing directory structural information as an XML document. The intent of DSML is to allow XML-based enterprise applications to leverage profile and resource information from a directory in their native environments. DSML allows XML and directories to work together and provides a common ground for all XML-based applications to better use directories. More information is available at `http://xml.coverpages.org/DSMLv2-draft14.pdf`. DSML v1 provides a means of representing directory information in the form of an XML document. DSML v2 goes further, providing a method for expressing directory queries and updates (and the results of those operations) as XML documents. DSML v2 is one of the major advances in the world of LDAP that's used to extend the reach of directories.

DSML is intended to be a simple XML schema definition that will enable directories to publish basic profile information in the form of an XML document so that it can be easily shared via native Internet protocols (such as HTTP or SMTP), as well as used by other applications. The principal goal is to ensure that directories are able to make a growing breed of XML-based applications directory aware.

It's not an initial goal of DSML to specify the attributes that all directories must contain or the method with which the directory information is accessed from the directory. The expectation is that standard protocols (such as LDAP), proprietary access protocols (such as Novell's NDAP), and proprietary APIs (such as Microsoft's ADSI) could produce DSML documents as an optional output. DSML holds the promise to advance business-to-business e-commerce by simplifying compatibility with other companies' applications. Microsoft is involved in DSML development via the DSML Services for Windows specifications and can serve as a great online resource for current developments in DSML.

A Note on Ambiguous Terminology

Because this specification discusses both XML and directories, you may confuse terminology from one domain with that from the other. In particular, the words *attribute* and *schema* have meaning in both the XML and directory domains. For this reason, this specification always qualifies the word *attribute* as either XML attribute or a directory attribute and likewise with the word *schema*.

The DSML Namespace URI

The vocabulary described in this specification is identified by this URI:

```
http://www.dsml.org/DSML
```

This is the DSML namespace URI.

In this specification, the prefix dsml is used on XML elements to indicate that they belong to the DSML namespace. The prefix (as with all XML namespace prefixes) is arbitrary, so you can use any suitable prefix (or the namespace declared as default). It's the URI that ultimately identifies the namespace, not the prefix.

Conceptual Overview

A DSML document describes directory *entries*, a directory *schema*, or both.

Each directory entry has a universally unique name called its *distinguished name*. A directory entry has a number of property-value pairs called directory *attributes*. Every directory entry is a member of a number of *object classes*. An entry's object classes constrain the directory attributes the entry may take. Such constraints are described in a directory *schema*, which may be included in the same DSML document or may be in a separate document.

Top-Level Structure

The document element of DSML is of the type dsml, which may have a child element of the type directory-entries. This element, in turn, has child elements of the type entry. The dsml element may also (if the document contains a directory schema) have a child element of the type directory-schema that, in turn, has child elements of the types class and attribute-type.

At the top-level, the structure of a DSML document is as shown in Listing 6-17.

Listing 6-17. *Top-Level Structure of a DSML Document*

```
<dsml:dsml xmlns:dsml="http://www.dsml.org/DSML">
  <!-- a document with only directory entries -->
  <dsml:directory-entries>
    <dsml:entry dn="...">...</dsml:entry>
    <dsml:entry dn="...">...</dsml:entry>
    <dsml:entry dn="...">...</dsml:entry>
    ...
  </dsml:directory-entries>
</dsml:dsml>
<dsml:dsml xmlns:dsml="http://www.dsml.org/DSML">
  <!-- a document with only a directory schema -->
  <dsml:directory-schema>
    <dsml:class id="..." ...>...</dsml:class>
    <dsml:attribute-type id="..." ...>...</dsml:attribute-type>
    ...
  </dsml:directory-schema>
</dsml:dsml>
<dsml:dsml xmlns:dsml="http://www.dsml.org/DSML">
  <!-- a document with both -->
  <dsml:directory-schema>
    <dsml:class id="..." ...>...</dsml:class>
    <dsml:attribute-type id="..." ...>...</dsml:attribute-type>
  </dsml:directory-schema>
  <dsml:directory-entries>
    <dsml:entry dn="...">...</dsml:entry>
    <dsml:entry dn="...">...</dsml:entry>
    <dsml:entry dn="...">...</dsml:entry>
    ...
  </dsml:directory-entries>
```

```
<dsml:dsml>
```

The top-level element `dsml` takes an optional XML attribute `complete`. A value of `true` indicates that the entries under `directory-entries` contain no external references. Either all `attribute-types` and `classes` referenced are found in the `directory-schema` section of the document or no references exist. A value of `false` indicates that at least one reference is to an external DSML document containing a directory schema. The default value is `true`.

Directory Entries

The following sections describe some of the entries, attributes, and object classes that can be stored in DSML.

The entry Element Type

Each entry represented in a DSML document is done so using an element of the type entry. The entry element contains elements representing the entry's directory attributes. The distinguished name of the entry is indicated by the XML attribute dn.

Note This specification doesn't provide a canonical form for distinguished names. Because normalization and ordering can vary between producers of DSML, some form of canonicalization would need to be performed by a consumer of DSML before string matching the values of the XML attribute dn.

It was decided (by the consortium, not the opressive powers of "The Man") to express the distinguished name as an XML attribute rather than a child element because of its identifying characteristic.

```
<dsml:entry dn="uid=prabbit,ou=development,o=bowstreet,c=us">
  <dsml:objectclass>
    <dsml:oc-value>top</dsml:oc-value>
    <dsml:oc-value>person</dsml:oc-value>
    <dsml:oc-value>organizationalPerson</dsml:oc-value>
    <dsml:oc-value>inetOrgPerson</dsml:oc-value>
  </dsml:objectclass>
  <dsml:attr name="sn"><dsml:value>Rabbit</dsml:value></dsml:attr>
  <dsml:attr name="uid"><dsml:value>prabbit</dsml:value></dsml:attr>
  <dsml:attr name="mail"><dsml:value>prabbit@dsml.org</dsml:value></dsml:attr>
  <dsml:attr name="givenname"><dsml:value>Peter</dsml:value></dsml:attr>
  <dsml:attr name="cn"><dsml:value>Peter Rabbit</dsml:value></dsml:attr>

</dsml:entry>
```

Entry Object Class

The object classes of an entry are represented by the oc-value child elements of an objectclass element. The content of each oc-value element indicates an object class to which the entry belongs. In the case where an object class has more than one name, only one name need be used. Both objectclass and oc-value have an optional XML attribute ref. An oc-value's ref is a URI reference to a class element that defines the object class. An objectclass's ref is a URI reference to an attribute-type defining the objectclass directory attribute. The latter wouldn't often be used but is provided to allow for extension of the objectclass directory attribute.

```
<dsml:objectclass ref="#objectclass">
  <dsml:oc-value ref="#person">person</dsml:oc-value>
  <dsml:oc-value ref="#org-person">organizationalPerson</dsml:oc-value>
</dsml:objectclass>
```

Directory Attributes

Directory attributes (with the exception of objectclass) are represented by an attr element. This element has a mandatory XML attribute name that indicates the name of the directory attribute. (A directory attribute can have more than one name, but only one need be expressed in the name attribute.)

The value or values of a directory attribute are expressed in child elements of the type value.

■**Note** The content of value is PCDATA; hence, any XML markup (or characters that could be treated as markup, namely < or &) must be escaped via the CDATA section, a character reference, or a predefined entity.

Each attr element can have an optional ref XML attribute whose value is a URI reference (URI plus XPointer) pointing to an attribute-type definition in a directory-schema in the same or different DSML document.

For example, if a DSML document with a directory-schema accessible at the URL http://www.bowstreet.com/schemata/physical-attributes.dsml has the following attribute-type definition:

```
<dsml:attribute-type id="eye-color">
  <dsml:name>eyecolor</dsml:name>
  <dsml:description>The color of the person's eyes</dsml:description>
  ...
</dsml:attribute-type>
```

Then an entry in directory-entries may have a child element, like so:

```
<dsml:attr
    name="eyecolor"
    ref="http://www.bowstreet.com/schemata/physical-attributes.dsml#eye-color">
  <dsml:value>blue</dsml:value>
</dsml:attr>
```

Multivalued Attributes

Where an entry has multiple values for a particular attribute, that attr element has multiple value children.

```
<dsml:entry dn-"uid-prabbit,ou-development,o-bowstreet,c-us">
  <dsml:objectclass>
    <dsml:oc-value>top</dsml:oc-value>
    <dsml:oc-value>person</dsml:oc-value>
    <dsml:oc-value>organizationalPerson</dsml:oc-value>
    <dsml:oc-value>inetOrgPerson</dsml:oc-value>
  </dsml:objectclass>
  <dsml:attr name="sn"><dsml:value>Rabbit</dsml:value></dsml:attr>
  <dsml:attr name="uid"><dsml:value>prabbit</dsml:value></dsml:attr>
  <dsml:attr name="mail">
```

```
        <dsml:value>prabbit@dsml.org</dsml:value>
        <dsml:value>peterr@home.com</dsml:value>
    </dsml:attr>
    <dsml:attr name="givenname"><dsml:value>Peter</dsml:value></dsml:attr>
    <dsml:attr name="cn"><dsml:value>Peter Rabbit</dsml:value></dsml:attr>

</dsml:entry>
```

Binary Data

Directory attributes containing binary data are encoded using an encoding scheme identified by the XML attribute encoding on the value element. Currently, DSML supports only base64 as a value, but the encoding XML attribute is included in order to enable support for other encoding schemes in the future.

▓**Note** base64 encoding, as described in RFC 1521, allows for whitespace characters that are to be ignored by any decoding software. Furthermore, base64 encoding doesn't introduce < or & characters, and therefore no additional encoding is necessary to include base64 in XML character data.

The following shows an example of how to represent the encoding data within an XML document:

```
<dsml:attr name="cacertificate">
  <dsml:value encoding="base64">
    MIICJjCCAY+...
  </dsml:value>

</dsml:attr>
```

Directory Schema

The following sections describe the definition of schema via DSML.

Object Classes

Each directory entry has a number of object classes, indicated by elements of the type object-class.

An object class is defined with a class element in a directory-schema. The class element takes an ID XML attribute id to make referencing easier.

The object class definition for the person object class may look like this:

```
<dsml:class
    id="person"
    superior="#top"
    type="structural">
<dsml:name>person</dsml:name>
<dsml:description>...</dsml:description>
<dsml:object-identifier>2.5.6.6</object-indentifier>
<dsml:attribute ref="#sn" required="true"/>
<dsml:attribute ref="#cn" required="true"/>
<dsml:attribute ref="#userPassword" required="false"/>
<dsml:attribute ref="#telephoneNumber" required="false"/>
<dsml:attribute ref="#seeAlso" required="false"/>
<dsml:attribute ref="#description" required="false"/>

</dsml:class>
```

id (XML Attribute)

This is a locally unique identifier for the object class. This enables the object class to be referenced across the Web, in particular from the ref XML attribute of an entry's objectclass or a subclass's superior XML attribute.

superior (XML Attribute)

This is the URI reference of class(es) from which this one is derived.

type (XML Attribute)

This is one of structural, abstract, or auxiliary.

obsolete (XML Attribute)

This is one of true or false. This defaults to false.

name (Child Element)

This is the NAME of the object class.

description (Child Element)

This is the optional DESC of the object class.

object-identifier (Child Element)

This is the OID of the object class.

attribute (Child Element)

This is a directory attribute type that entries of this class may or must have.

ref (XML Attribute on the attribute Element)

This is the URI reference of the directory attribute type.

required (XML Attribute on the attribute Element)

This is one of true or false. It indicates whether entries of this class are required to have the directory attribute.

XML attributes were chosen in those cases where the information provides unique identification (using an ID attribute not only ensures uniqueness, but allows for ease of reference via XPointer), is an enumeration (which, in a DTD, can be contained only in attributes), or is a reference.

Attribute Type Definitions

You can define directory attribute types in a similar way to object classes. For example:

```
<dsml:attribute-type
    id="cn"
    superior="...#name">
  <dsml:name>cn</dsml:name>
  <dsml:description>...</dsml:description>
  <dsml:object-identifier>2.5.4.3</dsml:object-identifier>
</dsml:attribute-type>

<dsml:attribute-type
    id="mail">
  <dsml:name>mail</dsml:name>
  <dsml:description>...</dsml:description>
  <dsml:object-identifier>0.9.2342.19200300.100.1.3</dsml:object-identifier>
  <dsml:syntax bound="256">0.9.2342.19200300.100.3.5</dsml:syntax>

</dsml:attribute-type>
```

id (XML Attribute)

This is a locally unique identifier for the attribute type. This enables the attribute type to be referenced across the Web, in particular from the ref XML attribute of an entry's attr or a derived directory attribute's superior XML attribute.

superior (XML Attribute)

This is the URI reference of attribute type from which this one is derived.

obsolete (XML Attribute)

This is one of true or false. This defaults to false.

single-value (XML Attribute)

This is one of true or false. This defaults to false.

user-modification (XML Attribute)

This is one of `true` or `false`. This defaults to `true`.

name (Child Element)

This is the `NAME` of the attribute type.

description (Child Element)

This is the optional `DESC` of the attribute type.

object-identifier (Child Element)

This is the OID of the object class.

syntax (Child Element)

This is an OID indicating the allowed syntax of values of this attribute type.

bound (XML Attribute on Syntax)

This is the suggested minimum upper bound for the attribute type.

equality (Child Element)

This is an OID that indicates the equality matching rule.

ordering (Child Element)

This is an OID that indicates the equality matching rule.

substring (Child Element)

This is an OID that indicates the equality matching rule.

XML attributes were chosen in those cases where the information provides unique identification (using an ID attribute not only ensures uniqueness, but allows for ease of reference via XPointer), is an enumeration (which, in a DTD, can only be contained in attributes), or is a reference.

Conformance

DSML has important implications for security management, which application architects should be aware of when deciding to support DSML. While LDAP requires a special port to be opened up on firewalls, initial versions of DSML will use HTTP or HTTPS as a transport. Thus, DSML documents will traverse firewalls on the HTTP port. Proponents of DSML tout this as an advantage. Certainly, it simplifies firewall administration. On the other hand, some organizations may not like the idea of a newly empowered HTTP that gives hackers an opportunity to attack directories as well as Web sites. It's too early to say how organizations and developers will deal with this problem, but it's one that will have to be addressed.

In defining conformance, it's useful to divide DSML documents into the following four types:

1. Documents containing no directory schema or any references to an external schema

2. Documents containing no directory schema but containing at least one reference to an external schema

3. Documents containing only a directory schema

4. Documents containing both a directory schema and entries

A *producer* of DSML must be able to produce documents of type 1. A producer of DSML may, in addition, be able to produce documents of types 2 through 4. A producer that can produce documents of type 1 is a *level 1* producer. A producer that can produce documents of all four types is a *level 2* producer. Future specifications will provide a mechanism for specifying during a request to a level 2 producer which type of document is to be returned.

A *consumer* of DSML must be able to handle all four document types, but it doesn't need to be able to use the directory schema information (either local or externally referenced). A consumer that can handle DSML documents of all four types is a *level 1* consumer. A consumer that can additionally use the directory schema information (either local or externally referenced) is a *level 2* consumer.

Summary

After reading this chapter, you should have a basic understanding of some of the interfaces available to you for programming and scripting against your directory. You should also be aware of some of the organizations and standards that are currently being developed to extend the functionality of the directory into completely new areas of functionality.

■■■

## CHAPTER 7

Integrating at the System Level

You'll see the power of LDAP while integrating with existing systems within your environment. Integration takes existing functional environments, such as a mail system or your Web browsers, and leverages Lightweight Directory Access Protocol (LDAP) to make the application utilize data stored within your directory. The integration of LDAP and existing applications allows you to centralize common data that may be used by multiple systems into a single data store. Leveraging LDAP in this way will allow you to reduce dependency on multiple data stores and data formats in use by various applications.

I'll use Linux as a baseline for many of the following configurations, and the examples are simple and generic enough to demonstrate the capabilities of your OpenLDAP directory. When applicable, I'll also use Solaris. Realize that you can apply the integration examples in this chapter, with often minimal to no modification, to other systems. This chapter should serve as a baseline for integration and give you ideas on how LDAP may fit into the greater scheme of your system.

Introducing Network Information Services

To understand how LDAP ties into network information services, you must understand RFC 2307, *An Approach for Using LDAP As a Network Information Service*. Network information has traditionally been stored in local files on each host in your infrastructure. Data on network topology, supported services, and even users falls into this category. As I discussed earlier, the storage methods evolved over time to utilize services such as Network Information Services (NIS) and Domain Name Service (DNS). While this works for many applications, technology needs to evolve. The direction that was chosen for storing this information shifted from proprietary protocols and file formats to LDAP. RFC 2307 describes mechanisms for mapping relevant service information into LDAP Interchange Format (LDIF), which is then loaded into your LDAP directory.

In an NIS environment, systems can have the following roles:

Master server: This is a system that stores the master copy of the NIS database files, or *maps*, for the domain in the /var/yp/*DOMAIN* directory and propagates them at regular intervals to the slave servers. Only the master maps can be modified. Each domain can have only one master server.

Slave server: This is a system that obtains and stores copies of the master server's NIS maps. These maps are updated periodically over the network. If the master server is unavailable, the slave servers continue to make the NIS maps available to clients. Each domain can have multiple slave servers distributed throughout the network.

Client: This is any system that queries NIS servers for NIS database information. Clients don't store and maintain copies of the NIS maps locally for their domains.

Introducing Standard NIS Configurations

NIS was originally created to bring efficiency to maintaining a large number of hosts and files. The maintenance of /etc/hosts and /etc/passwd on a large system often becomes a burden. Centralizing this information, accessing this information, and keeping this information in sync are where NIS fits into the picture. NIS is an application layer service that's used on a variety of systems. It relies on Transmission Control Protocol (TCP) and Uniform Datagram Protocol (UDP) for transport and Remote Procedure Call (RPC) for passing information. NIS is a client-server model that relies on a client process requesting data from the server.

Network information was typically stored in flat text files, also known as *source files*, and then loaded into a simple database back end. This is evident in the basic implementations of NIS. The source files create a set of tables, or maps, that NIS will use to obtain required information. The basic NIS environment consists of a master host, which contains the authoritative information, and one or more slave servers. The process of keeping information in sync is called *propagation*, and this utilizes the yppush process. This is similar to the method of replication used in an LDAP environment.

You can create NIS maps with tools that convert the source files (which are just text files) into database format. Each NIS map has a name that programs use to access the required information.

When planning an NIS configuration, you must gauge your network administration needs with regard to the domain structure, the server disposition, your security concerns, and your network's physical structure. For each NIS domain you want to configure on your network, you'll need to follow a basic set of steps. First, decide which hosts on your network you want to include in this domain. Second, choose a domain name for the domain, and make a note of it for use later in the configuration process. Choose a host that has the characteristics described in master servers. Decide which host, if any, will act as a slave server. Finally, decide which hosts will be clients in this domain.

To fully demonstrate how to integrate LDAP and NIS, I'll start with a basic setup of an NIS master server, demonstrate synchronization services, and ultimately focus on a full LDAP integration.

The examples in this chapter will be based on a domain name that I've set to be YourCompany, on a master server named NISmaster, and on a slave server named NISslave. To follow along with the examples, on NISmaster, create the /var/yp/ypdomain file and add the line YourCompany. When you've done this, you can view the contents of this file.

```
$ cat /var/yp/ypdomain
YourCompany
```

Set your domain to YourCompany with the domainname command. Verify that this has taken effect by typing the command again without any options. YourCompany should be returned.

```
$ domainname YourCompany
$ domainname
YourCompany
```

NIS will be able to understand a large number of maps by default. I won't explain the specific maps and will use only a few as an example. The maps you'll be concerned with are passwd.byname, passwd.byuid, services, mail.aliases, and ypservers. These maps also have nicknames that will make administration easier. Mail.aliases has the nickname of aliases, and passwd.byname has the nickname of passwd. When viewing maps with the ypcat command, you can use these nicknames. For example, ypcat passwd is really the same as ypcat passwd.byname.

Upon the initial configuration, you're ready to set up your basic maps. You do this with the ypinit command.

```
$ cd /var/yp
$ ./ypinit -m
We now need to construct a list of hosts that run NIS servers.
Enter the names or addresses of these hosts one at a time,
Excluding this host, then simply hit <Enter> to end the list.
Name (<Enter> to exit): NISslave
Name (<Enter> to exit):
Parsing configuration files into databases.
```

The -m flag specified on the command line denotes that this will be the master server. After initializing your base set of information, you should be able to start your master server. The default startup scripts in your rc.d directory start up NIS services upon basic system startup. Or you can do this manually with the following command:

```
$ /usr/libexec/rpc.passwd /etc/passwd.nis -m passwd
```

You'll want to make sure your NIS services are running and communicating with the appropriate host. Since the master also functions as a client to itself, you can run the ypwhich command locally and make sure that the appropriate host is returned.

```
$ ypwhich
NISmaster
```

Once you've set up a basic NIS master server, you'll want to have NIS slaves communicating with it to obtain their information. On the NIS slaves, use the ypset command to point them to the appropriate NIS master.

```
NISslave$ ypset NISmaster
NISslave$ ypwhich
NISmaster
```

The ypinit command with the -s flag will initialize hosts as NIS slaves.

```
$ cd /var/yp
$ ./ypinit -s NISmaster
Transferring map passwd.byname from server NISmaster
Transferring map mail.aliases from server NISmaster
Transferring map group.byname from server NISmaster
...
```

Performing Synchronization with LDAP

The overall goal of setting up NIS services is to be able to obtain certain types of information from remote hosts instead of just local files. In the beginning, your hosts would read data from /etc/passwd, /etc/hosts, and other local sources. These files had no mechanism in place to keep them in sync. A user existing on HOST1 wouldn't necessarily have an account on HOST2 unless the system administrator manually provisioned it. With NIS, you have the capability of having the same account on both hosts.

Unfortunately, one drawback of NIS is that NIS uses only the maps. If other types of applications within your environment require the user of passwd and hosts files that only exist in NIS, they'd either have to use NIS to query the information or rely on something outside of NIS to generate them. This is where LDAP comes in.

The first method that was used to integrate LDAP and NIS was based on a synchronization model (see Figure 7-1).

Figure 7-1. *Synchronization model*

NIS clients still use the same sets of protocols to read information from the same sets of maps. These maps contain the same information. The difference, in a synchronization model, is that the maps are generated based on queries from an LDAP system. The queries are performed, and the same maps are generated as before. Nothing changes on the NIS side of the equation except the methods used to generate data. The authoritative source now becomes LDAP, but the information is still retrieved in the same legacy methods. Some initial implementations of the NIS/LDAP synchronization model relied on specific daemons to generate the particular maps. Tools are provided for converting the existing data into tables that would be stored in LDAP. Netscape and Sun Microsystems came up with a basic synchronization model against the Netscape Directory Server and the Solaris operating environment that expanded this basic model and replaced the NIS services with actual daemons that functioned like NIS clients and servers but retrieved information directly from LDAP.

Taking the example of the aliases file (the mail.aliases map), you can see the progression. In the beginning, the aliases file may look like this:

```
mailer-daemon: postmaster
postmaster: root
testuser: tom@sun4c.net
```

Through conversion, the resulting entry within LDAP may be the following:

```
dn: cn=mailer-daemon,ou=Aliases,dc=Your,dc=Company
cn: mailer-daemon
objectClass: nisMailAlias
objectClass: top
rfc822MailMember: postmaster

dn: cn=postmaster,ou=Aliases,dc=Your,dc=Company
cn: postmaster
objectClass: nisMailAlias
objectClass: top
rfc822MailMember: root

dn: cn=testuser,ou=Aliases,dc=Your,dc=Company
cn: testuser
objectClass: nisMailAlias
objectClass: top
rfc822MailMember: tom@sun4c.net
```

The idea with this aliases example shows that while the data may end up being stored as the original format, the authoritative source would be stored in LDAP. You'd use script to generate search filters against the LDAP system in order to generate the resulting /etc/aliases file. That is, a script can search LDAP as follows:

```
$ ldapsearch -h ldaphost -b ou=Aliases,dc=Your,dc=Company \
rfc822MailMember=* cn rfc822MailMember
```

The output of this command can be script that obtains the left side of the aliases file (cn) and the right side of the aliases file (rfc822MailMember). By creating data in your LDAP system but still relying on the old data formats and mechanisms, you've taken the first step in having some level of integration with LDAP.

Performing Direct Integration

The next step is to utilize a new set of standards and tools that forego traditional access mechanisms and read information directly through LDAP. The most common of these mechanisms is available via Pluggable Authentication Modules (PAMs). When used correctly, PAM provides many advantages for a system administrator, such as the following:

- You can use a common authentication scheme with a wide variety of applications.

- You can implement PAM with various applications without having to recompile the applications to specifically support PAM.

- The administrator and application developer get great flexibility and control over authentication.

- Application developers don't need to develop their program to use a particular authentication scheme. Instead, they can focus purely on the details of their program.

PADL software (http://www.padl.com) has made significant progress in integrating network services and LDAP. A set of migration tools is available from PADL that allows you to more easily migrate your existing system infrastructure to LDAP. If you want to forego some of the manual configurations required for many Linux or Solaris systems, you can use these migration tools. Some Linux distributions provide their own specific versions of these migration tools.

Check with your specific version of Linux to determine whether LDAP integration has any prerequisites. Older Linux systems, which are always evolving, require the installation of the nss_ldap and pam_ldap modules. The big process you'll need to deal with is the migration of information from existing files to LDAP information. You can use the MigrationTools package (which is PADL-specific; other distributions of Linux rely on a package called openldap-migration) for Linux to make this task easier. This package contains a set of scripts that can be used (as well as viewed for reference) that will make the manual tasks associated with LDAP integration a more automated process.

The core of the migration scripts relies on the migration_common.ph file. This is the common configuration file used by the scripts to define your system parameters. You'll need to edit this file to include the parameters valid for your system. Some parameters won't be used or are there with the assumption that certain services (outside of standard identity components) are being migrated. Examples of this include DEFAULT_MAIL_DOMAIN and DEFAULT_MAIL_HOST.

```
$DEFAULT_MAIL_DOMAIN = "yourcompany.com";
$DEFAULT_BASE = "dc=Your,dc=Company";
$DEFAULT_MAIL_HOST = "mailhost.yourcompany.com";
$EXTENDED_SCHEMA = 1;
```

This file controls the default settings for data that's to be migrated. DEFAULT_MAIL_DOMAIN is responsible for setting the default e-mail address of users within your domain. The DEFAULT_BASE parameter is just another reference to the base distinguished name (DN) of your system. These should always be consistent. Some systems attempt to grab this information based on the fully qualified domain name of your host or other identity parameters. Avoid these attempts at plug-and-play migration and manually configure this setting. The DEFAULT_MAIL_HOST parameter is the base host that's used to accept mail. I'll explain DEFAULT_MAIL_HOST and DEFAULT_MAIL_DOMAIN (and other similar parameters you will run across) in the "Using Sendmail" section later in this chapter. You can use the EXTENDED_SCHEMA setting to support object classes beyond the base configuration of your system.

You have the ability to migrate all your data into LDAP. Some of this information may be useful to have in LDAP, but other sets of data are more static and could just as easily be stored in the original flat text configuration files. However, it's a good idea to have a general level of consistency in your information, so storing bits and pieces of the same system components in multiple authoritative sources isn't the best idea.

The migrate_all_online.sh script migrates all your system data (primarily in the /etc directory) into LDAP.

```
$ ./migrate_all_online.sh
Enter the X.500 naming context you wish to import into: [dc=Your,dc=Company]
Enter the name of your LDAP server [ldapmaster]: localhost
Enter the manager DN: [cn=Directory manager]: cn=Directory manager
Enter the credentials to bind with: password
Do you wish to generate a DUAConfigProfile [yes|no]? no
```

The migration script should be run locally on the host storing the localized master set of information that will be used to store the resulting LDAP data. The manager DN being asked for should be consistent with the rootdn directive in your slapd.conf server configuration file. The password should be the same as the password specified in the rootpw directive. The DUAConfigProfile should be set to no, as this imports all new configuration data into your LDAP system. The full migration of all data by the scripts themselves is always a bit danger-ous, because many available scripts and migration tools aren't created against your specific environment and may cause conflicts. Trusting scripts to blindly add data to your system is asking for trouble. Having data exported into LDIF files for viewing before a forced import is the best method of migrating any information.

Manually running each migration script can export LDIF files that can be examined, modified, and then added using the standard set of LDAP tools. Similar packages and tools exist for Debian and other Linux distributions. I'll use the Mandrake package as a baseline in these examples.

You can search the text of the migration_common.ph file using the grep command to see what variables can be modified and to get a good idea of where you're starting.

```
[root@ldaphost MigrationTools-45]# grep ^\\$ migration_common.ph \
| grep -v classmap
$NETINFOBRIDGE = (-x "/usr/sbin/mkslapdconf");
$DEFAULT_MAIL_DOMAIN = "padl.com";
$DEFAULT_BASE = "dc=padl,dc=com";
$DEFAULT_MAIL_HOST = "mail.padl.com";
$EXTENDED SCHEMA = 0;
```

Upon modification of this common file, your results will change.

```
[root@ldaphost MigrationTools-45]# grep ^\\$ migration_common.ph \
| grep -v classmap
$NETINFOBRIDGE = (-x "/usr/sbin/mkslapdconf");
$DEFAULT_MAIL_DOMAIN = "yourcompany.com";
$DEFAULT_BASE = "dc=Your,dc=Company";
$DEFAULT_MAIL_HOST = "mail.yourcompany.com";
$EXTENDED_SCHEMA = 1;
```

Once you've made your modifications, you're able to run the various migration tools that have been provided for your convenience. The migrate_base.pl script creates the base contain-ers (organizational units) within LDAP for storing your newly migrated system information.

Listing 7-1 shows the contents of the migrate_base.pl script.

Listing 7-1. migrate_base.pl

```
#!/usr/bin/perl
#
# $Id: migrate_base.pl,v 1.4 1998/10/20 14:38:52 lukeh Exp $
#
# Copyright (c) 1997 Luke Howard.
# All rights reserved.
#
```

```
# Redistribution and use in source and binary forms, with or without
# modification, are permitted provided that the following conditions
# are met:
# 1. Redistributions of source code must retain the above copyright
#    notice, this list of conditions and the following disclaimer.
# 2. Redistributions in binary form must reproduce the above copyright
#    notice, this list of conditions and the following disclaimer in the
#    documentation and/or other materials provided with the distribution.
# 3. All advertising materials mentioning features or use of this software
#    must display the following acknowledgment:
#        This product includes software developed by Luke Howard.
# 4. The name of the other may not be used to endorse or promote products
#    derived from this software without specific prior written permission.
#
# THIS SOFTWARE IS PROVIDED BY THE LUKE HOWARD "AS IS" AND
# ANY EXPRESS OR IMPLIED WARRANTIES, INCLUDING, BUT NOT LIMITED TO, THE
# IMPLIED WARRANTIES OF MERCHANTABILITY AND FITNESS FOR A PARTICULAR PURPOSE
# ARE DISCLAIMED.  IN NO EVENT SHALL LUKE HOWARD BE LIABLE
# FOR ANY DIRECT, INDIRECT, INCIDENTAL, SPECIAL, EXEMPLARY, OR CONSEQUENTIAL
# DAMAGES (INCLUDING, BUT NOT LIMITED TO, PROCUREMENT OF SUBSTITUTE GOODS
# OR SERVICES; LOSS OF USE, DATA, OR PROFITS; OR BUSINESS INTERRUPTION)
# HOWEVER CAUSED AND ON ANY THEORY OF LIABILITY, WHETHER IN CONTRACT, STRICT
# LIABILITY, OR TORT (INCLUDING NEGLIGENCE OR OTHERWISE) ARISING IN ANY WAY
# OUT OF THE USE OF THIS SOFTWARE, EVEN IF ADVISED OF THE POSSIBILITY OF
# SUCH DAMAGE.
#
#
# LDIF entries for base DN
#
#

require 'migrate_common.ph';

$PROGRAM = "migrate_base.pl";
$NAMINGCONTEXT = &getsuffix($PROGRAM);

$classmap{'o'} = 'organization';
$classmap{'dc'} = 'domain';
$classmap{'l'} = 'locality';
$classmap{'ou'} = 'organizationalUnit';
$classmap{'c'} = 'country';
$classmap{'nismapname'} = 'nisMap';
$classmap{'cn'} = 'container';
```

```perl
sub gen_suffix
{
 @dn_components = split(/,/, $DEFAULT_BASE);
 for ($dnloc = $#dn_components; $dnloc >= 0; $dnloc--)
  {
  &base_ldif;
  }
}

sub base_ldif
{
 # we don't handle multivalued RDNs here; they're unlikely
 # in a base DN.
 # Don't escape commas either XXX
 local ($rdn) = $dn_components[$dnloc];
 local ($remaining_dn) = join(',', @dn_components[($dnloc + 1)..$#dn_components]);
 ldif_entry($rdn, $remaining_dn);
}

sub ldif_entry
{
# remove leading, trailing whitespace
 local ($lhs, $rhs) = @_;
 local ($type, $val) = split(/\=/, $lhs);
 local ($dn);

 if ($rhs ne "") {
  $dn = $lhs . ',' . $rhs;
 } else {
  $dn = $lhs;
 }

 $type =~ s/$\s*//;
 $type =~ s/^\s*//;
 $type =~ tr/A-Z/a-z/;
 $val =~ s/$\s*//;
 $val =~ s/^\s*//;

 print "dn: $dn\n";
 print "$type: $val\n";
 print "objectClass: top\n";
 print "objectClass: $classmap{$type}\n";
 if ($EXTENDED_SCHEMA) {
  if ($DEFAULT_MAIL_DOMAIN) {
   print "objectClass: domainRelatedObject\n";
   print "associatedDomain: $DEFAULT_MAIL_DOMAIN\n";
  }
 }
```

```perl
    print "\n";
}

sub gen_namingcontexts
{
 # uniq naming contexts
 local (@ncs, $map, $nc);
 foreach $map (keys %NAMINGCONTEXT) {
  $nc = $NAMINGCONTEXT{$map};
  if (!grep(/^$nc$/, @ncs)) {
   push(@ncs, $nc);
   &ldif_entry($nc, $DEFAULT_BASE);
  }
 }
}

sub main
{
 if ($ARGV[0] ne "-n") {
  &gen_suffix();
 }
 &gen_namingcontexts();
}

&main;
```

The resulting output is as follows:

```
[root@ldaphost MigrationTools-45]# ./migrate_base.pl
dn: dc=Your,dc=Company
dc: Your
objectClass: top
objectClass: domain
objectClass: domainRelatedObject
associatedDomain: yourcompany.com

dn: ou=Hosts,dc=Your,dc=Company
ou: Hosts
objectClass: top
objectClass: organizationalUnit
objectClass: domainRelatedObject
associatedDomain: yourcompany.com

dn: ou=Rpc,dc=Your,dc=Company
ou: Rpc
objectClass: top
objectClass: organizationalUnit
objectClass: domainRelatedObject
associatedDomain: yourcompany.com
```

```
dn: ou=Services,dc=Your,dc=Company
ou: Services
objectClass: top
objectClass: organizationalUnit
objectClass: domainRelatedObject
associatedDomain: yourcompany.com

dn: nisMapName=netgroup.byuser,dc=Your,dc=Company
nismapname: netgroup.byuser
objectClass: top
objectClass: nisMap
objectClass: domainRelatedObject
associatedDomain: yourcompany.com

dn: ou=Mounts,dc=Your,dc=Company
ou: Mounts
objectClass: top
objectClass: organizationalUnit
objectClass: domainRelatedObject
associatedDomain: yourcompany.com

dn: ou=Networks,dc=Your,dc=Company
ou: Networks
objectClass: top
objectClass: organizationalUnit
objectClass: domainRelatedObject
associatedDomain: yourcompany.com

dn: ou=People,dc=Your,dc=Company
ou: People
objectClass: top
objectClass: organizationalUnit
objectClass: domainRelatedObject
associatedDomain: yourcompany.com

dn: ou=Group,dc=Your,dc=Company
ou: Group
objectClass: top
objectClass: organizationalUnit
objectClass: domainRelatedObject
associatedDomain: yourcompany.com

dn: ou=Netgroup,dc=Your,dc=Company
ou: Netgroup
objectClass: top
objectClass: organizationalUnit
objectClass: domainRelatedObject
associatedDomain: yourcompany.com
```

```
dn: ou=Protocols,dc=Your,dc=Company
ou: Protocols
objectClass: top
objectClass: organizationalUnit
objectClass: domainRelatedObject
associatedDomain: yourcompany.com

dn: ou=Aliases,dc=Your,dc=Company
ou: Aliases
objectClass: top
objectClass: organizationalUnit
objectClass: domainRelatedObject
associatedDomain: yourcompany.com

dn: nisMapName=netgroup.byhost,dc=Your,dc=Company
nismapname: netgroup.byhost
objectClass: top
objectClass: nisMap
objectClass: domainRelatedObject
associatedDomain: yourcompany.com
```

Whether you use all the integration tools to directly access LDAP or use them as a set of suggestions to implement a synchronization strategy, it's good to understand and implement the ideas and schema to have a good level of RFC 2307 standardization. As shown in Listing 7-1, each of the specific containers is reserved for a specific purpose. This gives you the ability to restrict your queries (by specifying the appropriate base DN) to a specific set of data. Thus, if you want to write a script that queries only the hosts within your infrastructure, you can set the base DN to ou=Hosts,dc=Your,dc=Company and search for objectclass=* instead of having to parse all the data if it was stored in a single organizational unit.

Most of the tools you'll be using require command-line inputs. You use the command-line inputs to provide the input that's being translated from its original data format into LDIF. To convert the /etc/aliases file (used by e-mail systems), you'll use the migrate_aliases.pl script shown in Listing 7-2.

The original /etc/aliases file you'll be using as an example may look like this:

```
mailer-daemon: postmaster
postmaster: root
testuser: tom@sun4c.net
```

Listing 7-2 shows the contents of the migrate_aliases.pl script.

Listing 7-2. migrate_aliases.pl

```perl
#!/usr/bin/perl
#
# $Id: migrate_aliases.pl,v 1.5 1999/07/24 06:29:19 lukeh Exp $
#
# Copyright (c) 1997 Luke Howard.
# All rights reserved.
#
```

```
#
# alias migration tool
# thanks to Dave McPike
#

require 'migrate_common.ph';

$PROGRAM = "migrate_aliases.pl";
$NAMINGCONTEXT = &getsuffix($PROGRAM);

&parse_args();
&open_files();

while(<INFILE>)
{
 chop;
 next unless ($_);
 next if /^#/;
 s/#(.*)$//;
```

```
 local($name, $memberstr) = split(/:/,$_,2);
 if ($use_stdout) {
  &dump_alias(STDOUT, $name, $memberstr);
 } else {
  &dump_alias(OUTFILE, $name, $memberstr);
 }
}

sub dump_alias
{
 local($HANDLE, $name, $memberstr) = @_;
 local(@aliases) = split(/,/, $memberstr);
 print $HANDLE "dn: cn=$name,$NAMINGCONTEXT\n";
 print $HANDLE "cn: $name\n";
 print $HANDLE "objectClass: nisMailAlias\n";
 print $HANDLE "objectClass: top\n";
 foreach $_ (@aliases) {
  s/^\s+//g;
  print $HANDLE "rfc822MailMember: $_\n";
 }
 print $HANDLE "\n";
}

close(INFILE);
if (OUTFILE != STDOUT) { close(OUTFILE); }
```

The execution of the script and resulting data are as follows:

```
[root@ldaphost MigrationTools-45]# ./migrate_aliases.pl /etc/aliases
dn: cn=mailer-daemon,ou=Aliases,dc=Your,dc=Company
cn: mailer-daemon
objectClass: nisMailAlias
objectClass: top
rfc822MailMember: postmaster

dn: cn=postmaster,ou=Aliases,dc=Your,dc=Company
cn: postmaster
objectClass: nisMailAlias
objectClass: top
rfc822MailMember: root

dn: cn=testuser,ou=Aliases,dc=Your,dc=Company
cn: testuser
objectClass: nisMailAlias
objectClass: top
rfc822MailMember: tom@sun4c.net
```

The migration of user information works in a similar way. The original /etc/passwd on your system may look like the following:

```
root:x:0:0:root:/root:/bin/bash
bin:x:1:1:bin:/bin:/sbin/nologin
daemon:x:2:2:daemon:/sbin:/sbin/nologin
adm:x:3:4:adm:/var/adm:/sbin/nologin
tom:x:90:0::/home/tom:/bin/sh
```

The complementary /etc/shadow file would be as follows:

```
root:$1$S_òwtköb$tzeauc.vfXDFno7gVnDkO.:12156:0:99999:7:::
bin:*:12156:0:99999:7:::
daemon:*:12156:0:99999:7:::
adm:*:12156:0:99999:7:::
tom:$1$FGOK1GLf$9ORWJILp/a49mdFKygx8k/:12156:0:99999:7:::
```

Upon running this script, you'll have LDIF profiles of the information that can be used as a baseline for any other user information you may want to add.

Listing 7-3 shows the contents of the migrate_passwd.pl script.

Listing 7-3. migrate_passwd.pl

```perl
#!/usr/bin/perl
#
# $Id: migrate_passwd.pl,v 1.7 1999/06/22 01:10:05 lukeh Exp $
#
# Copyright (c) 1997 Luke Howard.
# All rights reserved.
#
# Redistribution and use in source and binary forms, with or without
# modification, are permitted provided that the following conditions
# are met:
# 1. Redistributions of source code must retain the above copyright
#    notice, this list of conditions and the following disclaimer.
# 2. Redistributions in binary form must reproduce the above copyright
#    notice, this list of conditions and the following disclaimer in the
#    documentation and/or other materials provided with the distribution.
# 3. All advertising materials mentioning features or use of this software
#    must display the following acknowledgment:
#        This product includes software developed by Luke Howard.
# 4. The name of the other may not be used to endorse or promote products
#    derived from this software without specific prior written permission.
#
# THIS SOFTWARE IS PROVIDED BY THE LUKE HOWARD "AS IS" AND
# ANY EXPRESS OR IMPLIED WARRANTIES, INCLUDING, BUT NOT LIMITED TO, THE
# IMPLIED WARRANTIES OF MERCHANTABILITY AND FITNESS FOR A PARTICULAR PURPOSE
# ARE DISCLAIMED.  IN NO EVENT SHALL LUKE HOWARD BE LIABLE
# FOR ANY DIRECT, INDIRECT, INCIDENTAL, SPECIAL, EXEMPLARY, OR CONSEQUENTIAL
# DAMAGES (INCLUDING, BUT NOT LIMITED TO, PROCUREMENT OF SUBSTITUTE GOODS
# OR SERVICES; LOSS OF USE, DATA, OR PROFITS; OR BUSINESS INTERRUPTION)
# HOWEVER CAUSED AND ON ANY THEORY OF LIABILITY, WHETHER IN CONTRACT, STRICT
```

```perl
# LIABILITY, OR TORT (INCLUDING NEGLIGENCE OR OTHERWISE) ARISING IN ANY WAY
# OUT OF THE USE OF THIS SOFTWARE, EVEN IF ADVISED OF THE POSSIBILITY OF
# SUCH DAMAGE.
#
#
# Password migration tool. Migrates /etc/shadow as well, if it exists.
#
# Thanks to Peter Jacob Slot <peter@vision.auk.dk>.
#

require 'migrate_common.ph';

$PROGRAM = "migrate_passwd.pl";
$NAMINGCONTEXT = &getsuffix($PROGRAM);

&parse_args();
&read_shadow_file();
&open_files();

while(<INFILE>)
{
    chop;
    next if /^#/;
    next if /^\+/;
    local($user, $pwd, $uid, $gid, $gecos, $homedir, $shell) = split(/:/);

    if ($use_stdout) {
    &dump_user(STDOUT, $user, $pwd, $uid, $gid, $gecos, $homedir, $shell);
    } else {
    &dump_user(OUTFILE, $user, $pwd, $uid, $gid, $gecos, $homedir, $shell);
    }
}

sub dump_user
{
 local($HANDLE, $user, $pwd, $uid, $gid, $gecos, $homedir, $shell) = @_;
 local($name,$office,$wphone,$hphone)=split(/,/,$gecos);
 local($sn);
 local($givenname);
 local($cn);
 local(@tmp);

 if ($name) { $cn = $name; } else { $cn = $user; }

 $_ = $cn;
 @tmp = split(/\s+/);
 $sn = $tmp[$#tmp];
 pop(@tmp);
 $givenname=join(' ',@tmp);
```

```
print $HANDLE "dn: uid=$user,$NAMINGCONTEXT\n";
print $HANDLE "uid: $user\n";
print $HANDLE "cn: $cn\n";

if ($EXTENDED_SCHEMA) {
 if ($wphone) {
  print $HANDLE "telephonenumber: $wphone\n";
 }
 if ($office) {
  print $HANDLE "roomnumber: $office\n";
 }
 if ($hphone) {
  print $HANDLE "homephone: $hphone\n";
 }
 if ($givenname) {
  print $HANDLE "givenname: $givenname\n";
 }
 print $HANDLE "sn: $sn\n";
 if ($DEFAULT_MAIL_DOMAIN) {
  print $HANDLE "mail: $user@","$DEFAULT_MAIL_DOMAIN\n";
 }
 print $HANDLE "objectClass: person\n";
 print $HANDLE "objectClass: organizationalPerson\n";
 print $HANDLE "objectClass: inetOrgPerson\n";
}

print $HANDLE "objectClass: account\n";
print $HANDLE "objectClass: posixAccount\n";
print $HANDLE "objectClass: top\n";

if ($DEFAULT_REALM) {
 print $HANDLE "objectClass: kerberosSecurityObject\n";
      print $HANDLE "krbname: $user\@$DEFAULT_REALM\n";
}

if ($shadowUsers{$user} ne "") {
 &dump_shadow_attributes($HANDLE, split(/:/, $shadowUsers{$user}));
} else {
 print $HANDLE "userPassword: {crypt}$pwd\n";
}

if ($shell) {
 print $HANDLE "loginShell: $shell\n";
}

if ($uid ne "") {
 print $HANDLE "uidNumber: $uid\n";
} else {
 print $HANDLE "uidNumber:\n";
}
```

```perl
 if ($gid ne "") {
  print $HANDLE "gidNumber: $gid\n";
 } else {
  print $HANDLE "gidNumber:\n";
 }

 if ($homedir) {
  print $HANDLE "homeDirectory: $homedir\n";
 } else {
  print $HANDLE "homeDirectory:\n";
 }

 if ($gecos) {
  print $HANDLE "gecos: $gecos\n";
 }

 print $HANDLE "\n";
}

close(INFILE);
if (OUTFILE != STDOUT) { close(OUTFILE); }

sub read_shadow_file
{
 open(SHADOW, "/etc/shadow") || return;
 while(<SHADOW>) {
  chop;
  ($shadowUser) = split(/:/, $_);
  $shadowUsers{$shadowUser} = $_;
 }
 close(SHADOW);
}

sub dump_shadow_attributes
{
 local($HANDLE, $user, $pwd, $lastchg, $min, $max,
   $warn, $inactive, $expire, $flag) = @_;

 print $HANDLE "objectClass: shadowAccount\n";
 if ($pwd) {
  print $HANDLE "userPassword: {crypt}$pwd\n";
 }
 if ($lastchg) {
  print $HANDLE "shadowLastChange: $lastchg\n";
 }
 if ($min) {
  print $HANDLE "shadowMin: $min\n";
 }
```

```
    if ($max) {
     print $HANDLE "shadowMax: $max\n";
    }
    if ($warn) {
     print $HANDLE "shadowWarning: $warn\n";
    }
    if ($inactive) {
     print $HANDLE "shadowInactive: $inactive\n";
    }
    if ($expire) {
     print $HANDLE "shadowExpire: $expire\n";
    }
    if ($flag) {
     print $HANDLE "shadowFlag: $flag\n";
    }
}
```

The result of running this script is as follows:

```
[root@ldaphost MigrationTools-45]# ./migrate_passwd.pl /etc/passwd
dn: uid=root,ou=People,dc=Your,dc=Company
uid: root
cn: root
sn: root
mail: root@yourcompany.com
mailRoutingAddress: root@mail.yourcompany.com
mailHost: mail.yourcompany.com
objectClass: mailRecipient
objectClass: person
objectClass: organizationalPerson
objectClass: inetOrgPerson
objectClass: account
objectClass: posixAccount
objectClass: top
objectClass: kerberosSecurityObject
objectClass: shadowAccount
userPassword: {crypt}$1$S_òwtköb$tzeauc.vfXDFno7gVnDkO.
shadowLastChange: 12156
shadowMax: 99999
shadowWarning: 7
krbName: root@YOURCOMPANY.COM
loginShell: /bin/bash
uidNumber: 0
gidNumber: 0
homeDirectory: /root
gecos: root
```

```
dn: uid=bin,ou=People,dc=Your,dc=Company
uid: bin
cn: bin
sn: bin
mail: bin@yourcompany.com
mailRoutingAddress: bin@mail.yourcompany.com
mailHost: mail.yourcompany.com
objectClass: mailRecipient
objectClass: person
objectClass: organizationalPerson
objectClass: inetOrgPerson
objectClass: account
objectClass: posixAccount
objectClass: top
objectClass: kerberosSecurityObject
objectClass: shadowAccount
userPassword: {crypt}*
shadowLastChange: 12156
shadowMax: 99999
shadowWarning: 7
krbName: bin@YOURCOMPANY.COM
loginShell: /sbin/nologin
uidNumber: 1
gidNumber: 1
homeDirectory: /bin
gecos: bin

dn: uid=daemon,ou=People,dc=Your,dc=Company
uid: daemon
cn: daemon
sn: daemon
mail: daemon@yourcompany.com
mailRoutingAddress: daemon@mail.yourcompany.com
mailHost: mail.yourcompany.com
objectClass: mailRecipient
objectClass: person
objectClass: organizationalPerson
objectClass: inetOrgPerson
objectClass: account
objectClass: posixAccount
objectClass: top
objectClass: kerberosSecurityObject
objectClass: shadowAccount
userPassword: {crypt}*
shadowLastChange: 12156
shadowMax: 99999
shadowWarning: 7
```

```
krbName: daemon@YOURCOMPANY.COM
loginShell: /sbin/nologin
uidNumber: 2
gidNumber: 2
homeDirectory: /sbin
gecos: daemon

dn: uid=adm,ou=People,dc=Your,dc=Company
uid: adm
cn: adm
sn: adm
mail: adm@yourcompany.com
mailRoutingAddress: adm@mail.yourcompany.com
mailHost: mail.yourcompany.com
objectClass: mailRecipient
objectClass: person
objectClass: organizationalPerson
objectClass: inetOrgPerson
objectClass: account
objectClass: posixAccount
objectClass: top
objectClass: kerberosSecurityObject
objectClass: shadowAccount
userPassword: {crypt}*
shadowLastChange: 12156
shadowMax: 99999
shadowWarning: 7
krbName: adm@YOURCOMPANY.COM
loginShell: /sbin/nologin
uidNumber: 3
gidNumber: 4
homeDirectory: /var/adm
gecos: adm

dn: uid=tom,ou=People,dc=Your,dc=Company
uid: tom
cn: tom
sn: tom
mail: tom@yourcompany.com
mailRoutingAddress: tom@mail.yourcompany.com
mailHost: mail.yourcompany.com
objectClass: mailRecipient
objectClass: person
objectClass: organizationalPerson
objectClass: inetOrgPerson
objectClass: account
objectClass: posixAccount
```

```
objectClass: top
objectClass: kerberosSecurityObject
objectClass: shadowAccount
userPassword: {crypt}$1$FGOK1GLf$9ORWJILp/a49mdFKygx8k/
shadowLastChange: 12156
shadowMax: 99999
shadowWarning: 7
krbName: tom@YOURCOMPANY.COM
loginShell: /bin/sh
uidNumber: 90
gidNumber: 0
homeDirectory: /home/tom
```

Realize that the migration tools that are provided should serve only as guidelines for you. In other words, the object classes, schema, and general information that are outputted should be used as an example and not necessarily imported directly into your LDAP system. The user records that you've just generated, for example, may not comply with your existing directory information tree (DIT), customized schema, or naming convention. You may already have users in your directory, and you wouldn't want to have any sort of conflicting namespace. However, if you have a common identifier between your existing user records and the information generated by these scripts, you can modify the output (or create an additional script) to match the independent records and add new information to an existing user base. For example, take the Linux account tom shown previously. The generated DN is as follows:

```
dn: uid=tom,ou=People,dc=Your,dc=Company
```

Within the record, you see uidnumber: 90. Your existing user profile for this user may already be uid=tom_jackiewicz,ou=People,ou=California,dc=Your,dc=Company. Maybe this record already had the uidnumber stored within it. You can use this to match data, thus giving you the ability to take the information generated for uid=tom,ou=People,dcYour,dc=Company and append it to the uid=tom_jackiewicz,ou=People,ou=California,dc=Your,dc=Company record that already exists.

You can also store group information in LDAP. The migrate_group.pl script is provided for you to create the appropriate LDIF file.

Listing 7-4 shows the contents of the migrate_group.pl script.

Listing 7-4. migrate_group.pl

```perl
#!/usr/bin/perl
#
# $Id: migrate_group.pl,v 1.6 1998/10/01 13:14:27 lukeh Exp $
#
# Copyright (c) 1997 Luke Howard.
# All rights reserved.
#
# Redistribution and use in source and binary forms, with or without
# modification, are permitted provided that the following conditions
# are met:
```

```
# 1. Redistributions of source code must retain the above copyright
#    notice, this list of conditions and the following disclaimer.
# 2. Redistributions in binary form must reproduce the above copyright
#    notice, this list of conditions and the following disclaimer in the
#    documentation and/or other materials provided with the distribution.
# 3. All advertising materials mentioning features or use of this software
#    must display the following acknowledgment:
#        This product includes software developed by Luke Howard.
# 4. The name of the other may not be used to endorse or promote products
#    derived from this software without specific prior written permission.
#
# THIS SOFTWARE IS PROVIDED BY THE LUKE HOWARD "AS IS" AND
# ANY EXPRESS OR IMPLIED WARRANTIES, INCLUDING, BUT NOT LIMITED TO, THE
# IMPLIED WARRANTIES OF MERCHANTABILITY AND FITNESS FOR A PARTICULAR PURPOSE
# ARE DISCLAIMED.  IN NO EVENT SHALL LUKE HOWARD BE LIABLE
# FOR ANY DIRECT, INDIRECT, INCIDENTAL, SPECIAL, EXEMPLARY, OR CONSEQUENTIAL
# DAMAGES (INCLUDING, BUT NOT LIMITED TO, PROCUREMENT OF SUBSTITUTE GOODS
# OR SERVICES; LOSS OF USE, DATA, OR PROFITS; OR BUSINESS INTERRUPTION)
# HOWEVER CAUSED AND ON ANY THEORY OF LIABILITY, WHETHER IN CONTRACT, STRICT
# LIABILITY, OR TORT (INCLUDING NEGLIGENCE OR OTHERWISE) ARISING IN ANY WAY
# OUT OF THE USE OF THIS SOFTWARE, EVEN IF ADVISED OF THE POSSIBILITY OF
# SUCH DAMAGE.
#
#
# Group migration tool
#
#

require 'migrate_common.ph';

$PROGRAM = "migrate_group.pl";
$NAMINGCONTEXT = &getsuffix($PROGRAM);

&parse_args();
&open_files();

while(<INFILE>)
{
 chop;
 next if /^#/;
 next if /^\+/;

 local($group, $pwd, $gid, $users) = split(/:/);
```

```perl
  if ($use_stdout) {
   &dump_group(STDOUT, $group, $pwd, $gid, $users);
  } else {
   &dump_group(OUTFILE, $group, $pwd, $gid, $users);
  }
}

sub dump_group
{
 local($HANDLE, $group, $pwd, $gid, $users) = @_;

 local(@members) = split(/,/, $users);

 print $HANDLE "dn: cn=$group,$NAMINGCONTEXT\n";
 print $HANDLE "objectClass: posixGroup\n";
 print $HANDLE "objectClass: top\n";
 print $HANDLE "cn: $group\n";
 if ($pwd) {
  print $HANDLE "userPassword: {crypt}$pwd\n";
 }

 print $HANDLE "gidNumber: $gid\n";

 @members = uniq($group, @members);
 foreach $_ (@members) {
  print $HANDLE "memberUid: $_\n";
 }

 print $HANDLE "\n";
}

close(INFILE);
if (OUTFILE != STDOUT) { close(OUTFILE); }
```

Your original /etc/group file may look like this:

```
root:x:0:root
bin:x:1:root,bin,daemon
daemon:x:2:root,bin,daemon
sys:x:3:root,bin,adm
adm:x:4:root,adm,daemon
```

After migration, the LDIF would look like Listing 7-5.

Listing 7-5. *The Group LDIF*

```
[root@ldaphost MigrationTools-45]# ./migrate_group.pl /etc/group
dn: cn=root,ou=Group,dc=Your,dc=Company
objectClass: posixGroup
objectClass: top
cn: root
userPassword: {crypt}x
gidNumber: 0

dn: cn=bin,ou=Group,dc=Your,dc=Company
objectClass: posixGroup
objectClass: top
cn: bin
userPassword: {crypt}x
gidNumber: 1
memberUid: daemon
memberUid: root

dn: cn=daemon,ou=Group,dc=Your,dc=Company
objectClass: posixGroup
objectClass: top
cn: daemon
userPassword: {crypt}x
gidNumber: 2
memberUid: bin
memberUid: root

dn: cn=sys,ou=Group,dc=Your,dc=Company
objectClass: posixGroup
objectClass: top
cn: sys
userPassword: {crypt}x
gidNumber: 3
memberUid: adm
memberUid: bin
memberUid: root

dn: cn=adm,ou=Group,dc=Your,dc=Company
objectClass: posixGroup
objectClass: top
cn: adm
userPassword: {crypt}x
gidNumber: 4
memberUid: daemon
memberUid: root
```

Groups are often problematic within LDAP (especially when integrating with multiple systems and different group hierarchies) because not all applications use the same type of group. The search string required for retrieving the previous group information would be (objectclass=posixGroup); however, many applications are, by default, configured to retrieve information via the query (objectclass=groupofuniquenames). Think about the applications using groups, the filters being used, and how groups will be used before storing a large mess of information in your system. The overall structure within your company, the individual process groups within Unix and Windows systems, and the grouping of information within certain applications all fall into the generic scope of a group. However, your organization may find it useful to combine all this data or keep information completely separate. For example, if someone wants to search your LDAP system for the adm group defined previously, they may not want to retrieve your entire corporate taxonomy.

Additional problems can occur if you're migrating generic groups used across certain systems into your LDAP directory. If the group administrators is a generic definition used across multiple applications with different members, it's not in your best interest to have a generic definition that could conflict. Storing only groups that are necessary and setting a naming standard for the groups best serves your user community.

Although it may seem logical and familiar to create profiles for information that's commonly stored in LDAP, such as users, group, and aliases, storing additional information outside this basic scope requires additional guidance. The problem of storing application (or in this case, service) data within LDAP is that there has rarely been guidance or schema predefined for your use. As a result, information had been inconsistent depending on the implementers. For these purposes, you benefit from the definitions of certain resource data and RFC 2307. For information outside this scope, it may benefit from the recent standardization of data.

Take, for example, the /etc/fstab file, which defines your disk layout. While not normally a candidate for being stored in LDAP, migration tools now give you this ability. The benefit may be the ability to audit system disk configurations via LDAP instead of requiring administrators to log into each host and read localized data. If you wanted to store this information in LDAP, the definition of the information in the schema requires a bit of excess planning. With the attributes already defined for you, it gives you a starting point. The original file in /etc may look like this:

```
LABEL=/                 /                ext3    defaults                   1 1
LABEL=/boot             /boot            ext3    defaults                   1 2
none                    /dev/pts         devpts  gid=5,mode=620             0 0
LABEL=/home             /home            ext3    defaults                   1 2
none                    /proc            proc    defaults                   0 0
none                    /dev/shm         tmpfs   defaults                   0 0
LABEL=/usr              /usr             ext3    defaults                   1 2
LABEL=/var              /var             ext3    defaults                   1 2
/dev/hda7               swap             swap    defaults                   0 0
/dev/cdrom              /mnt/cdrom       iso9660 noauto,owner,kudzu,ro 0 0
```

You can run the provided migration script, migrate_fstab.pl, to convert this information to LDIF, which can then be stored in LDAP. Listing 7-6 shows the contents of the migrate_fstab.pl script.

Listing 7-6. `migrate_fstab.pl`

```perl
#!/usr/bin/perl
#
# $Id: migrate_fstab.pl,v 1.3 1998/10/01 13:14:26 lukeh Exp $
#
# Copyright (c) 1997 Luke Howard.
# All rights reserved.
#
# Redistribution and use in source and binary forms, with or without
# modification, are permitted provided that the following conditions
# are met:
# 1. Redistributions of source code must retain the above copyright
#    notice, this list of conditions and the following disclaimer.
# 2. Redistributions in binary form must reproduce the above copyright
#    notice, this list of conditions and the following disclaimer in the
#    documentation and/or other materials provided with the distribution.
# 3. All advertising materials mentioning features or use of this software
#    must display the following acknowledgment:
#        This product includes software developed by Luke Howard.
# 4. The name of the other may not be used to endorse or promote products
#    derived from this software without specific prior written permission.
#
# THIS SOFTWARE IS PROVIDED BY THE LUKE HOWARD "AS IS" AND
# ANY EXPRESS OR IMPLIED WARRANTIES, INCLUDING, BUT NOT LIMITED TO, THE
# IMPLIED WARRANTIES OF MERCHANTABILITY AND FITNESS FOR A PARTICULAR PURPOSE
# ARE DISCLAIMED.  IN NO EVENT SHALL LUKE HOWARD BE LIABLE
# FOR ANY DIRECT, INDIRECT, INCIDENTAL, SPECIAL, EXEMPLARY, OR CONSEQUENTIAL
# DAMAGES (INCLUDING, BUT NOT LIMITED TO, PROCUREMENT OF SUBSTITUTE GOODS
# OR SERVICES; LOSS OF USE, DATA, OR PROFITS; OR BUSINESS INTERRUPTION)
# HOWEVER CAUSED AND ON ANY THEORY OF LIABILITY, WHETHER IN CONTRACT, STRICT
# LIABILITY, OR TORT (INCLUDING NEGLIGENCE OR OTHERWISE) ARISING IN ANY WAY
# OUT OF THE USE OF THIS SOFTWARE, EVEN IF ADVISED OF THE POSSIBILITY OF
# SUCH DAMAGE.
#
#
# fstab migration tool
# These classes were not published in RFC 2307.
# They are used by MacOS X Server, however.
#

require 'migrate_common.ph';

$PROGRAM = "migrate_fstab.pl";
$NAMINGCONTEXT = &getsuffix($PROGRAM);

&parse_args();
&open_files();
```

```perl
while(<INFILE>)
{
 chop;
 next if /^#/;
 s/#(.*)$//;

 local($fsname, $dir, $type, $opts, $freq, $passno) = split(/\s+/);
 if ($use_stdout) {
  &dump_mount(STDOUT, $fsname, $dir, $type, $opts, $freq, $passno);
 } else {
  &dump_mount(OUTFILE, $fsname, $dir, $type, $opts, $freq, $passno);
 }
}

sub dump_mount
{
 local($HANDLE, $fsname, $dir, $type, $opts, $freq, $passno) = @_;
 local (@options) = split(/,/, $opts);
 print $HANDLE "dn: cn=$fsname,$NAMINGCONTEXT\n";
 print $HANDLE "cn: $fsname\n";
 print $HANDLE "objectClass: mount\n";
 print $HANDLE "objectClass: top\n";
 print $HANDLE "mountDirectory: $dir\n";
 print $HANDLE "mountType: $type\n";
 if (defined($freq)) {
  print $HANDLE "mountDumpFrequency: $freq\n";
 }
 if (defined($passno)) {
  print $HANDLE "mountPassNumber: $passno\n";
 }
 foreach $_ (@options) {
  print $HANDLE "mountOption: $_\n";
 }
 print $HANDLE "\n";
}

close(INFILE);
if (OUTFILE != STDOUT) { close(OUTFILE); }
```

The result of running this script is as follows:

```
[root@ldaphost MigrationTools-45]# ./migrate_fstab.pl /etc/fstab
dn: cn=LABEL=/,ou=Mounts,dc=Your,dc=Company
cn: LABEL=/
objectClass: mount
objectClass: top
mountDirectory: /
mountType: ext3
```

```
mountDumpFrequency: 1
mountPassNo: 1
mountOption: defaults

dn: cn=LABEL=/boot,ou=Mounts,dc=Your,dc=Company
cn: LABEL=/boot
objectClass: mount
objectClass: top
mountDirectory: /boot
mountType: ext3
mountDumpFrequency: 1
mountPassNo: 2
mountOption: defaults

dn: cn=none,ou=Mounts,dc=Your,dc=Company
cn: none
objectClass: mount
objectClass: top
mountDirectory: /dev/pts
mountType: devpts
mountDumpFrequency: 0
mountPassNo: 0
mountOption: gid=5
mountOption: mode=620

dn: cn=LABEL=/home,ou=Mounts,dc=Your,dc=Company
cn: LABEL=/home
objectClass: mount
objectClass: top
mountDirectory: /home
mountType: ext3
mountDumpFrequency: 1
mountPassNo: 2
mountOption: defaults

dn: cn=none,ou=Mounts,dc=Your,dc=Company
cn: none
objectClass: mount
objectClass: top
mountDirectory: /proc
mountType: proc
mountDumpFrequency: 0
mountPassNo: 0
mountOption: defaults
```

```
dn: cn=none,ou=Mounts,dc=Your,dc=Company
cn: none
objectClass: mount
objectClass: top
mountDirectory: /dev/shm
mountType: tmpfs
mountDumpFrequency: 0
mountPassNo: 0
mountOption: defaults

dn: cn=LABEL=/usr,ou=Mounts,dc=Your,dc=Company
cn: LABEL=/usr
objectClass: mount
objectClass: top
mountDirectory: /usr
mountType: ext3
mountDumpFrequency: 1
mountPassNo: 2
mountOption: defaults

dn: cn=LABEL=/var,ou=Mounts,dc=Your,dc=Company
cn: LABEL=/var
objectClass: mount
objectClass: top
mountDirectory: /var
mountType: ext3
mountDumpFrequency: 1
mountPassNo: 2
mountOption: defaults

dn: cn=/dev/hda7,ou=Mounts,dc=Your,dc=Company
cn: /dev/hda7
objectClass: mount
objectClass: top
mountDirectory: swap
mountType: swap
mountDumpFrequency: 0
mountPassNo: 0
mountOption: defaults

dn: cn=/dev/cdrom,ou=Mounts,dc=Your,dc=Company
cn: /dev/cdrom
objectClass: mount
objectClass: top
mountDirectory: /mnt/cdrom
mountType: iso9660
mountDumpFrequency: 0
```

```
mountPassNo: 0
mountOption: noauto
mountOption: owner
mountOption: kudzu
mountOption: ro
```

While it's good to see the format of data that the migration scripts provide, you can also see that the specific host that these disk configurations apply to doesn't apply across all potential systems in your environment. Creating additional organization units per host or references to various types of standard disk configurations from other host profiles is necessary in a large environment.

The process of converting host information (stored in /etc/hosts) follows the same basic idea. Take the following /etc/hosts file as an example:

```
# Do not remove the following line, or various programs
# that require network functionality will fail.
127.0.0.1       ldaphost.yourcompany.com
127.0.0.1       ldaphost localhost.localdomain localhost
192.168.10.40            randomhost
```

Listing 7-7 shows the contents of the migrate_hosts.pl script.

Listing 7-7. migrate_hosts.pl

```perl
#!/usr/bin/perl
#
# $Id: migrate_hosts.pl,v 1.4 1998/10/01 13:14:28 lukeh Exp $
#
# Copyright (c) 1997 Luke Howard.
# All rights reserved.
#
# Redistribution and use in source and binary forms, with or without
# modification, are permitted provided that the following conditions
# are met:
# 1. Redistributions of source code must retain the above copyright
#    notice, this list of conditions and the following disclaimer.
# 2. Redistributions in binary form must reproduce the above copyright
#    notice, this list of conditions and the following disclaimer in the
#    documentation and/or other materials provided with the distribution.
# 3. All advertising materials mentioning features or use of this software
#    must display the following acknowledgment:
#        This product includes software developed by Luke Howard.
# 4. The name of the other may not be used to endorse or promote products
#    derived from this software without specific prior written permission.
#
```

```
# THIS SOFTWARE IS PROVIDED BY THE LUKE HOWARD "AS IS" AND
# ANY EXPRESS OR IMPLIED WARRANTIES, INCLUDING, BUT NOT LIMITED TO, THE
# IMPLIED WARRANTIES OF MERCHANTABILITY AND FITNESS FOR A PARTICULAR PURPOSE
# ARE DISCLAIMED.  IN NO EVENT SHALL LUKE HOWARD BE LIABLE
# FOR ANY DIRECT, INDIRECT, INCIDENTAL, SPECIAL, EXEMPLARY, OR CONSEQUENTIAL
# DAMAGES (INCLUDING, BUT NOT LIMITED TO, PROCUREMENT OF SUBSTITUTE GOODS
# OR SERVICES; LOSS OF USE, DATA, OR PROFITS; OR BUSINESS INTERRUPTION)
# HOWEVER CAUSED AND ON ANY THEORY OF LIABILITY, WHETHER IN CONTRACT, STRICT
# LIABILITY, OR TORT (INCLUDING NEGLIGENCE OR OTHERWISE) ARISING IN ANY WAY
# OUT OF THE USE OF THIS SOFTWARE, EVEN IF ADVISED OF THE POSSIBILITY OF
# SUCH DAMAGE.
#
#
# hosts migration tool
#
#

require 'migrate_common.ph';

$PROGRAM = "migrate_hosts.pl";
$NAMINGCONTEXT = &getsuffix($PROGRAM);

&parse_args();
&open_files();

while(<INFILE>)
{
    chop;
 next unless ($_);
 next if /^#/;
 s/#(.*)$//;
 local($hostaddr, $hostname, @aliases) = split(/\s+/);

 if ($use_stdout) {
  &dump_host(STDOUT, $hostaddr, $hostname, @aliases);
 } else {
  &dump_host(OUTFILE, $hostaddr, $hostname, @aliases);
 }
}


sub dump_host
{
 local($HANDLE, $hostaddr, $hostname, @aliases) = @_;
 local($dn);
 return if (!$hostaddr);
```

```
print $HANDLE "dn: cn=$hostname,$NAMINGCONTEXT\n";
print $HANDLE "objectClass: top\n";
print $HANDLE "objectClass: ipHost\n";
print $HANDLE "objectClass: device\n";
print $HANDLE "ipHostNumber: $hostaddr\n";
print $HANDLE "cn: $hostname\n";
@aliases = uniq($hostname, @aliases);
foreach $_ (@aliases) {
 if ($_ ne $hostname) {
  print $HANDLE "cn: $_\n";
 }
}
print $HANDLE "\n";
}


close(INFILE);
if (OUTFILE != STDOUT) { close(OUTFILE); }
```

Listing 7-8 shows the command and resulting LDIF entry.

Listing 7-8. *Host LDIF*

```
[root@ldaphost MigrationTools-45]# ./migrate_hosts.pl /etc/hosts
dn: cn=ldaphost.yourcompany.com,ou=Hosts,dc=Your,dc=Company
objectClass: top
objectClass: ipHost
objectClass: device
ipHostNumber: 127.0.0.1
cn: ldaphost.yourcompany.com
cn: ldaphost
cn: localhost
cn: localhost.localdomain

dn: cn=randomhost,ou=Hosts,dc=Your,dc=Company
objectClass: top
objectClass: ipHost
objectClass: device
ipHostNumber: 192.168.10.40
cn: randomhost
```

The resulting LDIF entry will be suitable as a template for basic host information and can be expanded to include other information that may be suitable. For example, in an environment that requires extensive auditing of host information, you may want to take the example in Listing 7-8 and expand it to include the MAC address, system owner, system description, and other information that may be specific to other applications that require this data.

It's always a good idea to have some of the information that I discussed in your directory before deploying other LDAP management tools. That is, if you already have templates for information defined, it's much easier to make applications comply with what you already have instead of you having to comply with nonstandard application templates. If an application that's already deployed within your environment uses a completely different format for host information, it'd be more difficult to modify your tools to retrieve this information.

Another type of information that can be migrated, along with system services and generic templates for service-style information, are your remote procedure call (RPC) definitions. Having the ability to publish your available services with LDAP and the RPC portmapper itself is also a good thing to have for a system audit.

The following is an example (incomplete) /etc/rpc file:

```
portmapper  100000      portmap sunrpc rpcbind
rstatd      100001      rstat rup perfmeter rstat_svc
```

Listing 7-9 shows the contents of the migrate_rpc.pl script.

Listing 7-9. migrate_rpc.pl

```perl
#!/usr/bin/perl
#
# $Id: migrate_rpc.pl,v 1.4 1998/10/01 13:14:36 lukeh Exp $
#
# Copyright (c) 1997 Luke Howard.
# All rights reserved.
#
# Redistribution and use in source and binary forms, with or without
# modification, are permitted provided that the following conditions
# are met:
# 1. Redistributions of source code must retain the above copyright
#    notice, this list of conditions and the following disclaimer.
# 2. Redistributions in binary form must reproduce the above copyright
#    notice, this list of conditions and the following disclaimer in the
#    documentation and/or other materials provided with the distribution.
# 3. All advertising materials mentioning features or use of this software
#    must display the following acknowledgment:
#        This product includes software developed by Luke Howard.
# 4. The name of the other may not be used to endorse or promote products
#    derived from this software without specific prior written permission.
#
# THIS SOFTWARE IS PROVIDED BY THE LUKE HOWARD "AS IS" AND
# ANY EXPRESS OR IMPLIED WARRANTIES, INCLUDING, BUT NOT LIMITED TO, THE
# IMPLIED WARRANTIES OF MERCHANTABILITY AND FITNESS FOR A PARTICULAR PURPOSE
# ARE DISCLAIMED.  IN NO EVENT SHALL LUKE HOWARD BE LIABLE
# FOR ANY DIRECT, INDIRECT, INCIDENTAL, SPECIAL, EXEMPLARY, OR CONSEQUENTIAL
# DAMAGES (INCLUDING, BUT NOT LIMITED TO, PROCUREMENT OF SUBSTITUTE GOODS
# OR SERVICES; LOSS OF USE, DATA, OR PROFITS; OR BUSINESS INTERRUPTION)
# HOWEVER CAUSED AND ON ANY THEORY OF LIABILITY, WHETHER IN CONTRACT, STRICT
# LIABILITY, OR TORT (INCLUDING NEGLIGENCE OR OTHERWISE) ARISING IN ANY WAY
# OUT OF THE USE OF THIS SOFTWARE, EVEN IF ADVISED OF THE POSSIBILITY OF
# SUCH DAMAGE.
#
#
```

```perl
# Rpc migration tool
#
#

require 'migrate_common.ph';

$PROGRAM = "migrate_rpc.pl";
$NAMINGCONTEXT = &getsuffix($PROGRAM);

&parse_args();
&open_files();

while(<INFILE>)
{
 chop;
 next unless ($_);
 next if /^#/;
 s/#(.*)$//;
 local($rpcname, $rpcnumber, @aliases) = split(/\s+/);

 if ($use_stdout) {
  &dump_rpc(STDOUT, $rpcname, $rpcnumber, @aliases);
 } else {
  &dump_rpc(OUTFILE, $rpcname, $rpcnumber, @aliases);
 }
}

sub dump_rpc
{
 local($HANDLE, $rpcname, $rpcnumber, @aliases) = @_;

 return if (!$rpcname);

 print $HANDLE "dn: cn=$rpcname,$NAMINGCONTEXT\n";
 print $HANDLE "objectClass: oncRpc\n";
 print $HANDLE "objectClass: top\n";
 print $HANDLE "oncRpcNumber: $rpcnumber\n";
 print $HANDLE "cn: $rpcname\n";
 @aliases = uniq($rpcname, @aliases);
 foreach $_ (@aliases) {
  print $HANDLE "cn: $_\n";
 }
 print $HANDLE "\n";
}

close(INFILE);
if (OUTFILE != STDOUT) { close(OUTFILE); }
```

Listing 7-10 shows the process and possible result of migration.

Listing 7-10. *RPC LDIF*

```
[root@ldaphost MigrationTools-45]# ./migrate_rpc.pl /etc/rpc
dn: cn=portmapper,ou=Rpc,dc=Your,dc=Company
objectClass: oncRpc
objectClass: top
description: RPC portmapper
oncRpcNumber: 100000
cn: portmapper
cn: portmap
cn: rpcbind
cn: sunrpc

dn: cn=rstatd,ou=Rpc,dc=Your,dc=Company
objectClass: oncRpc
objectClass: top
description: RPC rstatd
oncRpcNumber: 100001
cn: rstatd
cn: perfmeter
cn: rstat
cn: rstat_svc
cn: rup
```

Your standard TCP/IP services stored in /etc/services are also available for migration. However, keep in mind that just because it's possible to migrate a file, it's not always the best scenario. These files may differ from host to host and can change during patch updates. An example /etc/services file looks like this:

```
ftp-data    20/tcp
ftp-data    20/udp
ftp         21/tcp
ftp         21/udp        fsp fspd
ssh         22/tcp        # SSH Remote Login Protocol
ssh         22/udp        # SSH Remote Login Protocol
cfengine    5308/tcp      # CFengine
cfengine    5308/udp      # CFengine
telnet      23/tcp
telnet      23/udp
```

Listing 7-11 shows the contents of the migrate_services.pl script.

Listing 7-11. migrate_services.pl

```perl
#!/usr/bin/perl
#
# $Id: migrate_services.pl,v 1.4 1998/10/01 13:14:37 lukeh Exp $
#
# Copyright (c) 1997 Luke Howard.
# All rights reserved.
#
# Redistribution and use in source and binary forms, with or without
# modification, are permitted provided that the following conditions
# are met:
# 1. Redistributions of source code must retain the above copyright
#    notice, this list of conditions and the following disclaimer.
# 2. Redistributions in binary form must reproduce the above copyright
#    notice, this list of conditions and the following disclaimer in the
#    documentation and/or other materials provided with the distribution.
# 3. All advertising materials mentioning features or use of this software
#    must display the following acknowledgment:
#        This product includes software developed by Luke Howard.
# 4. The name of the other may not be used to endorse or promote products
#    derived from this software without specific prior written permission.
#
# THIS SOFTWARE IS PROVIDED BY THE LUKE HOWARD "AS IS" AND
# ANY EXPRESS OR IMPLIED WARRANTIES, INCLUDING, BUT NOT LIMITED TO, THE
# IMPLIED WARRANTIES OF MERCHANTABILITY AND FITNESS FOR A PARTICULAR PURPOSE
# ARE DISCLAIMED.  IN NO EVENT SHALL LUKE HOWARD BE LIABLE
# FOR ANY DIRECT, INDIRECT, INCIDENTAL, SPECIAL, EXEMPLARY, OR CONSEQUENTIAL
# DAMAGES (INCLUDING, BUT NOT LIMITED TO, PROCUREMENT OF SUBSTITUTE GOODS
# OR SERVICES; LOSS OF USE, DATA, OR PROFITS; OR BUSINESS INTERRUPTION)
# HOWEVER CAUSED AND ON ANY THEORY OF LIABILITY, WHETHER IN CONTRACT, STRICT
# LIABILITY, OR TORT (INCLUDING NEGLIGENCE OR OTHERWISE) ARISING IN ANY WAY
# OUT OF THE USE OF THIS SOFTWARE, EVEN IF ADVISED OF THE POSSIBILITY OF
# SUCH DAMAGE.
#
# services migration tool
#
#

require 'migrate_common.ph';

$PROGRAM = "migrate_services.pl";
$NAMINGCONTEXT = &getsuffix($PROGRAM);

&parse_args();
&open_files();
```

```
while(<INFILE>)
{
 chop;
 next unless ($_);
 next if /^#/;
 s/#(.*)$//;
 local($servicename, $portproto, @aliases) = split(/\s+/);

 if ($use_stdout) {
  &dump_service(STDOUT, $servicename, $portproto, @aliases);
 } else {
  &dump_service(OUTFILE, $servicename, $portproto, @aliases);
 }
}

sub dump_service
{
 local($HANDLE, $servicename, $portproto, @aliases) = @_;

 local($port, $proto) = split(/\//, $portproto);

 return if (!$servicename);

 print $HANDLE "dn: cn=$servicename+ipServiceProtocol=$proto, \
$NAMINGCONTEXT\n";
    print $HANDLE "objectClass: ipService\n";
    print $HANDLE "objectClass: top\n";
    print $HANDLE "ipServicePort: $port\n";
    print $HANDLE "ipServiceProtocol: $proto\n";
    print $HANDLE "cn: $servicename\n";
    @aliases = uniq($servicename, @aliases);
    foreach $_ (@aliases) {
        print $HANDLE "cn: $_\n";
    }
    print $HANDLE "\n";
}

close(INFILE);
if (OUTFILE != STDOUT) { close(OUTFILE); }
```

Listing 7-12 shows the process and possible result of this migration.

Listing 7-12. *Result*

```
[root@ldaphost MigrationTools-45]# ./migrate_services.pl /etc/services
dn: cn=ftp-data,ou=Services,dc=Your,dc=Company
objectClass: ipService
objectClass: top
ipServicePort: 20
ipServiceProtocol: udp
ipServiceProtocol: tcp
cn: ftp-data

dn: cn=ftp,ou=Services,dc=Your,dc=Company
objectClass: ipService
objectClass: top
ipServicePort: 21
ipServiceProtocol: udp
ipServiceProtocol: tcp
cn: ftp
cn: fspd
cn: fsp

dn: cn=ssh,ou=Services,dc=Your,dc=Company
objectClass: ipService
objectClass: top
ipServicePort: 22
ipServiceProtocol: udp
ipServiceProtocol: tcp
cn: ssh

dn: cn=telnet,ou=Services,dc=Your,dc=Company
objectClass: ipService
objectClass: top
ipServicePort: 23
ipServiceProtocol: udp
ipServiceProtocol: tcp
cn: telnet

dn: cn=smtp,ou=Services,dc=Your,dc=Company
objectClass: ipService
objectClass: top
ipServicePort: 25
ipServiceProtocol: udp
ipServiceProtocol: tcp
cn: smtp
cn: mail
```

```
dn: cn=cfengine,ou=Services,dc=Your,dc=Company
objectClass: ipService
objectClass: top
ipServicePort: 5308
ipServiceProtocol: udp
ipServiceProtocol: tcp
cn: cfengine
```

Although the most relevant information from the file is shown in LDIF format, you can see that some comments that were included in the original no longer exist. It may be beneficial, especially for the sake of less-seasoned system administrators, to add comments and descriptions back into the LDIF. You can use these fields, while not necessary for system-level applications, in any interfaces that you create for retrieving and administering this information.

Configuring the LDAP Client (Host)

You'll need to configure each system that will rely on information from LDAP as a client. Even the server that will be authoritative for this LDAP information will need to be configured as a client accessing itself. You'll need to start by modifying the /etc/ldap.conf configuration file that's present in your Linux host.

```
# @(#)$Id: ldap.conf,v 1.24 2001/09/20 14:12:26 lukeh Exp $
#
# This is the configuration file for the LDAP nameservice
# switch library and the LDAP PAM module.
#
# PADL Software
# http://www.padl.com
#

# Your LDAP server. Must be resolvable without using LDAP.
host 127.0.0.1
```

Your LDAP host will be the value of the host directive. It's a good idea to standardize the configuration of your ldap.conf file. Even if you're making configurations on the master LDAP system (and the host will be binding to itself), you should specify the specific IP address of the LDAP system itself. Relying on local won't work on other systems in your environment.

```
# The distinguished name of the search base.
base dc=example,dc=com
```

For these purposes, you'll be specifying the base directive as dc=Your,dc=Company.

```
# Another way to specify your LDAP server is to provide an
# uri with the server name. This allows to use
# Unix Domain Sockets to connect to a local LDAP Server.
#uri ldap://127.0.0.1/
#uri ldaps://127.0.0.1/
#uri ldapi://%2fvar%2frun%2fldapi_sock/
# Note: %2f encodes the '/' used as directory separator
```

The configuration files support various methods of specifying the LDAP system to which you'll be connecting. Additionally, you can use and expand the uri directive and notation to increase the scope of your LDAP searches.

```
# The LDAP version to use (defaults to 3
# if supported by client library)
#ldap_version 3
```

The default version of the LDAP protocol you'll be using is LDAPv3.

```
# The distinguished name to bind to the server with.
# Optional: default is to bind anonymously.
#binddn cn=proxyuser,dc=example,dc=com
```

```
# The credentials to bind with.
# Optional: default is no credential.
#bindpw secret
```

```
# The distinguished name to bind to the server with
# if the effective user ID is root. Password is
# stored in /etc/ldap.secret (mode 600)
#rootbinddn cn=manager,dc=example,dc=com
```

Because LDAP integration replaces the standard mechanisms of reading local files and databases on your Unix system, you have the ability to increase the security of your system profiles. Where traditional files that you're migrating are world-readable by design, thus giving everyone access to this information, LDAP allows you to restrict this information to be readable only by certain bind DNs in your system. However, by default, an anonymous query can retrieve this information.

The rootbinddn directive sets the LDAP equivalent of root on your host. This DN will, by default, give someone with the password excessive access rights on your host. While the password for this DN is protected by file permissions, storing this information on multiple hosts isn't advised because your LDAP environment, with its control over many new things, may be compromised. This can lead to a cracker having full control over your environment, and it defeats many of the benefits of using new security features in LDAP. The primary reasons this account and password are configured are to be able to perform certain privileged system operations, such as changing passwords, and performing more significant system configurations. During integration, it's a good idea to log the operations that this account is performing and create individual user accounts (tied to the host) with access controls that allow these operations. For example, on LDAPSLAVE10, the rootbinddn may be cn=ldapslave10-manager,dc=your,dc=compancn=ldapslave10-manager,dc=your,dc=company. That way, operations you see while auditing log files show you where any questionable operations originated. This suggestion applies to any superuser accounts you may need to use.

You can also omit this configuration option on many client machines. You can specify the root account only on certain trusted hosts with increased host security and a controlled environment of administrators.

```
# The port.
# Optional: default is 389.
#port 389
# The search scope.
#scope sub
#scope one
#scope base
```

The LDAP port and search specifications are also definable within the configuration file.

```
# Search timelimit
#timelimit 30

# Bind timelimit
#bind_timelimit 30
```

You can modify time limits for your LDAP binds and transactions within the configuration file to allow you to tune your system appropriately.

```
# Idle timelimit; client will close connections
# (nss_ldap only) if the server has not been contacted
# for the number of seconds specified below.
#idle_timelimit 3600
```

Because the greatest overhead in a network transaction is establishing the original connectivity, clients often establish one (or more) connections to the remote host and keep the connection alive. This will typically increase system performance. However, if a connection has been idle for a certain amount of time, it's a good idea to refresh the connection by closing it and reopening it again. In some buggy interfaces, the connection is often still open but no longer able to retrieve LDAP information.

```
# Filter to AND with uid=%s
#pam_filter objectclass=account

# The user ID attribute (defaults to uid)
#pam_login_attribute uid
```

User profiles within LDAP will differ depending on your environment. As I demonstrated during the migration of standard user profiles, the base configurations of a system won't always work. You're able to, within the ldap.conf configuration file, specify how a user is defined and what attribute will be used to log into a system. The generic uid attribute, in the existing environment, won't always translate directly to the login name within a Linux host. You may see that the uid attribute is used as a generic profile identifier, and the loginname attribute may be used to define the Linux login name. You can specify these parameters as follows:

```
# Search the root DSE for the password policy (works
# with Netscape Directory Server)
#pam_lookup_policy yes
```

```
# Check the 'host' attribute for access control
# Default is no; if set to yes, and user has no
# value for the host attribute, and pam_ldap is
# configured for account management (authorization)
# then the user will not be allowed to login.
#pam_check_host_attr yes

# Group to enforce membership of
#pam_groupdn cn=PAM,ou=Groups,dc=example,dc=com

# Group member attribute
#pam_member_attribute uniquemember
```

The pam_groupdn directive is useful when an LDAP server provides authentication information to a pool of clients but only when the user should be authorized on a set of clients. This directive can provide the same functionality of NIS netgroups, as shown in Listing 7-13.

Listing 7-13. *PAM Configurations*

```
# Specify a minimum or maximum UID number allowed
#pam_min_uid 0
#pam_max_uid 0

# Template login attribute, default template user
# (can be overridden by value of former attribute
# in user's entry)
#pam_login_attribute userPrincipalName
#pam_template_login_attribute uid
#pam_template_login nobody

# HEADS UP: the pam_crypt, pam_nds_passwd,
# and pam_ad_passwd options are no
# longer supported.

# Do not hash the password at all; presume
# the directory server will do it, if
# necessary. This is the default.
#pam_password clear

# Hash password locally; required for University of
# Michigan LDAP server, and works with Netscape
# Directory Server if you're using the UNIX-Crypt
# hash mechanism and not using the NT Synchronization
# service.
#pam_password crypt
# Remove old password first, then update in
# cleartext. Necessary for use with Novell
# Directory Services (NDS)
#pam_password nds
```

```
# Update Active Directory password, by
# creating Unicode password and updating
# unicodePwd attribute.
#pam_password ad

# Use the OpenLDAP password change
# extended operation to update the password.
#pam_password exop
```

PAM-specific configurations are also made within the ldap.conf configuration file. Within these PAM configurations, you specify values to enable your systems to function appropriately. One issue that you'll encounter during configuration in a centralized environment is that if multiple passwords are used across systems, a good chance exists that multiple formats for storing these passwords are being used. Imagine the scenario where you have a legacy system that stores information on {crypt}, and newer systems rely on {SSHA}. While newer systems may have the ability to read multiple formats, the legacy systems would instantly be confused (and stop functioning) if the password they encounter is stored in a format that isn't understood. Verify the methods of encryption that each of your systems uses, and determine a common denominator that's functional across the greatest number of systems, as shown in Listing 7-14.

Listing 7-14. *NSS Configurations*

```
# RFC2307bis naming contexts
# Syntax:
# nss_base_XXX          base?scope?filter
# where scope is {base,one,sub}
# and filter is a filter to be &'d with the
# default filter.
# You can omit the suffix eg:
# nss_base_passwd       ou=People,
# to append the default base DN but this
# may incur a small performance impact.
#nss_base_passwd        ou=People,dc=example,dc=com?one
#nss_base_shadow        ou=People,dc=example,dc=com?one
#nss_base_group         ou=Group,dc=example,dc=com?one
#nss_base_hosts         ou=Hosts,dc=example,dc=com?one
#nss_base_services      ou=Services,dc=example,dc=com?one
#nss_base_networks      ou=Networks,dc=example,dc=com?one
#nss_base_protocols     ou=Protocols,dc=example,dc=com?one
#nss_base_rpc           ou=Rpc,dc=example,dc=com?one
#nss_base_ethers        ou=Ethers,dc=example,dc=com?one
#nss_base_netmasks      ou=Networks,dc=example,dc=com?ne
#nss_base_bootparams    ou=Ethers,dc=example,dc=com?one
#nss_base_aliases       ou=Aliases,dc=example,dc=com?one
#nss_base_netgroup      ou=Netgroup,dc=example,dc=com?one
```

This section relates directly to the containers that were created during the migration process. It allows you to move configurations elsewhere if the default configurations being used don't work for your environment. However, if integrating LDAP with other applications is necessary, it's good to use the defaults. Other applications can hard-code these location values within their configurations. Storing these organizational units deep within an LDAP tree may create unnecessary complexity.

The ?one flag at the end of the container defines the search scope being used for each of the searches being performed. This is helpful because a global search scope won't be easily used on all systems, especially those with flatter namespaces and larger databases.

Listing 7-15 shows how to map data between NSS and PAM objects to attributes and object classes within the directory.

Listing 7-15. *Mapping Information*

```
# attribute/objectclass mapping
# Syntax:
#nss_map_attribute      rfc2307attribute      mapped_attribute
#nss_map_objectclass    rfc2307objectclass    mapped_objectclass


# configure --enable-nds is no longer supported.
# For NDS now do:
#nss_map_attribute uniqueMember member

# configure --enable-mssfu-schema is no longer supported.
# For MSSFU now do:
#nss_map_objectclass posixAccount User
#nss_map_attribute uid msSFUName
#nss_map_attribute uniqueMember posixMember
#nss_map_attribute userPassword msSFUPassword
#nss_map_attribute homeDirectory msSFUHomeDirectory
#nss_map_objectclass posixGroup Group
#pam_login_attribute msSFUName
#pam_filter objectclass=User
#pam_password ad

# configure --enable-authpassword is no longer supported
# For authPassword support, now do:
#nss_map_attribute userPassword authPassword
#pam_password nds
# For IBM SecureWay support, do:
#nss_map_objectclass posixAccount aixAccount
#nss_map_attribute uid userName
#nss_map_attribute gidNumber gid
#nss_map_attribute uidNumber uid
#nss_map_attribute userPassword passwordChar
#nss_map_objectclass posixGroup aixAccessGroup
#nss_map_attribute cn groupName
#nss_map_attribute uniqueMember member
#pam_login_attribute userName
#pam_filter objectclass=aixAccount
#pam_password clear
```

As I discussed earlier, the default attributes used for information may not be relevant for your system configuration, and it may be necessary to change the attributes that are being used to store certain information. Listing 7-16 shows the configurations you'll need to modify in order to utilize some of the security features of OpenLDAP.

Listing 7-16. *Security Configurations*

```
# Netscape SDK LDAPS
#ssl on

# Netscape SDK SSL options
#sslpath /etc/ssl/certs/cert7.db

# OpenLDAP SSL mechanism
# start_tls mechanism uses the normal LDAP port, LDAPS typically 636
#ssl start_tls
#ssl on

# OpenLDAP SSL options
# Require and verify server certificate (yes/no)
# Default is "no"
#tls_checkpeer yes

# CA certificates for server certificate verification
# At least one of these are required if tls_checkpeer is "yes"
#tls_cacertfile /etc/ssl/ca.cert
#tls_cacertdir /etc/ssl/certs

# SSL cipher suite
# See man ciphers for syntax
#tls_ciphers TLSv1

# Client certificate and key
# Use these, if your server requires client authentication.
#tls_cert
#tls_key
ssl no
pam_password md5
```

You can use other configuration options to enable Secure Sockets Layer (SSL) and Transport Layer Security (TLS) if these are used within your environment.

Using the ldapclient Utility

You can use the ldapclient utility to initialize LDAP client machines, restore network service environment on LDAP clients, and list the contents of the LDAP client cache in human-readable format. This utility can output the appropriate LDIF files for initialization of an LDAP client or can directly connect to specific hosts and make the configurations for you.

```
/usr/sbin/ldapclient [-v| -q] init [-a proxyName=profile] \
[-adomainName=domain] [-a proxyDN=proxyDN] [-a proxyPassword=password] \
[-a certificatePath=path] LDAP_server_addr[:port_number]
/usr/sbin/ldapclient [-v| -q] manual [-a attrName=attrVal]
/usr/sbin/ldapclient [-v| -q] mod [-a attrName=attrVal]
/usr/sbin/ldapclient [-v| -q] list
/usr/sbin/ldapclient [-v| -q] uninit
/usr/sbin/ldapclient [-v| -q] genprofile -a profileName=profileName
[-a attrName=attrVal]
```

You can run the utility in the init, manual, or mod form. In the init form, ldapclient retrieves profile information from an LDAP server (specified by the server_addr parameter) and makes the appropriate changes in the configurations for functionality. In manual mode, the configuration options for the host configuration are specified on the command line, and profiles that may existing in your LDAP server aren't used. You can use the mod mode to make changes to a host that has already been configured using the manual directive. If any file is modified during installation, it will be backed up to /var/ldap/restore. The files that are typically modified during initialization are the same ones that would be modified during any NIS or NIS+ initialization. These files are as follows:

- /etc/nsswitch.conf

- /etc/defaultdomain (if it exists)

- /var/yp/binding/`domainname` (for an NIS or YP client)

- /var/nis/NIS_COLD_START (for an NIS+ client)

- /var/ldap/ldap_client_file (for an existing LDAP client)

- /var/ldap/ldap_client_cred (for an existing LDAP client)

The list form of the ldapclient utility is used to list the LDAP client configuration. The output will be human readable. LDAP configuration files are typically readable except by LDAP administrators.

The uninit form of the ldapclient utility uninitializes the network service environment, restoring it to the state it was in prior to the last execution of ldapclient using init or manual. The restoration will succeed only if the machine was initialized with the init or manual form of ldapclient, as it uses the backup files created by these options.

The genprofile option writes an LDIF-formatted configuration profile based on the attributes specified on the command line to standard output. This profile can then be loaded into an LDAP server to be used as the client profile, which can be downloaded by means of the ldapclient init command. You can load the LDIF-formatted profile to the directory server through ldapadd (1) or through any server-specific import tool.

To access the information stored in the directory, clients can either authenticate to the directory or use an unauthenticated connection. The LDAP client is configured to have a credential level of either anonymous or proxy. In the first case, the client doesn't authenticate to the directory. In the second case, client authenticates to the directory using a proxy identity.

The following command-line modes (as discussed previously) for the ldapclient utility are supported:

- `init`: Initialize client from a profile on a server.

- `manual`: Manually initialize the client with the specified attribute values.

- `mod`: Modify attribute values in the configuration file after a manual initialization of the client.

- `list`: Write the contents of the LDAP client cache to standard output in human-readable form.

- `uninit`: Uninitialize an LDAP client, assuming that `ldapclient` was used to initialize the client.

- `genprofile`: Generate a configuration profile in LDIF format that can then be stored in the directory for clients to use, with the `init` form of this command.

The following attributes are supported:

`AttributeMap`: This specifies a mapping from an attribute defined by a service to an attribute in an alternative schema. You can use this to change the default schema used for a given service. The syntax of `attributeMap` is defined in the profile Internet Engineers Task Force (IETF) draft. You can specify this option multiple times. The default value for all services is `NULL`. In the example `attributeMap: passwd:uid=employeeNumber`, the LDAP client would use the LDAP attribute `employeeNumber` rather than `uid` for the `passwd` service. This is a multivalued attribute.

`AuthenticationMethod`: This specifies the default authentication method used by all services unless overridden by the `serviceAuthenticationMethod` attribute. You can specify multiple values, using a comma-separated list. The default value is `none`. For those services that use `credentialLevel` and `credentialLevel` of anonymous, this attribute is ignored. Services such as `pam_ldap` will use this attribute, even if `credentialLevel` is anonymous. The supported authentication methods were described previously.

`BindTimeLimit`: This is the maximum time in seconds that a client should spend performing a bind operation. Set this to a positive integer. The default value is 30.

`CertificatePath`: This is the certificate path for the location of the certificate database. The value is the path where security database files reside. This is used for TLS support, which is specified in the `authenticationMethod` and `serviceAuthenticationMethod` attributes. The default is `/var/ldap`.

`CredentialLevel`: This specifies the credential level the client should use to contact the directory. The credential levels supported are either anonymous or proxy. If a proxy credential level is specified, then the `authenticationMethod` attribute must be specified to determine the authentication mechanism. Further, if the credential level is proxy and at least one of the authentication methods requires a bind DN, the `proxyDN` and `proxyPassword` attribute values must be set.

`DefaultSearchBase`: This specifies the default search base DN. This has no default. You can use the `serviceSearchDescriptor` attribute to override `defaultSearchBase` for given services.

defaultSearchScope=one | sub: This specifies the default search scope for the client's search operations. This default can be overridden for a given service by specifying a serviceSearchDescriptor. The default is a one-level search.

DomainName: This specifies the DNS domain name. This becomes the default domain for the machine. The default is the current domain name. This attribute is used only in client initialization.

followReferrals=true | false: This specifies the referral setting. A setting of true implies that referrals will be automatically followed; false results in referrals not being followed. The default is true.

ObjectclassMap: This specifies a mapping from an objectclass defined by a service to an objectclass in an alternative schema. You can use this to change the default schema used for a given service. The syntax of objectclassMap is defined in the profile IETF draft. You can specify this option multiple times. The default value for all services is NULL. In the example, objectclassMap=passwd:posixAccount=unixAccount, the LDAP client would use the LDAP objectclass of unixAccount rather than the posixAccount for the passwd service. This is a multivalued attribute.

PreferredServerList: This specifies the space-separated list of preferred server IP addresses to be contacted before servers specified by the defaultServerList attribute. The port number is optional. If not specified, the default LDAP server port number 389 is used, except when TLS is specified in the authentication method. In this case, the default LDAP server port number is 636. You can also use fully qualified hostnames. If you use fully qualified hostnames, you must configure nsswitch.conf to use files or DNS, not LDAP, to resolve host lookup. If you fail to configure nsswitch.conf properly, then your system or certain processes can hang if you use a hostname value.

ProfileName: This specifies the profile name. For ldapclient init, this attribute is the name of an existing profile that may be downloaded periodically depending on the value of the profileTTL attribute. For ldapclient genprofile, this is the name of the profile to be generated. The default value is default.

ProfileTTL: This specifies the TTL value in seconds for the client information. This is relevant only if the machine was initialized with a client profile. If you don't want ldap_cachemgr (1M) to attempt to refresh the LDAP client configuration from the LDAP server, set profileTTL to zero. Valid values are either zero (for no expiration) or a positive integer in seconds. The default value is 12 hours.

ProxyDN: This specifies the bind DN for the proxy identity. This option is required if the credential level is proxy and at least one of the authentication methods requires a bind DN. It has no default value.

ProxyPassword: This specifies the client proxy password. This option is required if the credential level is proxy and at least one of the authentication methods requires a bind DN. It has no default.

SearchTimeLimit: This specifies the maximum number of seconds allowed for an LDAP search operation. The default is 30 seconds. The server may have its own search time limit.

ServiceAuthenticationMethod: This specifies authentication methods to be used by a service. You can specify multiple values with a comma-separated list. The default value is no service authentication methods, in which case each service would default to the authenticationMethod value. The supported authentications were described previously. Three services support this feature: passwd-cmd, keyserv, and pam_ldap. The passwd-cmd service defines the authentication method to be used by passwd (1) to change the user's password and other attributes. The keyserv service identifies the authentication method to be used by the chkey (1) and newkey (1M) utilities. The pam_ldap service defines the authentication method to be used for authenticating users when pam_ldap (5) is configured. If this attribute isn't set for any of these services, the authenticationMethod attribute defines the authentication method. This is a multivalued attribute.

ServiceCredentialLevel: This specifies the credential level to be used by a service. You can specify multiple values in a space-separated list. The default value for all services is NULL. The supported credential levels are anonymous or proxy. At present, no service uses this attribute. This is a multivalued attribute.

ServiceSearchDescriptor: This overrides the default base DN for LDAP searches for a given service. The format of the descriptors also allows you to override the default search scope and search filter for each service. The syntax of serviceSearchDescriptor is defined in the profile IETF draft. The default value for all services is NULL. This is a multivalued attribute. In the example serviceSearchDescriptor=passwd:ou=people,dc=a1,dc=acme,dc=com?one, the LDAP client would do a one-level search in the ou=people,dc=a1,dc=acme,dc=com service rather than the ou=people,defaultSearchBase for the passwd service.

The ldapclient utility supports the following command-line options:

- -a: Specify attrName and its value.

- -q: Quiet mode. No output is generated.

- -v: Verbose output.

It supports the following operands:

DefaultServerList: This is a space-separated list of server IP addresses. The port number is optional. If not specified, the default LDAP server port number 389 is used except when TLS is specified in the authentication method, in which case the default LDAP server port number is 636.

You can also use fully qualified hostnames. If you use fully qualified hostnames, you must configure nsswitch.conf to use files or DNS, not LDAP, to resolve host lookup. If you fail to configure nsswitch.conf properly, then your system or certain processes can hang if you use a hostname value.

To initialize a new host using the default profile stored on your LDAP service (at 192.168.10.10), you'd use the following command.

```
example# ldapclient init 192.169.10.10
```

The following example shows how to set up a client using only one server. The authentication method is set to none, and the search base is set to dc=Your,dc=Company.

```
example# ldapclient manual -a authenticationMethod=none \
-a defaultSearchBase=dc=Your,dc=Company \
-a defaultServerList=192.168.10.10
```

The following example shows how to set up a client using only one server. The credential level is set to proxy. The authentication method of is sasl/CRAM_MD5, with the option not to follow referrals. The domain name is domainname.YourCompany.com, and the LDAP server is running on port number 386 at IP address 192.168.10.10.

```
example# ldapclient manual \
-a credentialLevel=proxy \
-a authenticationMethod=sasl/CRAM_MD5 \
-a proxyPassword=secret \
-a proxyDN=cn=proxyagent,ou=profile,dc=domainname,dc=Your,dc=Company \
-a defaultSearchBase=dc=domainname,dc=Your,dc=Company \
-a domainName=domainname.YourCompany.com \
-a followReferrals=false \
-a defaultServerList=192.168.10.10:386
```

Configuring NSS

Your host needs to be configured, via Name Service Switch, to use LDAP. Your base configuration is stored in /etc/nsswitch.conf. The default file on a system within LDAP could look like the following:

```
passwd:    db files nisplus nis
shadow:    db files nisplus nis
group:     db files nisplus nis
hosts:     nisplus [NOTFOUND=return] files dns
```

This configuration tells your host where to look for various types of information. For example, it looks for a host via nisplus, then local files, and then dns. The NOTFOUND option lets you stop if the previous option wasn't returned. To reduce your master server's dependency on network services, its critical systems (and itself) should be stored within the /etc/hosts file. If certain critical hosts in your environment, such as LDAP slaves, aren't in this file, you'll have too much dependency on DNS and other network services for your environment to function. Reducing this dependency also speeds up certain operations. This is advised only for static data, because many configurations are dynamic and cause conflict if there are IP conflicts because of external DNS changes.

For your system to know to use LDAP to retrieve information, you add the line ldap to your configuration file. The resulting file looks like the following:

```
passwd:    ldap files
shadow:    ldap files
group:     ldap files
hosts:     ldap dns [NOTFOUND=return] files dns
```

The basic idea is to use LDAP whenever the information is available and to fall back on other sources of data if it's not. The specific options to use within this file depend on services available within your environment, which is the authoritative source for information. Retrieving host information via LDAP may not be the best thing for your particular environment. The specific search order also depends on how services are configured, because NIS may be the authoritative source for some users with LDAP storing information only for certain external users or role accounts.

Because pure LDAP integration with products is relatively new, consider integration with the existing migration tools and software optional, not a requirement. That is, just because you can do something using LDAP, it may not always be the best option for you. DNS, for example, has established tools and a proven set of APIs that already work well. Moving this information to LDAP may not give you any benefits. Certain flat text files that are relatively static (but may be appended during patches or operating system upgrades) are already maintained well as files. Administrators rarely modify these files manually. Therefore, storing this data via LDAP (and having hosts rely on this data) may conflict with system patches and system upgrades, as no mechanisms currently exist that update these files via LDAP.

Configuring PAM

You'll be making many system modifications in order to utilize PAM LDAP modules. The configuration file for the pam_ldap.so module is /etc/pam_ldap.conf.

```
Ldaphost$ cat /etc/pam_ldap.conf
uri ldaps://ldap.example.com/
base dc=example,dc=com
pam_password exop
```

The uri directive points PAM to your LDAP server. Your base DN is configured using the base directive. The directive pam_password exop tells pam-ldap to change passwords in a way that allows OpenLDAP to apply the hashing algorithm specified in /etc/ldap/slapd.conf, instead of attempting to hash locally and write the result directly into the database.

The base configurations for PAM are stored in /etc/pam.d. They define the libraries and other information necessary for utilizing various system services, such as authentication. The base configuration file on your existing Linux system may look like this:

```
#%PAM-1.0
auth       required      /lib/security/pam_env.so
auth       sufficient    /lib/security/pam_unix.so likeauth nullok
auth       required      /lib/security/pam_deny.so
auth       required      /lib/security/pam_nologin.so
account    required      /lib/security/pam_unix.so
password   required      /lib/security/pam_cracklib.so retry=3 type=
password   sufficient    /lib/security/pam_unix.so nullok use_authtok md5 shadow
password   required      /lib/security/pam_deny.so

session    required      /lib/security/pam_limits.so
session    required      /lib/security/pam_unix.so
```

To give LDAP capabilities to your hosts via PAM requires modification of the /etc/pam.d/ system-auth configuration file. The basic idea is to use pam_ldap.so for functions that will utilize LDAP, as follows:

```
auth          sufficient    /lib/security/pam_ldap.so use_first_pass
```

Add this line after the base configurations that already exist. In the case of auth, you'd add it before the last deny line.

```
auth          required      /lib/security/pam_deny.so
```

You append the account directive as follows upon the addition of LDAP support:

```
account       required      /lib/security/pam_unix.so
account       sufficient    /lib/security/pam_ldap.so
```

The other directives may look like the following upon completion:

```
password      required      /lib/security/pam_cracklib.so retry=3 \
minlen=4 dcredit=0 ucredit=0
password      sufficient    /lib/security/pam_unix.so nullok use_authtok md5 shadow
password      sufficient    /lib/security/pam_ldap.so use_authtok
password      required      /lib/security/pam_deny.so

session       required      /lib/security/pam_limits.so
session       required      /lib/security/pam_unix.so
session       optional      /lib/security/pam_ldap.so
```

These configurations insert LDAP support via pam_ldap.so so that it's utilized during certain system procedures. Much like older NIS configurations, you're able to utilize local files first and then retrieve additional information using LDAP. Additional modules exist that will add other functionality to your system. PAM serves as a great solution for customizing system authentication methods that were previously hard-coded. Upon configuring PAM to use LDAP, software that supports PAM will be able to use LDAP. Viewing system and LDAP logs to verify how certain software components utilize this and what data they require may be necessary when issues arise. You may require some attributes that you haven't defined in your schema for certain software and that would be queried unsuccessfully against your LDAP host. Legacy software won't be able to utilize PAM and will react strangely to your new system configurations.

Specific configurations related to specific system services and function are included in /etc/pam.d as well. The passwd command, for example, utilizes /etc/pam.d/passwd, and sudo utilizes /etc/pam.d/sudo. You also need to insert the pam_ldap.so value into these specific files to enable these programs to utilize LDAP. You need to add new lines for all the directives (auth, account, password, and session) to reference new information much in the same way they were inserted in the base configuration file.

Setting Up Security

When implementing any centralized authentication system, control of authentication and authorization is passed onto the new system. Security products, such as those available from RSA, need to take this into account. Before, a user could be added and removed from local password files, but this is no longer the case. Base configurations allow any user able to authenticate to log into any host that utilizes these centralized systems. PAM allows you to modify the /etc/ldap.conf configuration file to check for attributes that control host access. You need to add the following line:

```
pam_check_host_attr yes
```

This option will, upon user authentication, check for the host attribute within a user's LDAP profile to see if the Fully Qualified Domain Name (FQDN) of the specific hosts exists. While not necessary for all hosts, systems that require a higher security level benefit from this option. Be careful in the case of users with no host attributes, because you could be denying them access to all servers. You can create manual functions to manage these scenarios.

Additionally, because information is now stored in LDAP, you should apply access controls to allow only specific accounts and hosts to retrieve certain information via LDAP.

Using Sendmail

Sendmail is the most popular Mail Transfer Agent (MTA) in use today. An MTA transfers mail between computers and starts working as soon as your Mail User Agent (MUA) sends a message. Sendmail, qmail, and Postfix are examples of popular MTAs that are probably used within your company. Microsoft Outlook, Eudora, and pine are examples of MUAs. In corporate environments, it's common to have a single system that has the capabilities (though separate) of an MUA and MTA. Lotus Notes is an example of such a system. Because of the popularity of sendmail and its historical dependence on flat files stored on the server, I'll discuss integrating this MTA with OpenLDAP.

In a traditional Sendmail environment, information associated with the lookup and routing of user Simple Mail Transfer Protocol (SMTP) information has been individually stored on each Sendmail server in the form of database maps or flat files. While this doesn't pose a problem for a single server, multiple Sendmail services had to somehow keep these files in synchronization with each other or required the e-mail administrator to update these files on each server individually. LDAP enables Sendmail to access a cross-platform, standards-based central repository of user information. Another key benefit of LDAP is that now companies can use standards-based tools, using almost any development language that's LDAP-enabled, to create a customized directory of information for company-wide access by all applications (not limited to e-mail).

Additionally, e-mail systems (in the world of TCP/IP) were quite primitive and didn't allow for the advanced routing of e-mails. When a mail to Tom_Jackiewicz@host1.YourCompany.com was sent, host1.YourCompany.com accepted the message, and the process was over. As e-mail systems scaled and more hosts were added, the routing of the message was contained within your e-mail address. This led to Susan_Surapruik@host25.YourCompany.com. This became a hassle and custom solutions were developed to allow for all people to exist at @YourCompany.com without having specific routing information contained within the e-mail address. One of the first standard ways of doing this was with LDAP. Using LDAP, a standard mail exchange (MX) record could be set up for a single domain, and routing was performed internally, without requiring the sender to have any knowledge of the routing required for a mail message to end up in the recipient's mailbox.

Figure 7-2 shows "modern" mail routing as it existed before LDAP became an integral component of e-mail systems. (Note that I won't discuss legacy X.400 and X.500 electronic mail systems in this chapter.)

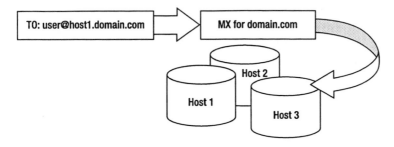

Figure 7-2. *"Modern" mail routing*

In this example, e-mail is sent to a user at a specific host. The MX for this domain (or for that specific host) is contacted, and e-mail is routed to the final destination. It was necessary for the sender to know which host the recipient existed on in order for the mail to be handled appropriately. If e-mail for user@host1.domain.com was mistakenly sent to user@host2.domain.com, the message would be invalid and inappropriately handled. Enabling LDAP support within Sendmail allowed you to store alias maps and other information used to route e-mail within your central directory.

Enabling the Software

You need to verify that the Sendmail you'll be working with is compiled with support for LDAP. To do this, execute the following command:

```
$ sendmail -d0.1 -bv root
Version 8.12.8
 Compiled with: DNSMAP HESIOD HES_GETMAILHOST LDAPMAP LOG MAP_REGEX
                MATCHGECOS MILTER MIME7TO8 MIME8TO7 NAMED_BIND NETINET NETINET6
                NETUNIX NEWDB NIS PIPELINING SASL SCANF STARTTLS TCPWRAPPERS
                USERDB USE_LDAP_INIT


============ SYSTEM IDENTITY (after readcf) ============
      (short domain name) $w = ldaphost
  (canonical domain name) $j = ldaphost.yourcompany.com
         (subdomain name) $m = yourcompany.com
              (node name) $k = ldaphost.yourcompany.com
=======================================================


Notice: -bv may give misleading output for non-privileged user
can not chdir(/var/spool/mqueue/): Permission denied
Program mode requires special privileges, e.g., root or TrustedUser.
$
```

In the output, you can see that the version of Sendmail you're working with has been compiled with LDAPMAP, which gives you native support for LDAP.

To compile Sendmail with LDAP support, do this:

```
APPENDDEF(`confMAPDEF', `-DLDAPMAP')
APPENDDEF(`confINCDIRS', `-I/path/to/openldap-1.2.11/include')
APPENDDEF(`confLIBSDIRS', `-L/path/to/openldap-1.2.11/libraries')
APPENDDEF(`confLIBS', `-lldap -llber')
```

The first line tells Sendmail to include the -DldapMAP option in the build process. The second and third lines tell Sendmail where to find the OpenLDAP include and libraries directories so that the necessary files can be located while building the Sendmail executable.

The following is the base configuration you need to add to your sendmail.mc configuration file:

```
LDAPROUTE_DOMAIN('yourcompany.com')dnl
Define(confLDAP_DEFAULT_SPEC,
-h ldap.yourcompany.com
-b dc=yourcompany.com
```

To define a group of hosts, use this:

```
Define(`confLDAP_CLUSTER', `Servers')
```

To enable LDAP aliases, use this:

```
Define(`ALIAS_FILE', `ldap:')
```

To enable other lookups, use this:

```
FEATURE(`access_db', `LDAP')
FEATURE(`virtusertable', `LDAP')
```

To enable classes, use this:

```
RELAY_DOMAIN_FILE(`@LDAP')
```

Invoke Sendmail in test mode to verify that the LDAP maps are being processed correctly. You can do this while Sendmail is running in daemon mode with no problems.

```
example: sendmail -bt
```

Sendmail will return a > prompt and wait for user input. Use /parse jradford@foo.com, and observe the last line Sendmail returns. The final result is a triple returning the mailer, host, and recipient, as follows:

```
mailer esmtp, host mailhost1.foo.com, user my_user@foo.com
```

The mailer is esmtp (or smtp), the host is mailhost1.foo.com (as set by the mail host's LASER attribute for the jradford entry), and the final username (as set by the mailroutingaddress LASER attribute) is the clean e-mail address of the user within your domain, such as tom@yourcompany.com. The returned mail host DNS name will now be looked up in DNS for valid MX records and be delivered based upon these returned values from DNS. To exit from test mode, simply press Ctrl+D.

Building the Binaries

From the root of the Sendmail archive, execute the `build` command to compile the Sendmail binaries and the appropriate support programs. You should see the `-dldapMAP` and `-lldap -llber` options on the command line while Sendmail is compiling.

```
[root@ldap02 sendmail-8.12.11]# pwd
/usr/src/sendmail-8.12.11
[root@ldap02 sendmail-8.12.11]# ./Build
Making all in:
/usr/src/sendmail-8.12.11/libsm
...
```

Migrating Information

During the migration of basic system information earlier, you already migrated various alias information into your system. The /etc/aliases file you migrated looked like the following:

```
dn: cn=mailer-daemon,ou=Aliases,dc=Your,dc=Company
cn: mailer-daemon
objectClass: nisMailAlias
objectClass: top
rfc822MailMember: postmaster

dn: cn=postmaster,ou=Aliases,dc=Your,dc=Company
cn: postmaster
objectClass: nisMailAlias
objectClass: top
rfc822MailMember: root

dn: cn=testuser,ou=Aliases,dc=Your,dc=Company
cn: testuser
objectClass: nisMailAlias
objectClass: top
rfc822MailMember: tom@sun4c.net
```

By initially defining the `ALIAS_FILE` directive with a pointer to LDAP, you enable the default search that Sendmail performs.

```
define(`ALIAS_FILE', `ldap:')
```

This creates the default search parameters as follows:

```
ldap -k (&(objectClass=sendmailMTAAliasObject)
              (sendmailMTAAliasGrouping=aliases)
              (|(sendmailMTACluster=${sendmailMTACluster})
                (sendmailMTAHost=$j))
              (sendmailMTAKey=%0))
          -v sendmailMTAAliasValue
```

You can see that the object classes that were migrated were generic, but the format was clear. Other data files that Sendmail is familiar with are similar. The following is a base example:

```
dn: sendmailMTAKey=postmaster,dc=Your,dc=Company
objectclass: sendmailMTA
objectclass: sendmailMTAAlias
objectclass: sendmailMTAAliasObject
sendmailMTAAliasGrouping: aliases
sendmailMTACluster: Servers
sendmailMTAKey: postmaster
sendmailMTAAlias: tjackiewicz

dn: sendmailMTAKey=testuser,dc=Your,dc=Company
objectclass: sendmailMTA
objectclass: sendmailMTAAlias
objectclass: sendmailMTAAliasObject
sendmailMTAAliasGrouping: aliases
sendmailMTACluster: Servers
sendmailMTAKey: testuser
sendmailMTAAlias: tom@sun4c.net
```

While avoiding a conflict, you have the flexibility of taking the existing set of information that has been migrated and appending the object classes that Sendmail understands. Or, you could modify the search filters used within Sendmail to perform searches based on the information you've already populated into your system. You can expand the definitions beyond Sendmail's own way of using LDAP by modifying the initial definitions. You do this as follows:

```
define(`ALIAS_FILE', `ldap:-k (&(objectClass=nisMailAlias) \
(mail=%0)) -v mgr pRFC822MailMember')
```

This will create a custom search that Sendmail will then perform to obtain the appropriate set of DNs that will be used for aliases. Although in the default example Sendmail expected certain values, you can consider this a suggestion and use your own schema. The new definition you've created will search for the object class of nisMailAlias that you created during migration.

Besides aliases and users, Sendmail uses other data for storing routing and delivery information that it will use internally. Table 7-1 lists all Sendmail maps.

Table 7-1. *Values for* sendmailMTAMapName

FEATURE()	sendmailMTAMapName
access_db	access
authinfo	authinfo
bitdomain	bitdomain
domaintable	domain
genericstable	generics
mailertable	mailer
uucpdomain	uucpdomain
virtusertable	virtuser

Each feature of Sendmail and the maps will expand to a base definition that can, as you saw with the alias data, be used as-is or modified to be more compliant with your system infrastructure.

By setting FEATURE(`mailertable', `LDAP'), the following sendmailMTAMap would be used:

```
Kmailertable ldap -k (&(objectClass=sendmailMTAMapObject)
                        (sendmailMTAMapName=mailer)
                        (|(sendmailMTACluster=${sendmailMTACluster})
                          (sendmailMTAHost=$j))
                        (sendmailMTAKey=%0))
                    -1 -v sendmailMTAMapValue
```

The following is an example LDAP LDIF entry:

```
dn: sendmailMTAMapName=mailer, dc=your,dc=company
        objectClass: sendmailMTA
        objectClass: sendmailMTAMap
        sendmailMTACluster: Servers
        sendmailMTAMapName: mailer


        dn: sendmailMTAKey=yourcompany.com, sendmailMTAMapName=mailer, dc=your, \
dc=company
        objectClass: sendmailMTA
        objectClass: sendmailMTAMap
        objectClass: sendmailMTAMapObject
        sendmailMTAMapName: mailer
        sendmailMTACluster: Servers
        sendmailMTAKey: yourcompany.com
        sendmailMTAMapValue: relay:[smtp.yourcompany.com]
```

As with other maps, you can modify values to include your own specific searches. However, with features that are more specific to Sendmail (and not global sets of data such as users, groups, and aliases) you should keep the original values. If you need to create your own, you do so but define the feature as follows:

```
FEATURE(`mailertable', `ldap:-1 -k (&(objectClass=customClass) \
(key=%0)) -v value')
```

You'll also want to include the following lines, depending on your specific configuration needs and operating system:

```
OSTYPE(line)dsl
MAILER(smtp)
MAILER(local)
```

You must define an operating system environment for your configuration. These configurations are stored within the ostype directory and define various base components of your system. Many of these configurations are the same, but the definitions exist for future compatibility. You should define the OSTYPE option immediately after any version information and before any other definitions. The MAILER definitions define what type of functionality your system will support. The MAILER(local) configuration defines local and prog mailers—basically your local delivery agents. The MAILER(smtp) configuration sets up support for SMTP, support for extended SMTP (esmtp), SMTP support for 8-bit data, support for on-demand delivery, and support for relaying. Additionally, you can set up support for legacy mailers such as UUCP or specific implementations of other applications that may work with your Sendmail system (such as QuickPage or Cyrus).

Classes, which function like macros within Sendmail, are also candidates for storage within your directory. Within base Sendmail configurations, classes are defined with the lead character of F, as follows:

```
F{ClassName}mapkey@mapclass:mapspec
```

mapkey is optional, and if not provided, the map key will be empty. You can use this with LDAP to read classes from LDAP. Note that the lookup happens only when sendmail is initially started. As with other definitions that I've previously discussed, you can use the special value `@LDAP' to use the default LDAP schema. For example, take a look at the definition for RELAY_DOMAIN_FILE in the following line:

```
RELAY_DOMAIN_FILE(`@LDAP')
```

This definition puts all the attribute sendmailMTAClassValue values of LDAP records with objectClass sendmailMTAClass and an attribute sendmailMTAClassName of 'R' into the class $={R}. The default set of queries being performed against LDAP is as follows:

```
F{R}@ldap:-k (&(objectClass=sendmailMTAClass)
            (sendmailMTAClassName=R)
            (|(sendmailMTACluster=${sendmailMTACluster})
              (sendmailMTAHost=$j)))
        -v sendmailMTAClassValue
```

Table 7-2 shows the full set of classes and resulting sendmailMTAClassNames.

Table 7-2. *Sendmail Class Names*

Command	sendmailMTAClassName
CANONIFY_DOMAIN_FILE()	Canonify
EXPOSED_USER_FILE()	E
GENERICS_DOMAIN_FILE()	G
LDAPROUTE_DOMAIN_FILE()	LDAPRoute
LDAPROUTE_EQUIVALENT_FILE()	LDAPRouteEquiv
LOCAL_USER_FILE()	L
MASQUERADE_DOMAIN_FILE()	M
MASQUERADE_EXCEPTION_FILE()	N
RELAY_DOMAIN_FILE()	R
VIRTUSER_DOMAIN_FILE()	VirtHost

You can create custom classes as follows:

```
F{ClassName}@LDAP
```

The resulting LDIF for your default class definition is as follows:

```
dn: sendmailMTAClassName=R, dc=your,dc=company
objectClass: sendmailMTA
objectClass: sendmailMTAClass
sendmailMTACluster: Servers
sendmailMTAClassName: R
sendmailMTAClassValue: sendmail.org
sendmailMTAClassValue: yourcompany.com
sendmailMTAClassValue: 10.56.23
```

As with other definitions, you can customize the set of information that Sendmail will utilize to create this information by expanding from the @LDAP definition to include other information.

Setting Up LDAP Routing

The basic functionality that LDAP initially gave Sendmail (and other mail systems) was the ability to route mail based on an attribute information contained within a user's profile (or DN). This was the "killer app" that gave LDAP global acceptance. So far I've discussed storing profile information that Sendmail uses internally within your LDAP directory, but haven't discussed the feature of actually utilizing mail routing information via LDAP. You enable this basic feature using the following:

```
FEATURE(`ldap_routing')
LDAPROUTE_DOMAIN('yourcompany.com')
LDAPROUTE_EQUIVALENT()
LDAPROUTE_EQUIVALENT_FILE()
```

Using this feature enables the routing of user mail to a particular host or moves it completely out of the environment using an alternate e-mail address. Enabling the ldap_routing feature allows Sendmail to route mail via LDAP information. LDAPROUTE_DOMAIN sets the base domain for which this is done. For example, if your company has the domain of yourcompany.com, this is the base domain that will be controlled via LDAP. You can specify alternate domains and subdomains with the LDAPROUTE_EQUIVALENT and LDAPROUTE_EQUIVALENT_FILE features, which will allow you to, for example, control mail for randomhost1.yourcompany.com or differentdepartment.yourcompany.com.

The LDAP routing feature can, like other definitions that are stored within LDAP, utilize extra parameters to fully customize the behavior of your LDAP searches. You do this as follows:

```
FEATURE(`ldap_routing', <mailHost>, <mailRoutingAddress>, <bounce>, <detail>)
```

In this example, <mailHost> is a map definition that describes how to look up an alternative mail host for a particular address. <mailRoutingAddress> is a map definition that describes how to look up an alternative address for a particular address; the <bounce> argument, if present and not the word passthru, dictates that mail should be bounced if neither a mailHost nor mailRoutingAddress is found. <detail> indicates what actions to take if the address contains +detail information. `strip' tries the lookup with the +detail and, if no matches are found, strips the +detail and tries the lookup again; `preserve' does the same as `strip', but if a mailRoutingAddress match is found, the +detail information is copied to the new address.

The default `<mailHost>` map definition is as follows:

```
ldap -1 -v mailHost -k (&(objectClass=inetLocalMailRecipient)
                          (mailLocalAddress=%0))
```

The default `<mailRoutingAddress>` map definition is as follows:

```
ldap -1 -v mailRoutingAddress -k (&(objectClass=inetLocalMailRecipient)
                                    (mailLocalAddress=%0))
```

The following possibilities exist as a result of an LDAP lookup on an address:

```
mailHost is        mailRoutingAddress is    Results in
-----------        ---------------------    ----------
set to a           set                      mail delivered to
"local" host                                mailRoutingAddress

set to a           not set                  delivered to
"local" host                                original address

set to a           set                      mailRoutingAddress
remote host                                 relayed to mailHost

set to a           not set                  original address
remote host                                 relayed to mailHost

not set            set                      mail delivered to
                                            mailRoutingAddress

not set            not set                  delivered to
                                            original address *OR*
                                            bounced as unknown user
```

The following are examples of users you'd have within your environment that utilize this information:

```
dn: uid=tjackiewicz,ou=People,dc=your,dc=company
objectclass: inetlocalmailrecipient
maillocaladdress: tom@yourcompany.com
mailroutingaddress: tom@mailhost8.yourcompany.com
```

This record would enable the delivery of mail directed at tom@yourcompany.com to tom@mailhost8.yourcompany.com. What this means is that whenever your Sendmail system accepted mail for this address, it'd know that the real address that needs to be used is stored in the mailroutingaddress attribute. This mailroutingaddress would be used, and the mail would be routed to the appropriate mail host. This is a legacy configuration, because LDAP now enables you to route mail using mailhost attributes instead of storing the routing information within the e-mail address itself. LDAP entries that define mail recipients within your directory need to have the objectClass of inetLocalMailRecipient defined, and the address needs to be listed in the mailLocalAddress attribute. If present, there must be only one `mailhost` attribute, and it must contain a fully qualified host name as its value. Similarly, if present, there must be only one `mailRoutingAddress` attribute, and it must contain an RFC 822–compliant address.

The following example demonstrates mail routing:

```
dn: uid=susan_surapruik, ou=People,dc=your,dc=company
objectClass: inetLocalMailRecipient
mailLocalAddress: susan_surapruik@yourcompany.com
mailHost: smart.yourcompany.com
```

This particular entry understands that the ultimate destination of susan_surapruik@yourcompany.com relies on the `mailhost` attribute. Upon a Sendmail system receiving this mail and looking up the entry within LDAP, the system would then route information to `smart.yourcompany.com`. Upon receipt of this mail at the destination mail host, `smart.yourcompany.com` would understand that the mail is local and is to be delivered (or, depending on configurations, handled and routed again). The susan_surapruik@yourcompany.com e-mail address would be retained.

You can combine these routing and mail-handling features. If you need to change the previous address for susan_surapruik upon receipt at the mail host, the entry would look like this:

```
dn: uid=susan_surapruik, ou=People,dc=your,dc=company
objectClass: inetLocalMailRecipient
mailLocalAddress: susan_surapruik@yourcompany.com
mailHost: smart.yourcompany.com
mailroutingaddress: susan@surapruik.yourcompany.com
```

This particular example would still send mail to the same `smart.yourcompany.com` host, but instead of retaining the original address, it'd rewrite it to be the address stored within the `mailroutingaddress` attribute.

As you can see, the use of LDAP now gives Sendmail the powerful features necessary to handle large e-mail environments while maintaining simplicity in the naming conventions that are used and distributed to the people outside your company. No longer is it necessary to have host-based routing and different e-mail addresses for each mail system within your environment.

Summary

After reading this chapter, you should become a bit more familiar with what is takes to integrate OpenLDAP into your environment. IETF drafts, RFCs, and migration information is available to you in this book as well as online and should serve as a guide for populating information into your directory.

■■■

## CHAPTER 8

Integrating OpenLDAP with Applications, User Systems, and Client Tools

Although not quite as complicated as the process of deploying Lightweight Directory Access Protocol (LDAP) and integrating it with your operating system and back-end applications, the ability to integrate LDAP with some of your existing clients and applications will quickly show you the benefits of LDAP within your environment. Many tools today utilize LDAP in some capacity, from Web browsers to mail clients. You can even use a base set of graphical user interface (GUI) tools to browse your LDAP structure for information.

You'll be configuring many types of applications that fall into the LDAP-enabled category. Just like integration at a system level (discussed in the previous chapter), you'll see a definite evolution in how applications support LDAP.

Originally, applications needed a certain level of LDAP synchronization, and they relied on native files and authentication technology. That is, Web servers such Apache or e-mail applications such as Sendmail synchronized via LDAP and stored information locally; in other words, they generated data via an LDAP interface. As applications evolved and LDAP became more of a requirement in corporate infrastructures, applications gained better native LDAP support.

Preparing for Integration

You must take various steps before configuring a client application against your server. Much like the configurations discussed in the previous chapter on server integration, you need to understand the configurations on which your LDAP server will depend. That is, if your client is expecting a certain set of attributes to describe a subset of data, you must understand how this information is configured on the server side. Some applications don't allow you to configure the way information is queried, which could stop you in your tracks or require you to work with the system administrators to gain interoperability.

Understanding how clients interact with your system is the most important step in preparing for integration. The following are some of the specific types of information you'll want to understand and research:

- Is the client requesting specific attributes? As I just mentioned, certain clients associate certain field names with specific LDAP attributes. For example, is the e-mail address expected to be rfc822mailrecipient or mail? Can you configure this for a specific search, or is this information hard-coded?

- Are wildcards automatically appended to searches? That is, when searching for uid=3261, will the search automatically become uid=3261*?

- How does the client handle referrals? Are they ignored, returned as errors, or followed?

- Is the client making any updates to the system that are unexpected?

- Is the client requesting specific object classes? That is, when configuring an application, are there any custom schema requirements for which your client is looking?

Between versions (even minor versions), clients often change how they interact with a system. Keep this in mind when making modifications. For example, Internet Explorer 3.02 performs searches differently than Internet Explorer 4.0 does, and they may not be documented well or may be hidden somewhere in the release notes. Also, some clients handle error messages, such as a "DSA is unwilling to perform" error, in different ways. The interpretation of error messages is a significant problem. For example, when error 10 (a referral) is returned to a client, some handle it appropriately, and others look at this as a significant failure and return no information.

Integrating Apache

Apache can use LDAP to extend its functionality. The Apache Web server has long supported LDAP for authentication and access control as an alternative to text files stored within its configurations. Two LDAP modules exist for this purpose. Unfortunately, these modules perform authentication in a manner that's both a security risk and nonportable. The process involves searching an entry, retrieving its password, and checking for a match against the password supplied. The crypt mechanism for password storage (like in older versions of Unix) is required for this level of integration. The Apache LDAP modules require that the userPassword attribute is either opened completely or restricted to a directory user whose username and password are listed in the Apache configuration files.

The Apache::AuthLDAP module for mod_perl leverages the power of the Net::LDAPapi module to provide extensible LDAP authentication and authorization handlers for Apache. This module has excellent performance and supports Apache on both Unix and Windows NT. It also supports LDAP over Secure Sockets Layer (SSL), as well as a mode that lets Microsoft FrontPage clients manage their Web permissions while still using LDAP for authentication. You can find Apache::AuthLDAP at http://perl.apache.org/ in the list of modules. Installation is relatively straightforward on any system where mod_perl and Net::LDAPapi have already been installed.

The module itself is actually divided into two parts. The first is the AUTH handler, which authenticates a user based on a given login name and password. The second part is the AUTHZ handler, which analyzes the require statements in an Apache access control file to provide access control. mod_perl must have both AUTH and AUTHZ handlers enabled in order to use this module.

The following is an example of an Apache access control file (in other words, access.conf or .htaccess) that restricts access for a particular area to people who can authenticate as someone with required attribute values:

```
<Directory /foo/bar>
# Authentication Realm and Type (only Basic supported)
AuthName "Foo Bar Authentication"
AuthType Basic
# Any of the following variables can be set. Defaults are listed
# to the right.
PerlSetVar BaseDN dc=Your,dc=Company                # Default:  Empty String ("")
PerlSetVar LDAPServer ldapserver.yourcompany.com # Default: localhost
PerlSetVar LDAPPort 389                             # Default: 389 (standard LDAP port)
PerlSetVar UIDAttr uid                              # Default: uid
PerlAuthenHandler Apache::AuthLDAP
# Require lines can be any of the following:
#
require valid-user          # Any Valid LDAP User
require user uid1 uid2 uid2  # Allow Any User in List
require ldapattrib val1 val2 # Allow Any User w/ Entry Containing
                            # Matching Attribute and Value
</Directory>
```

The Apache::AuthLDAP module supports access control based on Valid-User, User, Attribute, Groups, or Filter. Valid-User checks that a user exists in LDAP. User checks that a user exists in a static list. For example, the directive require user tjackiewicz would require that the user have the username of tjackiewicz for the authentication to pass. Attribute verifies that users contain a certain attribute within their profiles. Groups requires a user to exist within a particular group. Filter requires that a user exist as a result of a particular LDAP filter. For example, require group "cn=Managers,dc=Your,dc=Company" requires that the user exist within the group profile for managers. User-based access controls simply require that the user's login name matches one in the require line.

Finally, filter-based access controls allow complex LDAP search filters to be created to control access based on one or more attribute-value combinations. This is currently the only way to implement access controls with multiple conditions. For example, a filter requiring that an authorized user's entry must contain a profile attribute with the value app1 and a department attribute with a value of IT may look like this:

```
require filter (&(profile=app1)(department=IT))
```

Each of the attributes defined within the filter should be indexed for performance.

Entries in an LDAP directory may contain attributes with uniform resource indicator (URI) values. Such attributes usually contain the home page for the given directory entry. Web servers can use these attributes to rewrite URIs based on directory information. In general, URI rewriting based on LDAP entries can be a good replacement for rewriting based on passwd file entries for sites that distribute users' personal Web pages across multiple servers but don't want to interconnect them using a network filesystem or other means. For example, you could automatically redirect all queries to ~username on a Web server to a URI residing in the LDAP entry for username. One way to add this functionality to Apache would be to develop a module similar to mod_userdir bundled with Apache. Such a module would simply parse an existing URI, substituting the results from an LDAP query as necessary. Another way to add this functionality is to have a Common Gateway Interface (CGI) perform the URI rewriting.

Apache::TransLDAP is a reference implementation of a mod_perl Apache module that will rewrite URIs based on LDAP attributes. You can find it in the Apache module list at http://perl.apache.org/.

Listing 8-1 is a short example of how to use this module to rewrite URIs from /users/ username on the current server to the labeledURI attribute in the username's LDAP entry.

Listing 8-1. TransLDAP

```
# Set the TransHandler to be TransLDAP
PerlTransHandler Apache::TransLDAP
# Set Server and Search Information
PerlSetVar  LDAPServer ldapserver.yourcompany.com
PerlSetVar  LDAPBase "dc=your,dc=company"
PerlSetVar  UIDAttr "uid"
# This is the standard attribute for
# URIs within an LDAP entry
PerlSetVar  URIAttr "labeleduri"
# The Virtual Home Page URI
PerlSetVar  UserDir "/users/"
```

With this module enabled, each request to the Apache server will call the Apache::TransLDAP module as a Perl TRANS handler. To work, TRANS handlers must be enabled in mod_perl, and Net::LDAPapi must already be installed. For each request, the module will first check to see if the URI begins with UserDir. If not, it declines to make changes and passes control back to Apache. Otherwise, a connection is opened to the LDAP server to find the entry for the specified user. If an entry isn't found, or the entry doesn't contain a value for the required URI attribute, the module will pass control back to Apache without making changes. Upon success, the initial part of the URI is translated to the LDAP attribute's value. This new URI is then returned to the Web client as a redirect, with response code 301. Although the previous technique works well for redirecting based on attributes within users, you can also use it to create virtual home pages for organizations, groups, and other object classes within the directory.

One of the most powerful features of Apache and mod_perl is the ability to have Perl-based configuration sections within httpd.conf and other server configuration files. Combined with the Net::LDAPapi module, the Apache server has the ability to obtain configuration information from an LDAP server. You can easily compile this module on various platforms. In fact, it has been tested extensively under Solaris and verified to work under HP/UX 10, AIX, BSD/OS, and Red Hat Linux. Additionally, as of version 1.39, the module has been verified to work with Windows NT 4.0 and Perl 5.004+. This is most useful in using an LDAP directory to control configuration for a cluster of servers. Prior to actually configuring a server via LDAP and Perl, it's first necessary to create an object class on the directory server that contains the configuration attributes needed by the server. For this example, the following attributes could make up an object class used for location access controls:

```
LocationURI
AuthType
authName
require
validClusterNumber
```

Once you create the object class on the server, you can populate entries in the directory with the information that's shown in Listing 8-2.

Listing 8-2. *Apache Access Control Lists in LDAP*

```
dn: cn=apacheACL1,ou=Apache,ou=Config,dc=your,dc=company
objectClass: apacheACL
location: /protected
authType: basic
authName: Protected
require: valid-user

dn: cn=apacheACL2,ou=Apache,ou=Config,dc=your,dc=company
objectClass: apacheACL
location: /private
authType: basic
authName: Private
require: user tom susan napoleon
require: group people
```

These LDAP entries could then be read using a <Perl> section within the Apache configuration files. Such a section could look like Listing 8-3.

Listing 8-3. *Sample Code*

```
# Create a new connection and bind
my $ldap = new Net::LDAPapi($server);
$ldap->bind_s;

# Search the directory for objects of
# the type I'm looking for.
if ($ldap->search_s($BASE, LDAP_SCOPE_SUBTREE, \
  "objectclass=apacheACL", [], 0) == LDAP_SUCCESS)
{
# Get all returned entries.
  my $locations =
      $ldap->get_all_entries;
```

```
# Go through each entry returned and
# create an access control for that
# location based on information in the
# directory.
 foreach my $dn (keys %{$locations})
 {
   my %entry = %{$locations->{$dn}};

   # Here we actually build the ACL
   $Location{$entry{"location"}->[0]}=
   {
    AuthType=>$entry{"authType"}->[0],
    AuthName=>$entry{"authName"}->[0],
    Limit => {
      METHODS=> `GET POST',
      require=> [@$entry{"require"}],
    }
   };
 }
}
```

The segment in Listing 8-3 would allow the Web server to retrieve all access control information from the directory server. Multiple servers using the same code segment would have identical access controls, and localized changes could also be added to local configuration files without affecting global controls. You could even extend the object class schema used for this example to include a cluster identifier, thus allowing different clusters to read different configurations. The only part of the code you'd have to change to support such functionality is the search. You could also do this by having each cluster configured within different parts of the directory tree. In this case, you'd have to change $BASE in the previous example to correspond with the correct part of the tree.

Integrating Pine

Pine is a tool for reading, sending, and managing electronic messages. Computing and Communications at the University of Washington (http://www.washington.edu) developed Pine. Though originally designed for inexperienced e-mail users, Pine has evolved to support many advanced features and an ever-growing number of configuration and personal preferences. Pine is available for Unix as well as for personal computers running a Microsoft operating system (PC-Pine). I'll concentrate on the Unix version of Pine for the configurations I'll be discussing. Pine has been successfully built with OpenLDAP 2.0.*x*, with OpenLDAP 1.*x*, with the University of Michigan LDAP library (ldap-3.3), and with the Netscape Directory software development kit (SDK) 1.0 LDAP library.

When using OpenLDAP as the library (or the older University of Michigan library), set up the symlink so that it points to the base of the LDAP source tree. The ldap-setup script looks for the directory ldap/libraries/liblber and the libraries ldap/libraries/libldap.a and ldap/libraries/liblber.a during the initial setup. To use the Netscape Directory SDK library, make a directory called ldap in the top-level pine directory (where Pine's build script is located).

That directory should contain two subdirectories: include and libraries. The include directory is where you should put the include files from the Netscape SDK. The libraries directory is where you should put the library libldap.a.

Pine uses the LDAP v2 protocol. When using the LDAP v3 protocol, the results are returned in the UTF-8 character set. Pine isn't yet ready to deal with that, so it tells the server to use the LDAP v2 protocol.

The base configurations for Pine are stored in your home directory in the file .pinerc. This file contains all the basic configurations for your environment, including your username, e-mail folders, and any remote hosts you may want to contact during your session. The LDAP configurations are also stored within this configuration file. The protocols that Pine will be utilizing are Internet Message Access Protocol (IMAP), Simple Mail Transfer Protocol (SMTP), and LDAP. IMAP will allow you to retrieve messages via folders stored on an IMAP-compatible server. SMTP allows you to send outgoing mail from your client. LDAP will facilitate access to various address books (stored within LDAP directories) that may exist within your environment or, in some cases, on the Internet. You may need to make multiple configuration changes across different Pine configuration files. As I mentioned earlier, you should have the .pinerc file stored in your home directory (~/.pinerc).

The ~/.pinerc directory stores configurations for just your instance of Pine, and anything configured in this file will impact only your Pine session. The file could look something like Listing 8-4.

Listing 8-4. ~/.pinerc

```
# Pine configuration file
#
# This file sets the configuration options used by Pine and PC-Pine. These
# options are usually set from within Pine or PC-Pine. There may be a
# systemwide configuration file that sets the defaults for some of the
# variables. On Unix, run pine -conf to see how system defaults have been set.
# For variables that accept multiple values, list elements are separated by
# commas. A line beginning with a space or tab is considered to be a
# continuation of the previous line. For a variable to be unset, its value must
# be blank. To set a variable to the empty string, its value should be "".
# You can override system defaults by setting a variable to the empty string.
# Lines beginning with # are comments and are ignored by Pine.

# Overrides your full name from Unix password file. Required for PC-Pine.
personal-name=Tom Jackiewicz

# Sets domain part of From: and local addresses in outgoing mail.
user-domain=yourcompany.com

# List of SMTP servers for sending mail. If blank: Unix Pine uses sendmail.
smtp-server=smtp.yourcompany.com

# Path of (local or remote) INBOX, e.g. ={mail.somewhere.edu}inbox
# Normal Unix default is the local INBOX (usually /usr/spool/mail/$USER).
inbox-path={mail01.yourcompany.com:143/imap/user=tom_jackiewicz}INBOX
```

```
# Overrides default path for your sent-mail folder, e.g. =old-mail (using first
# folder collection dir) or ={host2}sent-mail or ="" (to suppress saving).
# Default: sent-mail (Unix) or SENTMAIL.MTX (PC) in default folder collection.
default-fcc={mail01.yourcompany.com:143/imap/user=tom_jackiewicz}sent-mail
# Overrides default path for saved-msg folder, e.g. =saved-messages (using 1st
# folder collection dir) or ={host2}saved-mail or ="" (to suppress saving).
# Default: saved-messages (Unix) or SAVEMAIL.MTX (PC) in default collection.
default-saved-msg-folder={mail01.yourcompany.com:143/imap/user=tom_jackiewicz}SAVE

# LDAP servers for looking up addresses.
ldap-servers=ldap.yourcompany.com:389 "/base=dc=your,dc=company"
```

In the configuration in Listing 8-4, I've removed various lines that don't specifically relate to Pine and external system integration (IMAP and LDAP). A default pine configuration will utilize local files for mailboxes and local resources (such as a locally installed sendmail binary) to function as a mail client. Local files are also used for address books and user lookups.

The file /etc/pine.conf.fixed, which is looked up first during the Pine session, looks like Listing 8-5 by default.

Listing 8-5. *Default* pine.conf.fixed *Configuration File*

```
#
# Pine systemwide enforced configuration file - customize as needed
#
# This file holds the systemwide-enforced values for Pine configuration
# settings. Any values set in it will override values set in the
# systemwide default configuration file (/etc/pine.conf) and
# the user's own configuration file (~/.pinerc).
# For more information on the format of this file, read the
# comments at the top of /etc/pine.conf
```

For systems with a static set of configurations that need to be enforced, the system administrator (root) creates this file, which provides defaults that override any configurations that may exist in a user's local configuration file. That is, if a default signature or SMTP server needs to be used, it'd be configured in this file. This removes flexibility for you to make your own client configurations and have Pine function in a way outside your system administrator's default configurations. Sometimes system administrators configure this file to ensure a static environment and a base set of servers for use, which helps in troubleshooting problems if an administrator knows there's only one place to look for configuration problems.

You can think of the /etc/pine.conf file as a set of suggestions from the administrators for your configurations. This file can contain the same set of information that the other configuration files contain, but any user with the ~/.pinerc file can overwrite the values stored here.

For the ~/.pinerc file, the user can change the settings directly from Pine by going into the Setup and then the Config area (press S and then press C). For LDAP settings, go into Setup and then Directory (press S and then press D). The following are the important settings for communicating with an LDAP server:

user-domain: This sets the domain name portion of your e-mail address. From tom@yourcompany.com, this would be yourcompany.com. Nonqualified e-mails sent from your client will default to this domain. That is, sending e-mail to just susan would default to susan@yourcompany.com.

customized-hdrs: This is the From header that will appear in the message you compose before you send it. If you don't specify this header, the username and full name are taken from the GECOS field of the Unix password file.

smtp-server: This is the hostname of the SMTP server that will be used to send mail. By default, the sendmail binaries are invoked directly by the application to send mail.

inbox-path: This contains the default path to your inbox. By default, this is a local file within your home directory. When integrating Pine with other systems, this can become a remote folder on an IMAP server.

folder-collections: This contains points to other folder collections you want to view. You should concern yourself with only two sets. The first is your inbox folders (personal folders you create in your inbox), and the second is your mailbox folders, which are default folders (in other words, Sent Items, Deleted Items, Drafts, Outbox, Public Folders, and so on). By default, these files are local files within your home directory. When integrating Pine with other systems, these can become remote folders on an IMAP server.

ldap-server: This is the hostname of your LDAP server in the LDAP URI format. That is, you can point to the server name, port, base distinguished name (DN), and other search information within this configuration.

From your shell, start Pine as follows:

```
$ pine
```

You'll be given a set of configuration choices. Press S to configure pine's options. Then press C to configure new options. The options I just discussed, and many others, are available from this configuration.

Another option (from the S menu) that's interesting is Z (RemoteConfigSetup). This is a command you'll probably want to use only once, if at all. It helps you transfer your Pine configuration data to an IMAP server, where it will be accessible from any of the computers you read mail from (using Pine). The idea behind a remote configuration is that you can change your configuration in one place and have that change show up on all the computers you use. This command doesn't show up on the menu at the bottom of the screen unless you press O (for Other Commands), but you don't need to press O to invoke the command.

The configuration to set up directories is also available from the standard S menu by pressing D. You can view existing configurations by pressing A to add a new directory to use for address book lookups. Listing 8-6 is an example of what you'll see when entering this configuration.

Listing 8-6. *Pine Configurations*

```
ldap-server          = ldaphost.yourcompany.com
search-base          = dc=your,dc=company
port                 = <No Value Set: using "389">
nickname             = Primary LDAP Server

Features             =
           Set    Feature Name
           ---    ----------------------
           [ ]    use-implicitly-from-composer
           [ ]    lookup-addrbook-contents
           [ ]    save-search-criteria-not-result
           [X]    disable-ad-hoc-space-substitution

search-type          =
           Set    Rule Values
           ---    ----------------------
           (*)    name
           ( )    surname
           ( )    givenname
           ( )    email
           ( )    name-or-email
           ( )    surname-or-givenname
           ( )    sur-or-given-or-name-or-email

search-rule          =
           Set    Rule Values
           ---    ----------------------
           ( )    contains
           (*)    equals
           ( )    begins-with
           ( )    ends-with

email-attribute      = <No Value Set: using "mail">
name-attribute       = cn
surname-attribute    = <No Value Set: using "sn">
givenname-attribute  = <No Value Set: using "givenname">

timelimit            = 300
sizelimit            = <No Value Set: using "0">

custom-search-filter = (&(objectclass=person)(mail=*)(sn=%s))

? Help     E Exit Setup    P Prev          - PrevPage A Add Value  % Print
```

In the previous configuration, you can see where configurations for your LDAP address book are. Older versions of Pine prefer to store configurations via IMAP folders. This was a legacy method that worked well for quite some time. The directives you'll be utilizing are as follows:

The ldap-server directive is the specific LDAP server you'll be using for your address book lookups. This takes the form of a standard hostname, not the LDAP URI format. For this example environment, you can use ldaphost.yourcompany.com.

The search-base directive is the base DN you'll be using for your address book lookups. For this environment, you'll use dc=your,dc=company.

The port directive is the default LDAP port is 389. You'll want to configure this option if your LDAP server is listening on a port other than 389.

The nickname directive is the nickname you'll use with your Pine client for searches. This is useful if you have multiple LDAP servers that you'll be using for searching if you want to configure different search filters against the same LDAP server. For this example environment, you can settle on "Primary LDAP Server" for the nickname.

Underneath the Features tab, you're able to configure the way your Pine client will act and utilize this LDAP address book information.

Underneath the Search-Type tab, you're able to configure the types of searches being performed. You're able to search by name, surname, givenname, email, name-or-email, surname-or-givenname, or sur-or-given-or-name-or-email. These are the default search options (and combinations of options) that your Pine client supports. I'll explain what these specific values map to in a moment. For this example environment, you can use the default of name for the search type.

The Search-Rule tab defines the type of search being used. You're given the options of contains, which is for substring searches; equals, for standard searches (=); and begins-with or ends-with, which are also variations of substring searches. For this environment, you can use equals.

The attributes that are mapped from the Search-Type tab can then be defined with the directives of email-attribute, name-attribute, surname-attribute, and givenname-attribute. For example, in a standard e-mail environment, the attribute name of mail is used for the e-mail attribute. If you want these values to change, you can define them here. For the name-attribute, for example, I'll be using cn.

You define timeout limits using the timelimit directive. This is the maximum time given to complete a search. This is defined in seconds.

You define the maximum number of entries returned from a search using the sizelimit directive. When the value isn't set or is set to 0, this means there's no maximum number of entries returned.

The previous directives make things easier for the novice LDAP user or a default LDAP environment. If you want to customize your filters, you'll want to modify the custom-search-filter directive. You can use standard LDAP search filters here, which can include ANDs, ORs, or a combination of values. You can use the %s attribute to store value given for the input during the invocation of the address book search.

Using the default configuration provided in this example, when you compose a new message and enter a name in the To box, Pine will first check your local address book for the nickname. If it doesn't find it, it will then run an LDAP query by default, using the default name you typed as the search string. Depending on the speed of the LDAP server, you should get a response relatively quickly. From the results you can choose the entry you were looking for and continue writing your e-mail. If you enter an e-mail address in the To box, it won't perform an LDAP search or any other address book search (in other words, susan@yourcompany) because it realizes you already know the e-mail address of the person to whom you want to send a message. If you just want to do a search, without actually composing a new message, you can go directly to your address book, select the LDAP server, and enter the search string from there (in other words, press M and then A). In case you don't want Pine to do an automatic LDAP lookup every time you compose a new message, you can change the parameter /impl=1 in the ldap-server setting to /impl=0. This will allow you to do a manual LDAP query if you want.

Integrating Samba

Samba is an open-source/free software suite that provides seamless file and print services to Server Message Block (SMB)/Common Internet File System (CIFS) clients. Samba is freely available under the GNU General Public License (GPL). Samba consists of two key programs: smbd and nmbd. They implement the four basic modern-day CIFS services, which are as follows:

- File and print services

- Authentication and authorization

- Name resolution

- Service announcement (browsing)

File and print services are, of course, the cornerstone of the CIFS suite. These are provided by smbd, the SMB daemon. smbd also handles "share mode" and "user mode" authentication and authorization. That is, you can protect shared file and print services by requiring passwords. In share mode (the simplest and least recommended scheme), a password can be assigned to a shared directory or printer (simply called a *share*). This single password is then given to everyone who is allowed to use the share. With user mode authentication, each user has a username and password, and the system administrator can grant or deny access on an individual basis. The OpenLDAP server needs to be configured to serve as a Security Access Manager (SAM) database. For Samba 2.2.4, you need to configure various things. Specifically, you need to import the Samba 2.2.4 LDAP v3 schema, you need to configure the base DN appropriately, and you need to import a minimum set of Samba-related DNs as part of the installation.

The Windows NT domain system provides a further level of authentication refinement for CIFS. The basic idea is that a user should have to log in only once to have access to all the authorized services on the network. The NT domain system handles this with an authentication server, called a *domain controller*. An NT domain (which shouldn't be confused with a Domain Name System [DNS] domain) is basically a group of machines that share the same domain controller.

The NT domain system deserves special mention because, until the release of Samba version 2, only Microsoft owned code to implement the NT domain authentication protocols. With version 2, Samba introduced the first non-Microsoft-derived NT domain authentication code.

The eventual goal, of course, is to completely mimic a Windows NT domain controller. When authenticating with Samba 2.2.4 and OpenLDAP, you'll store the following set of information:

- Windows user accounts using the sambaAccount object class (contained in samba.schema)

- Windows computer accounts (in other words, workstations) using the sambaAccount object class

- User-only user accounts using the shadowAccount object class (contained in nis.schema)

- User groups (Windows and Unix, as it doesn't make a difference to Samba 2.2.4) using the posixGroup object class

nmbd handles the other two CIFS pieces: name resolution and browsing. These two services basically involve the management and distribution of lists of NetBIOS names.

Name resolution takes two forms: broadcast and point-to-point. A machine can use either or both of these methods, depending upon its configuration. Broadcast resolution is the closest to the original NetBIOS mechanism. Basically, a client looking for a service named Trillian will call out "Yo! Trillian! Where are you?" and wait for the machine with that name to answer with an Internet Protocol (IP) address. This can generate a bit of broadcast traffic (a lot of shouting in the streets), but it's restricted to the local area network (LAN) so it doesn't cause too much trouble.

The other type of name resolution involves using a NetBIOS Name Service (NBNS) server. (Microsoft called its NBNS implementation WINS, for Windows Internet Name Service, and that acronym is more commonly used today.) Clients on different subnets can all share the same NBNS server, so, unlike broadcast, the point-to-point mechanism isn't limited to the LAN. In many ways the NBNS is similar to the DNS, but the NBNS name list is almost completely dynamic, and few controls ensure that only authorized clients can register names. Conflicts can, and do, occur fairly easily.

Finally, there's browsing. Samba's nmbd handles this. This isn't the Web browsing you know and love, but is a browsable list of services (file and print shares) offered by the computers on a network. This is similar to the remote procedure call (RPC)/portmapper services under Unix.

On a LAN, the participating computers hold an election to decide which of them will become the local master browser (LMB). The "winner" then identifies itself by claiming a special NetBIOS name (in addition to any other names it may have). The LMB's job is to keep a list of available services, and it's this list that appears when you click the Windows Network Neighborhood icon.

In addition to LMBs, domain master browsers (DMBs) coordinate browse lists across NT domains, even on routed networks. Using the NBNS, an LMB will locate its DMB to exchange and combine browse lists. Thus, the browse list is propagated to all hosts in the NT domain. Unfortunately, the synchronization times are spread apart a bit. It can take more than an hour for a change on a remote subnet to appear in the Network Neighborhood.

Samba comes with a variety of utilities. The most commonly used are as follows:

- smbclient: This is a simple SMB client, with an interface similar to that of the File Transfer Protocol (FTP) utility. It can be used from a Unix system to connect to a remote SMB share, to transfer files, and to send files to remote print shares (printers).

- nmblookup: This is the NetBIOS name service client. You can use mblookup to find NetBIOS names on a network, look up their IP addresses, and query a remote machine for the list of names the machine thinks it owns.

- swat: This is the Samba Web Administration Tool (SWAT). SWAT allows you to configure Samba remotely, using a Web browser.

You can download smbldap-tools (for Samba and LDAP interaction) at http://www.idealx.org. This is a good package that contains useful scripts for managing users and groups when you're using LDAP as a source of information for your environment. Samba 2.2.3 needs to be compiled with the -with-ldapsam option. You need to import the schema provided with these tools into your OpenLDAP schema directory. You do this via the slapd.conf file, as shown in Listing 8-7.

Listing 8-7. slapd.conf *for Samba*

```
# Schema and objectClass definitions
include   /etc/ldap/schema/core.schema
include   /etc/ldap/schema/cosine.schema
include   /etc/ldap/schema/nis.schema
include   /etc/ldap/schema/inetorgperson.schema
include   /etc/ldap/schema/misc.schema
include   /etc/ldap/schema/samba.schema
```

The main configuration file used for configurations is smb.conf. The file looks like Listing 8-8.

Listing 8-8. smb.conf *File*

```
[global]
workgroup = GROUP
security = user
wins support = yes
os level = 80
domain master = true
domain logons = yes
local master = yes
preferred master = true
passwd program = /usr/local/sbin/smbldap-passwd.pl -o %u
ldap suffix = dc=your,dc=company
ldap admin cn = cn=Directory Manager
ldap port = 389
ldap server = ldaphost.yourcompany.com
ldap ssl = No
add user script = /usr/local/sbin/smbldap-useradd.pl -w %u
domain admin group = @"Domain Admins"
```

```
logon path = \\%N\profiles\%u
logon drive = H:
logon home = \\homesrv\%u
logon script = logon.cmd
[netlogon]
comment = Network Logon Service
path = /data/samba/netlogon
guest ok = yes
writable = no
share modes = no
; share for storing user profiles
[profiles]
path = /data/samba/profiles
read only = no
create mask = 0600
directory mask = 0700
```

You can edit various defaults for the smbldap tools via the
/usr/local/sbin/smbldap_conf.pm configuration file. Listing 8-9 shows the default file, which
is followed by an explanation of the directives.

Listing 8-9. *LDAP Configurations for Samba*

```
########################################################################
#
# LDAP Configuration
#
########################################################################

# Notes: to use to dual LDAP servers back end for Samba, you must patch
# Samba with the dual-head patch from IDEALX. If not using this patch
# just use the same server for slaveLDAP and masterLDAP.
#
# Slave LDAP : needed for read operations
#
# Ex: $slaveLDAP = ``127.0.0.1'';
$slaveLDAP = ``localhost'';

#
# Master LDAP : needed for write operations
#
# Ex: $masterLDAP = ``127.0.0.1'';
$masterLDAP = ``localhost'';

#
# LDAP Suffix
#
# Ex: $suffix = ``dc=SMELUG,dc=ORG'';
$suffix = ``dc=SMELUG,dc=ORG'';
```

```
#
# Where are stored Users
#
# Ex: $usersdn = ``ou=Users,$suffix''; for ou=Users,dc=SMELUG,dc=ORG
$usersou = q(Users);

$usersdn = ``ou=$usersou,$suffix'';

#
# Where are stored Computers
#
# Ex: $computersdn = ``ou=Computers,$suffix''; for ou=Computers,dc=SMELUG,dc=ORG
$computersou = q(Computers);

$computersdn = ``ou=$computersou,$suffix'';

#
# Where are stored Groups
#
# Ex $groupsdn = ``ou=Groups,$suffix''; for ou=Groups,dc=SMELUG,dc=ORG
$groupsou = q(Groups);

$groupsdn = ``ou=$groupsou,$suffix'';

#
# Default scope Used
#
$scope = ``sub'';

#
# Credential Configuration
#
# Bind DN used
# Ex: $binddn = ``cn=Manager,$suffix''; for cn=Manager,dc=SMELUG,dc=org
$binddn = ``cn=Manager,$suffix'';
#
# Bind DN passwd used
# Ex: $bindpasswd = 'secret'; for 'secret'
#$bindpasswd = ``secret'';
$bindpasswd = ``smelug'';

#
# Notes: if using dual LDAP patch, you can specify to different configuration
# By default, we will use the same DN (so it will work for standard Samba
# release)
#
```

```
$slaveDN = $binddn;
$slavePw = $bindpasswd;
$masterDN = $binddn;
$masterPw = $bindpasswd;

#######################################################################
#
# Unix Accounts Configuration
#
#######################################################################

# Login defs
#
# Default Login Shell
#
# Ex: $_userLoginShell = q(/bin/bash);
$_userLoginShell = q(/bin/bash);

#
# Home directory prefix (without username)
#
#Ex: $_userHomePrefix = q(/home/);
$_userHomePrefix = q(/home/);

#
# Gecos
#
$_userGecos = q(System User);

#
# Default User (POSIX and Samba) GID
#
#$_defaultUserGid = 100;
$_defaultUserGid = 201;

#
# Default Computer (Samba) GID
#
$_defaultComputerGid = 553;

#
# Skel dir
#
$_skeletonDir = q(/etc/skel);
```

```
#########################################################################
#
# SAMBA Configuration
#
#########################################################################

#
# The UNC path to home drives location without the username last extension
# (will be dynamically prepended)
# Ex: q(\\\\My-PDC-netbios-name\\homes) for \\My-PDC-netbios-name\homes
$_userSmbHome = q(\\\\\SMELUG-PDC\\homes);

#
# The UNC path to profiles locations without the username last extension
# (will be dynamically prepended)
# Ex: q(\\\\My-PDC-netbios-name\\profiles) for \\My-PDC-netbios-name\\profiles
##$_userProfile = q(\\\\\GOULDNET\\profiles\\);
$_userProfile = q(\\\\\SMELUG-PDC\\);

#
# The default Home Drive Letter mapping
# (will be automatically mapped at logon time if home directory exist)
# Ex: q(U:) for U:
$_userHomeDrive = q(D:);

#
# The default user netlogon script name
# if not used, will be automatically username.cmd
#
##$_userScript = q(startup.cmd); # make sure script file is edited under dos
#$_userScript = q(STARTUP.BAT); # make sure script file is edited under dos


#########################################################################
```

Within the configuration file, you can modify various LDAP parameters and the way your system interacts with the directory. Separate slave and master LDAP servers (the slave for reads and the master for writes) are supported with the following directives so that referrals don't need to be supported:

```
$slaveLDAP = ``ldapslaveserver'';
$masterLDAP = ``ldapmasterserver'';
```

You can configure your base DN using the following directive:

```
$suffix = ``dc=Your,dc=Company'';
```

You can define separate containers for the various types of objects you'll be storing in your LDAP system (users, computers, and groups) in the following directives:

```
$usersou = q(Users);
$usersdn = ``ou=$usersou,$suffix'';
$computersou = q(Computers);
$computersdn = ``ou=$computersou,$suffix'';
$groupsou = q(Groups);
$groupsdn = ``ou=$groupsou,$suffix'';
```

The suffix is a variable that was previously defined as $suffix.

The following directive defines the scope of your searches:

```
$scope = ``sub'';
```

You can configure special users and passwords that you'll use to bind in the following directives:

```
$binddn = ``cn=Manager,$suffix'';
$bindpasswd = ``smelug'';
$slaveDN = $binddn;
$slavePw = $bindpasswd;
$masterDN = $binddn;
$masterPw = $bindpasswd;
```

You can define the defaults for your accounts, which would typically exist in /etc/passwd and other profile sources, in the following directives:

```
$_userLoginShell = q(/bin/bash);
$_userHomePrefix = q(/home/);
$_userGecos = q(System User);
$_defaultUserGid = 201;
$_defaultComputerGid = 553;
$_skeletonDir = q(/etc/skel);
```

You can set specific configurations for Samba account information using the following directives:

```
$_userSmbHome = q(\\\\SMELUG-PDC\\homes);
$_userProfile = q(\\\\SMELUG-PDC\\);
$_userHomeDrive = q(D:);
$_userScript = q(startup.cmd);
```

While application profiles need their own sets of schema and configuration trees, user profiles for SMB would just be complementary to the existing user environment you've created. For example, you may have accounts in LDAP for tjackiewicz and ssurapruik in LDAP as shown in Listing 8-10.

Listing 8-10. *Existing DNs in Your Directory*

```
dn: uid=tjackiewicz,ou=People,dc=your,dc=company
dn: uid=ssurapruik,ou=People,dc=your,dc=company
```

You'll need to modify the profiles to add object classes for posixAccount and sambaAccount and attributes that would be useful for configurations. The resulting accounts for Tom and Susan would end up like those in Listing 8-11.

Listing 8-11. *Resulting LDIFs After SMB Modification*

```
dn: uid=tjackiewicz,ou=People,dc=your,dc=company
objectclass: inetorgperson
objectclass: posixaccount
objectclass: sambaaccount
cn: Tom Jackiewicz
sn: Jackiewicz
uid: tjackiewicz
gidNumber: 100
homeDirectory: /home/tjackiewicz
loginShell: /bin/bash
description: Tom's account
acctflags: [UX]
homedrive: H:
smbhome: \\smbserver\home
profilepath: \\smbserver\profiles\tjackiewicz
scriptpath: tjackiewicz.cmd
uidnumber: 100
```

Integrating Eudora

Qualcomm Eudora is a common mail client you may run into within your existing environment. I'll use this as a base example for GUI mail client configurations. You can use Eudora's Web site at http://www.eudora.com as a reference for current configurations and any help you may need. It's strongly recommended that you use Eudora 4.2 or later before configuring it for LDAP interoperability.

Eudora gives you the ability to utilize directory services for address book lookups instead of relying on a local address book or proprietary database. It also gives you the ability to utilize, natively, remote directories providing yellow pages and white pages information such a Four11, BigFoot, and Yahoo. Eudora utilizes the following LDAP uniform resource locator (URL) format for referencing LDAP information:

```
ldap://host[:port]/[base][?fields-to-return]
```

This has the following parameters:

- host: Set this value to the LDAP server within your environment. For the example environment, I'll use ldaphost.yourcompany.com.

- port: Set this value to the port of the LDAP server within your environment. The default is 389.

- `base`: This value configures the base DN for your LDAP environment. For this environment, I'll use dc=your,dc=company.

- `fields-to-return`: These are the field names that are returned during your LDAP search. When multiple fields are returned, each should be separated by a comma, such as name1=value1,name2=value2.

If you want to connect to ldaphost.yourcompany.com on port 389 with a base DN of dc=your,dc=company and then return the values of cn, sn and mail, you'd use the following filter:

```
ldap://ldaphost.yourcompany.com:389/dc=Your,dc=Company?cn,sn,mail
```

Setting up filters for address book searches in Eudora is simple, because Eudora follows the standard LDAP URI format. In general, the various LDAP-capable clients (such as Communicator, Eudora, and Outlook 98/Express) vary greatly in the actual LDAP query they generate based on the user searching for a name. These variations in the query often result in a different set of "hits" being returned to the same query, depending on which client is being used. In many cases, despite the variations, the user will still likely find the person for whom they were looking. But this won't always be the case, particularly with Win Eudora (which generates such an open-ended query that often the search limits imposed will cause only a partial result to be returned to the user).

You can modify LDAP configurations for Eudora via the Esoteric Settings 4.*x* plug-in file within your Eudora installation folder. Copy the Esoteric Settings 4.*x* folder into the Eudora Stuff folder, and restart Eudora. Upon reloading the application, you'll be able to access LDAP configurations via the Special/Settings tab. You'll be presented with the following options:

- **Directory services host**: This is the LDAP server or remote yellow pages or white pages directory (as discussed previously).

- **Wordwise search filter template**: This is the attribute search filter you'll be using. For example, it could be (|(givenname=*^0*)(cn=*^0*)(givenname=*^0*)(sn=*^0*)).

When creating filters, the ^0 will be replaced by the input query during a dialog box. The * is a wildcard. You'll need to make sure that the remote server has substring indexing on the attributes you search via a wildcard.

With these configurations, LDAP will be utilized for lookups of information. To make LDAP the default protocol used to look up information, select Special ➤ Settings ➤ Hosts. In the Directory Services text box, you're able to input the same host you've configured as directory services host in the previous configuration as a complete LDAP URI. Through this tab, you can also configure your Post Office Protocol (POP) and SMTP servers.

Integrating Exchange

While still relatively immature for most Microsoft-based products, LDAP v2 is implemented in Microsoft Exchange 5.0 as a way to access information stored within its internal Microsoft Access database.

The gateway is configured and turned on by default. This configuration works well in the simplest of environments, but requires additional configuration when your LDAP environment is customized. You'll need to configure the authentication methods that users will use to securely access the directory. The authentication methods available to you are as follows:

- Clear text

- Clear text with SSL

- Both

If you require secure access to your directory, you should enable SSL access only. To enable SSL, you must register your Exchange Server and obtain a certificate from a certificate authority (CA), which can be a local or enterprise CA or a third party, such as VeriSign.

Next, you have to decide whether to permit anonymous access from users outside the organization. Depending on the configuration of your LDAP environment, critical data may or may not be exposed via an anonymous search. For example, if telephone numbers are considered intellectual property or have different security requirements, that may require authentication to see. Make sure all your LDAP clients follow security rules set within your company. With Exchange, you can't control overall access to the directory based on username and password, but you can selectively control access to attributes by anonymous or authenticated users or replicated sites. So an anonymous user could see the directory, but they'll see only the selected information. Other LDAP implementations offer more robust authentication. The ideal security would be public key, but this isn't available in current LDAP implementations.

You'll need to configure the search types that determine how the directory will treat substring searches—that is, partial and wildcard searches. Depending on your back-end server configurations, certain searches that contain wildcards aren't indexed and will cause significant delay on the client and server. For example, if a username search for uid=tjackiewicz will append an asterisk to the end of it, the search becomes uid=tjackiewicz*. Despite you inputting the entire search and not expecting a wildcard to be performed, the server will interpret the * as a wildcard search and take significantly longer to return results. The default treats any substring search as an initial search, providing better response to the user. Other default options involve allowing only initial searches (fast) or all substring searches (slow). Within this configuration, you can specify the maximum number of search results returned by the directory to the user. The default value is 100. You can raise or lower this number depending on how many directory entries you have or how much data you want to transmit to the user. In Exchange 5.5, you can configure the directory to return search results in chunks, such as 100 entries at a time.

The final step during your configuration is to select the idle timeout interval for LDAP connections. The default setting in Exchange 5.0 is ten minutes. This is extremely high, and you should change this to a small value (such as 30 seconds) to improve directory access and query response times.

For the sake of security, you'll need to access the Exchange Site Addressing configuration area to select which attributes you want internal users and the public to see in their search results. This is where you permit or deny access by attributing and publishing a subset of the Exchange global address list to the Internet as white pages, which are accessed by LDAP clients. (You can compare this feature to a meta-directory that serves as an intermediate layer between your authoritative data and a published set of information that exists on another server.)

Exchange doesn't permit you to dynamically extend your directory schema in 5.0, but it does provide ten custom directory attributes. More features will be available as the LDAP interoperability matures and becomes more standardized.

You'll need to make various decisions based on information available from your directory. For example, what will you do about users with several e-mail addresses in the directory? One solution is to publish only the user's Internet mail address to anonymous users. For internal users, you can publish all the addresses (cc:Mail, Microsoft Mail, X.400) if you're certain this wouldn't cause too much confusion. Senders would select the one address that would be handled correctly by their own messaging system. You can select any or all of the attributes in Exchange for public view, but be aware that not all LDAP clients support all attributes. In addition, some expect only certain attribute names or have other limitations that will prevent them from appropriately dealing with the information you provide. Most of the current LDAP-compliant clients can search and view Exchange's attributes, but may not fully support all the basic or extended operations. For example, the Exchange 5.0 LDAP server doesn't support "sounds like" or Boolean searching. If a client tries to invoke these methods, Exchange Server returns a protocol error to the user. Although you can specify which attributes can be seen by anonymous or authenticated users and for intersite replication, you can't restrict a specific user or group from accessing the directory.

Listing 8-12 is an example of how to identify and fetch user data in Internet Information Services (IIS) using Exchange and LDAP.

Listing 8-12. *Identifying and Fetching User Data in IIS*

```
<%

Dim LUser, strQuery, strServerName, oConn, oRS, GreetName, ITuser

LUser = Request.QueryString("LogonUser")
strServerName = Put here your Exchange Server Name

strQuery = "<LDAP://" & strServerName & ">;(uid=" & LUser & "); adspath,cn;subtree"

'Create ADO connection and set its properties
Set oConn = Server.CreateObject("ADODB.Connection")
oConn.Provider = "ADsDSOOBJECT"

'Pass the credentials to Exchange Server.
oConn.Properties("User_ID") = "IUSR_MAIL"
oConn.Properties("Password") = "IUSR_MAIL"
oConn.Properties("Encrypt Password") = False
oConn.Open "Active Directory Provider"

Set oRS = oConn.Execute(strQuery)

If oRS.BOF OR oRS.EOF Then
  Response.Write "Unable to retrieve information."
Else
  Response.Write "CN: " & oRS.Fields("cn").Value
End If
```

```
oRS.Close
oConn.Close
Set oRS = Nothing
Set oConn = Nothing

%>
```

Integrating LDAP Browsers

LDAP browsers are typically GUI tools that are alternatives to basic command-lines tools for viewing information that exists within your LDAP directory. While systems administrators often prefer command-line tools for looking at information, some LDAP users within your environment, such as junior administrators and those in your help desk, may prefer a more aesthetically pleasing approach. Many LDAP browsers are available to you by searching online. One of the most common tools available is LDAP Browser provided by Softerra via http://www.softerra.com. The LDAP browser is designed for viewing and searching entries inside an LDAP directory. It doesn't support creating, removing, editing, or importing data.

Softerra LDAP Browser provides a convenient Explorer-like interface for LDAP directory viewing and searching. It has been developed specifically for Win32 platforms and connects to any LDAP v2 and v3 servers. If you're a professional software developer or system administrator, LDAP Browser will let you view and analyze LDAP directories easily and comfortably under a Win32 platform. The browser has the same look and feel as LDAP Administrator, including all its interface improvement. It's much more powerful and convenient than the previous version (LDAP Browser 1.0 beta) because it has a full multithreaded engine, SSL support, directory search, favorites, improved LDAP v3 support, X.509 certificate viewer, and much more to facilitate your work with LDAP.

You can download this browser from Softerra's home page and install it on a number of platforms.

Another browser that's popular is creatively named LDAP Browser/Editor, which is available online at http://www.iit.edu/~gawojar/ldap/. This browser allows you to edit information, so it doesn't serve as just a read-only browser. It even includes modrdn functionality that isn't common among many other GUI-based LDAP clients.

Integrating Appliances

The latest trend in information technology has been the creation of an *appliance*. An appliance is typically an all-in-one solution to a problem that once fell into the realm of system administrators and application developers. That is, where you once had a machine running Solaris and Sendmail, you'd now have a rack-mounted unit that replaces the basic functionality of your Sendmail environment and gives your support staff a set of interfaces to view configurations and traffic flow online. In come the appliances, and out go the tasks of keeping your operating system and applications up-to-date. The reduction in the total cost of ownership of your environment is often a good enough reason to forego the traditional solutions deployed for e-mail systems and Web services. All the components of your infrastructure that once required significant training, maintenance, and an above-average level of expertise are now being transitioned to appliance-based solutions.

Vendors such as IronPort and Mirapoint provide appliances for e-mail that give you basic LDAP functionality out of the box. Mirapoint even provides an LDAP server in an appliance model. There's no typical configuration for any of the LDAP configurations you can have with an appliance or any set of standard rules that apply to each appliance you'll encounter. For-profit companies typically release appliances with no requirements set on them in order to standardize configurations or keep their profile data the same from version to version. You should read the manuals for each appliance you'll be configuring and ensure you aren't dependent on data that may exist in one version that may not be available in the next release. Just like configuring a new server, it may be best to wipe out configurations and start over during a major upgrade, as interoperability with LDAP is often dynamic in nature. The best thing to know and appreciate is that LDAP has become the common protocol, access method, and storage system that's used by everyone to standardize information.

Summary

In this chapter, I discussed various applications and the methods they use to integrate into an LDAP environment. This should give you a good start in understanding how some of the other applications in your environment will utilize LDAP.

Index

forums.apress.com

FOR PROFESSIONALS BY PROFESSIONALS™

JOIN THE APRESS FORUMS AND BE PART OF OUR COMMUNITY. You'll find discussions that cover topics of interest to IT professionals, programmers, and enthusiasts just like you. If you post a query to one of our forums, you can expect that some of the best minds in the business—especially Apress authors, who all write with *The Expert's Voice*™—will chime in to help you. Why not aim to become one of our most valuable participants (MVPs) and win cool stuff? Here's a sampling of what you'll find:

DATABASES
Data drives everything.

Share information, exchange ideas, and discuss any database programming or administration issues.

INTERNET TECHNOLOGIES AND NETWORKING
Try living without plumbing (and eventually IPv6).

Talk about networking topics including protocols, design, administration, wireless, wired, storage, backup, certifications, trends, and new technologies.

JAVA
We've come a long way from the old Oak tree.

Hang out and discuss Java in whatever flavor you choose: J2SE, J2EE, J2ME, Jakarta, and so on.

MAC OS X
All about the Zen of OS X.

OS X is both the present and the future for Mac apps. Make suggestions, offer up ideas, or boast about your new hardware.

OPEN SOURCE
Source code is good; understanding (open) source is better.

Discuss open source technologies and related topics such as PHP, MySQL, Linux, Perl, Apache, Python, and more.

PROGRAMMING/BUSINESS
Unfortunately, it is.

Talk about the Apress line of books that cover software methodology, best practices, and how programmers interact with the "suits."

WEB DEVELOPMENT/DESIGN
Ugly doesn't cut it anymore, and CGI is absurd.

Help is in sight for your site. Find design solutions for your projects and get ideas for building an interactive Web site.

SECURITY
Lots of bad guys out there—the good guys need help.

Discuss computer and network security issues here. Just don't let anyone else know the answers!

TECHNOLOGY IN ACTION
Cool things. Fun things.

It's after hours. It's time to play. Whether you're into LEGO® MINDSTORMS™ or turning an old PC into a DVR, this is where technology turns into fun.

WINDOWS
No defenestration here.

Ask questions about all aspects of Windows programming, get help on Microsoft technologies covered in Apress books, or provide feedback on any Apress Windows book.

HOW TO PARTICIPATE:

Go to the Apress Forums site at **http://forums.apress.com/**.
Click the New User link.

Printed in the United States
98533LV00005B/1-12/A